Ellen - The best ever. A great teacher, leader and friend!

George

Ellen - You are truly the best of the best!
Love ya - John

TEACHING AS LEADING

Profiles Of Excellence In The Open-Door College

TEACHING AS LEADING

*Profiles Of Excellence In
The Open-Door College*

By

George A. Baker III
John E. Roueche
Rosemary Gillett-Karam

THE COMMUNITY COLLEGE PRESS
A division of the American Association
of Community and Junior Colleges

Published by The Community College Press, a division of American Association of Community and Junior Colleges
National Center for Higher Education
One Dupont Circle, N.W., Suite 410
Washington, D.C. 20036

Phone: (202) 728-0200

ISBN 0-87117-199-0

Library of Congress Catalog Card Number: 89-85381

Table of Contents

Dedication

Ideas can open our cells. They can liberate us from the prisons we have ourselves built. In the laboratory of the scientist, the vision of the Poet, the memory of the historian, the discipline of the scholar, the imagination of the writer and the passion of the teacher. I went looking for......"The news of the mind." I found a kingdom of thought, rich in insights into our times.

Bill Moyers
A World of Ideas p. VII

And so did we! Thus we dedicate this work to the passion of the 869 award-winning instructors who so freely shared their "passion for teaching" with us.

GAB
JER
RG-K

CANADA

AWARD-WINNING INSTRUCTORS

Alberta

Mount Royal College
Donald N. Baker, President

Svea Craig-Mason
Melvin Pasternak
Robert Rose

Margaret Osborne
Mardy Roberts
Eva Rosenberg

Red Deer College
Edward J. Luterbach, President

Doug Girvan
Brad Hemstreet
Brian McDonald
Doug Swanson

Laurel Goodacre
Ed Kamps
Donna Storvik
Paul Williams

Southern Alberta Institute
  of Technology
W. G. Johnson, President

Chane Bush
David Pike

Bill Field

British Columbia

Selkirk College
Leo Perra, President

Lesley Anderson

Vancouver Community College
Paul Gallagher, President

John F. Parker

Ontario

Centennial College of Applied
    Arts & Technology
I. B. McCauley, President

Jack Spohn

Conestoga College of Applied
    Arts & Technology
John Tibbits, President

Bruce Bjorkquist

Humber College of Applied
    Arts & Technology
Robert A. Gordon, President

Joseph Kertes

Lambton College of Applied
    Arts & Technology
A. Wilkinson, President

Derwyn Smith

Mohawk College of Applied
    Arts & Technology
Keith L. McIntyre, President

Maureen Emmerson
Esther L. McIntosh
Jack O'Brien
Robert Tripe

Robert E. Malcomson
Jay Moore
Harry Sutcliffe

Sir Sandford Fleming College
Brian Desbiens, President

Angele Dion

David Long

St. Lawrence College Saint-Laurent
W.W. Cruden, President

Joe Jordan
William E. Tennant

Edward R. Lypchuk

Newfoundland

Newfoundland & Labrador Institute
    of Fisheries & Marine Technology
David A. Vardy, President

Edgar Churchill

Boyd Smith

Saskatchewan

Saskatchewan Institute of Art, Science
    & Technology - Kelsey Campus
Larry Dinter, President

Linda Brose

Ann M. Giesbrecht

Yukon

Yukon College
John E. Casey, Director

Mary Lou Smith

viii

UNITED STATES

Alabama

Bessemer State Technical College   Fred Kapp
W. Michael Bailey, President

Gadsden State Community College   George W. Terrell, Jr.
Robert W. Howard, President

George C. Wallace State Community   Mina L. Dickens   Linda Parish
  College
Nathan L. Hodges, President

J. F. Ingram State Technical College   Kenneth E. Scott   Bruce Thomas
Murry C. Gregg, President

Jefferson State Junior College   Janice Roberts
Judy M. Merritt, President

John C. Calhoun State Community   Elizabeth H. Brett   George O.
  College   Williams, Jr.
James R. Chasteen, President

Lurleen B. Wallace State Junior College   Bev Smith
William H. McWhorter, President

Arizona

Rio Salado Community College   Julie Bertch   René Díaz-Lefebvre
Charles Green, President   Laura Helminski   Helen Sprawls

Arkansas

East Arkansas Community College   Peter Haven   Jim McInturff
Bob C. Burns, President   Mary M. Weiner

Westark Community College   Don Bailey   Brenda Cantwell
Joel R. Stubblefield, President   Mike Cooper   Anita Hammack
                                                          Nancy Zechiedrich

California

Butte College   Dian Hasson   Katherine C. Newman
W. Lee Reeder, Superintendent/President

Cabrillo College   Charles F. Squatrito
Robert F. Agrella, Superintendent/
  President

California (cont.)

Cerritos College
Ernest A. Martinez, President

John Bogdanovich
James Fye
Connie Mantz
Nova Jean Weber

Hy L. Finkelstein
Joseph Girtner
Patricia Regan
Franklin Yee

Coastline Community College
William M. Vega, President

Joseph W. DeCarlo
Ning Yeh

Barbara J. Darby

Columbia College
W. Dean Cunningham, President

Richard L. Dyer

James R. Mendonsa

Cypress College
Kirk Avery, President

Charlene Felos
Robert Harkrider

Russell Flynn

DeAnza College
A. Robert DeHart, President

Sally Anderson
Charles B. Barker III
Joyce Colvard
Rena Frabony
Frank Soler
Barbara B. Travis

Chris Avery
Douglas T. Cheeseman
Gary Cummings
Michael Holler
Bruce J. Sturm
John W. Wanlass

Diablo Valley College
Phyllis Peterson, President

James M. Ardini

James J. Rawls

Foothill College
Thomas H. Clements, President

Marcia Frederick
Michiko Hiramatsu
Mike McHargue
Glenn Moffat
Miriam Rosenthal
Harry Saterfield
Angel Sierra
Margie Whalen

Catherine Germano
James Mauch
Larry Miller
Robert Pierce
Irv Roth
Bryan Shaner
Mona Spicer

Fullerton College
Philip Borst, President

Kathleen Engstrom
William Smith

Martin Hebeling

Gavilan College
John J. Holleman, Superintendent/
  President

Marilyn Abad-Cardinalli

Robert Funk

Grossmont Community College
Ivan L. Jones, President

William Bornhorst

X

California (cont.)

Hartnell Community College
James R. Hardt, Superintendent/
   President

Joanne Miller

Kearny Mesa Continuing Education Center
Robert L. Matthews, President

Claude E. Richards

Kings River Community College
Abel B. Sykes, Jr., President

Paul Kaser
Lawrence (Bud) West

Clark Skogsberg

Long Beach City College
Beverly O'Neill, Superintendent/
   President

F. Allen Bundy
Lowell Johnson
George Shaw
Joyce Witscher

David Frattalone
Robert Orr
Howard Shifflett

Los Angeles Harbor College
James L. Heinselman, President

Farah P. Fisher
Larry W. Heimgartner
Rodney Oakes
Robert Sager
JoRae Zuckerman

James H. Heffron
John C. McCarthy
James P. O'Brien
Robert G. Wrenn

Los Angeles Pierce College
David B. Wolf, President

Kathy Basil
Gail Hobbs
Ronald Smetzer
Paul Xanthos

Richard Follett
Robert Ono
Ann Watkins

Merced College
Tom K. Harris, Jr., Superintendent/
   President

Deanna Hauser

Modesto Junior College
Stanley L. Hodges, President

Ronald L. Alves
Sandra C. Bucknell
Richard F. Nimphius
Dorothy L. Scully
C. Wayne Wightman

Mark E. Bender
Edward F. Leal
Robert D. Raduechel
Stephen L. Stroud

Mt. San Antonio College
John D. Randall, Superintendent/
   President

Frank A. Acuna

Wayne J. Lutz

Palomar College
George R. Boggs, President

Gary Alderson
Karen Huffman

Ray Dahlin
Richard Norlin

California (cont.)

Rancho Santiago College — Terry W. Bales — Thomas J. Osborne
Robert D. Jensen, President

San Diego City College — Lawrence Forman
Jeanne Atherton, President

San Diego Miramar College — Dorothy K. Simpson
George F. Yee, President

Santa Barbara City College — Henry Bagish — Robert Casier
Peter R. MacDougall, — George Frakes — John Kay
  Superintendent/President — Barbara Lindemann — Elwood Schapansky

Santa Monica College — Edward Tarvyd
Richard L. Moore, Superintendent/
  President

Solano Community College — Sarah Phelan
Marjorie K. Blaha, Superintendent/
  President

Southwestern College — Irma Alvarez — Charlotte McGowan
Joseph M. Conte, Superintendent/ — Lucy T. Pryde — Jim Switzer
  President — Teresa A. Thomas

Colorado

Colorado Mountain College — William J. Hill
Dennis M. Mayer, President

Community College of Aurora — Cynthia A. Barnes — James Ford
Larry D. Carter, President

Community College of Denver — Melvin Carter — Linda Forkner
Byron McClenney, President — Barbara Gill — Robert Norden

Northeastern Junior College — Clay Prall
Marvin W. Weiss, President

Pueblo Community College — Mary Ann Burris
Tony Zeiss, President

Connecticut

Housatonic Community College
Vincent S. Darnowski, President

Ronald Abbe
John Conway
Walter Gerry
Glen Kindilien
Patricia Pifko

Natalie Bieber
Catherine Cron
Phyllis Gutowski
Norman Moore
Maria Roche

South Central Community College
Antonio Perez, President

Robert E. Tremblay

Delaware

Delaware Technical & Community College
John R. Kotula, President

Josephine S. Rolison

Florida

Brevard Community College
Maxwell C. King, President

John Willard

Broward Community College
Willis N. Holcombe, President

Joe Castillo

Barbara West

Central Florida Community College
William J. Campion, President

Kevin Mulholland

Florida Community College
   at Jacksonville
Charles Spence, President

Joan Bearden
Libby Holt
Larry Monts

Leo DeGoursey
Ethel (Pat) Jenkins
Christine Robinson

Manatee Community College
Stephen J. Korcheck, President

Robert D. Campbell

Miami-Dade Community College
Robert H. McCabe, President

Thelma Altshuler
Robert H. Calabrese
Joseph H. Gibson
James S. Gray
Jon Kitner
Oswaldo Lopez
Robert Moorman
Cecil B. Nichols
Ann G. Rose
Melvin Schwartz
Reina K. Welch

Robert Blitzer
Betty Ferguson
Jorge B. Gonzalez
Harold E. Harms
Marvin Langsam
Jane Mangrum
German Munoz
John H. Pryor, Jr.
Candido Sanchez
Sharon Thomas
Carolyn B. Wright

Okaloosa-Walton Community College
James R. Richburg, President

Wesley Johnstone

C. M. Duque Wilson

Florida (cont.)

Palm Beach Community College
Edward M. Eissey, President

Watson B. Duncan III

Richard E. Yinger

Seminole Community College
Earl S. Weldon, President

Jill D. Smith

St. Petersburg Junior College
Carl M. Kuttler, Jr., President

Donald J. Bergsma
Maria Chapin
Karen Estes
Helen W. Gilbart
Sylvia Holladay
Earl Kohler
Starr C. Weihe
Ray S. Wilson

Jean Bravick
Gladys Cummings
Willie B. Felton, Jr.
Robert Hackworth
Barbara Hull
Jerry Smith
Johnnie R. Williams

Valencia Community College
Paul C. Gianini, Jr., President

William M. McCord

Marlene Spencer

Georgia

Atlanta Metropolitan College
Edwin A. Thompson, President

Ronald P. Chandonia

Brunswick College
John W. Teel, President

Ronald Ridgley

John I I. Sterrett

Hawaii

Hawaii Community College
Patrick W. Naughton, Acting Provost

Jane Iida
James M. Yoshida

Kenneth K. Kameoka

Honolulu Community College
Peter Kessinger, Provost

Harvey Chun
Beng Poh Yoshikawa

David Cleveland

Kapiolani Community College
John Morton, Provost

Robert S. Chinen
R. Tim McCabe

Robert Fearrien

Kauai Community College
Y. David Iha, Provost

Andrew Bushnell
Brian Yamamoto

William Kikuchi

Idaho

College of Southern Idaho
Gerald R. Meyerhoeffer, President

Claudeen Buettner
Penny Glenn

James R. Gentry
Helen Hammond

XV

Illinois (cont.)

Triton College   Robert Anthony   Tom Secco
James Catanzaro, President   Melvin Swieton

Waubonsee Community College   Gibby Monokoski
John J. Swalec, President

Wilbur Wright College   Keith Dobberstein
Raymond F. LeFevour, President

Iowa

Hawkeye Institute of Technology   Gareth D. Downey   Robert G. Kimm
John E. Hawse, Superintendent/
   President

Iowa Lakes Community College   Jerry L. Larson   Burlin H. Matthews
Richard H. Blacker, President   David R. Peterson

Iowa Valley Community College District   Donald Benbow   Joseph White
John J. Prihoda, Superintendent/
   President

Muscatine Community College   Gerhard (Jeff) F. Koch
Victor F. McAvoy, President

Kansas

Coffeyville Community College   Lue Barndollar   Jim Criswell
Dan Kinney, President   Don Ellerman

Cowley County Community College   Carol Hobaugh-Maudlin   James Miesner
Patrick J. McAtee, President

Highland Community College   Ronald E. Goulet
Larry F. Devane, President

Johnson County Community College   Charles Bishop   Eugene Butler
Charles J. Carlsen, President   Harold Harp   Donna Krichiver
   Carolyn Neptune   Patrick Sweeney
   Roger Traver   Robin Woods
   Robert Xidis

Seward County Community College   Xyla Johnson
Theodore W. Wischropp, President

Kentucky

Ashland Community College
Anthony Newberry, President

Opal S. Conley

Elizabethton Community College
Charles Stebbins, President

James Murley

Hazard Community College
G. Edward Hughes, President

Richard Crowe

Valina Hurt

Jefferson Community College
Ronald J. Horvath, President

Margo Elliott
Richard Lyons
Mehale (Mike) Zalampas

Mary Jeanne Fletcher
M. Sherree Zalampas

Somerset Community College
Richard Carpenter, President

Najam Saeed

Sharon Whitehead

Maryland

Catonsville Community College
John M. Kingsmore, President

Leroy Giles

Raymond Quigley, Jr.

Cecil Community College
Robert L. Gell, President

Bonnie Giraldi

Chesapeake College
Robert C. Schleiger, President

Brenda Bloomgarden
Mercedes Lesser

Edna Marie Hudson

Community College of Baltimore
Joseph T. Durham, President

James E. Coleman
Thomas Hooe

Beverly Gold

Essex Community College
John Ravekes, President

Peter D. Adams

Edward Sherwin

Frederick Community College
Lee J. Betts, President

Shirley J. Davis
Charles R. Luttrell

Phyllis R. Hamilton

Hagerstown Junior College
Norman P. Shea, President

Steve Zabetakis

Howard Community College
Dwight A. Burrill, President

Susan R. Bard
Jerrold Casway
Susan Frankel
Patricia Turner

Mark M. Canfield
Valerie Costantini
Linda L. Johnston

Maryland (cont.)
Montgomery College   Thomas E. Kenney
Robert E. Parilla, President

Massachusetts
Cape Cod Community College   Brenda Boleyn
Philip R. Day, Jr., President

Middlesex Community College   Regina Goodwin   Dale Trudo
Evan S. Dobelle, President

Springfield Technical Community College   Roberta R. Nichols   Stephen G. Weisner
Andrew M. Scibelli, President

Michigan
Glen Oaks Community College   David C. Greenhoe   Daryl E. Herrmann
Philip G. Ward, President   Donald H. VanZuilen

Lake Michigan College   Alice Rasmussen   Robert Schodorf
Anne E. Mulder, President   K. Sundaram   Sheran Wallis

Mid Michigan Community College   James H. VanderMey
Eugene F. Schorzmann, President

Monroe County Community College   John W. Staas
Gerald D. Welch, President

Oakland Community College   Dennis H. Fiems   Sandra L. Langeland
R. Stephen Nicholson, Chancellor

Schoolcraft College   Lincoln T. Lao   Arthur J. Lindenberg
Richard W. McDowell, President   Janina Udrys

Washtenaw Community College   George Agin   Janet Hastings
Gunder A. Myran, President   Ruth Hatcher   Daniel Minock
                                           Dean Russell   J. Robert Wotring

Minnesota
University of Minnesota Technical   David Harmon   David McCarthy
   College-Waseca   Mark Wilson
Edward C. Frederick, Chancellor

Mississippi

Copiah-Lincoln Community College
Billy B. Thames, President

Roy W. Daughdrill
Faye M. Hill
Phyllis Hayes Lanier
Thomas A. Ross III
Edwin L. Smith

Danny T. Harrell
Melnèe K. Jaudon
Kay Rayborn
Carolyn V. Smith

East Central Community College
Eddie M. Smith, President

Alfred H. Bailey
Thomas W. Thrash

Bruce Guraedy
Ovid S. Vickers

Itawamba Community College
W. O. Benjamin, President

Kenneth R. Bishop

Meridian Community College
William F. Scaggs, President

Wilhelmine Damon
Sue Key

Shirley Nell Goodman

Mississippi Gulf Coast Community College
Barry L. Mellinger, President

Joan E. Fitch
Jon R. Lewis
Patricia A. Odom
Charles R. Shows
Charles L. Sullivan

Teresa M. Griffis
Nelda J. Lott
David C. Schwab
T. Ralph Smith

Missouri

Penn Valley Community College
Zelema Harris, President

Lloyd Daniel

Ron Taylor

St. Louis Community College
  at Florissant Valley
Michael T. Murphy, President

Carol A. Berger
Larry Byers
Michael J. Fuller
Emily M. Liebman

Kenneth B. Boyer
Carol A. Edwards
Stan Kary
Frank Stanton

St. Louis Community College
  at Forest Park
Vernon O. Crawley, President

Jack E. Miller

St. Louis Community College
  at Meramec
Gwendolyn Stephenson, President

Rosemary H. Thomas

Montana

Dawson Community College
Donald H. Kettner, President

Peter J. Degel
Thomas A. Ree

Norman D. Krueger

Nebraska

Central Community College
Joseph W. Pruesser, President

David Fulton
Latham Mortensen

Mary Lou Holmberg

Nebraska (cont.)

McCook Community College	Jerda Garey	
Robert G. Smallfoot, President		
Metropolitan Community College	Keith W. Deiml	Robert Gronstal
J. Richard Gilliland, President	Marian O. Paul	James Trebbien
Mid-Plains Technical Community College	Marilyn McGahan	Eloise Schwab
William G. Hasemeyer, Area President		
Western Nebraska Community College	Willie L. Quindt	
John N. Harms, President		

New Jersey

Camden County College	John deFrancesco	Edith Goodman
Robert Ramsay, President	Joseph Haro	Betty Joynes
	Gwendolyn E. Weiant	
Cumberland County College	Sharon Kewish	Carol A. Kozak
Philip S. Phelon, President		

New Mexico

Dona Ana Branch Community College	Rebecca Boggs	Eula Fern Thompson
Donaciano E. Gonzalez, Provost	John F. Walker	
Eastern New Mexico University—Clovis	Don (Red) Nevins	John O'Connell
Jay Gurley, Provost	Joe Ortiz	Chris Walters
New Mexico Military Institute	William E. Gibbs	Darlene Logan
Gerald Childress, Superintendent		
New Mexico State University	Janine T. Erbes	David Leas
at Alamogordo	David H. Townsend	
Charles R. Reidlinger, Provost		
San Juan College	Melvona Boren	Estelle Morin
James C. Henderson, President	David Nickoley	

New York

Broome Community College	David Walsh	
Donald A. Dellow, President		

New York (cont.)

Genesee Community College
Stuart Steiner, President

Ruth Andes
Donna Blake
Frances Hoeft
Donald Petote
Edward Stringham
Carl Wahlstrom
Margaret Williams

Theodore Ashizawa
Judith DePalma
Bernard Hoerbelt
Mary Platt
Clinton Tallman
Alan Williams

Hudson Valley Community College
Joseph J. Bulmer, President

Sally Bauer
Ronald E. Dow
Norman R. Swanson

Catherine Davis
Barbara M. Houser

Niagara County Community College
Donald Donato, President

Gail Bolster
Alex Greenberg
James Mezhir

Gene Carella
Bryce McMichael
Patricia Wille

Onondaga Community College
Bruce Leslie, President

Diane Case
Marcia Walton

John Panagakis

Schenectady County Community College
Peter Burnham, President

Peter Cousins
Martin Weinstein

James Parent

Suffolk County Community College
Robert T. Kreiling, President

Celeste Berner
Tak-Tow Chen
Richard Fox
Carolyn A. Gould
Raymond A. McCartney
Laurette Pavi
Louis S. Rupnick
Jacqueline Schillig
Paschal Ungarino

Sari G. Byrd
Kevin Foley
Richard E. Gambrell
Darlene Hochman
Merilyn Merenda
Mary H. Phillips
Steven Saltzman
Morton D. Strassberg

Tompkins-Cortland Community College
Eduardo J. Marti, President

Joseph N. Dabes
Sandra Pollack

Kenneth P. McEwan

Westchester Community College
Joseph N. Hankin, President

John Ahern
Greta Cohan
William V. Costanzo
Albert Liberi
Linda C. Sledge
Maryanne Vent

Stanley M. Behr
Iris M. Cook
Elaine Klein
Shirley G. Lim
Sinforosa Tan
Eileen Walsh

North Carolina

Alamance Community College
W. Ronald McCarter, President

David M. Payne
Norman Svee

Doris R. Schomberg

Blue Ridge Technical College
David W. Sink, Jr., President

David M. Holcombe
Benjamin F. Streets III

Earl D. Medlin

Central Carolina Community College
Marvin R. Joyner, President

Linda B. Dalrymple
Charles G. Wadsworth

Nancy S. Turner

Central Piedmont Community College
Ruth G. Shaw, President

Ray V. Caldwell
James H. Sasser
Beverly E. Terry

R. Gene Reid
George J. Soos
Thomas M. Vance

College of the Albemarle
J. Parker Chesson, Jr., President

Wilma W. Harris
Robert O. Stephens

Faye E. Hoffman

Fayetteville Technical Community College
R. Craig Allen, President

Ann N. Ashford
Darl H. Champion

Marie Cash
Marsha Ralph

Guilford Technical Community College
Raymond J. Needham, President

Rita C. Gress
Mildred R. Mallard
Barbara VanDusen

Walter F. Hawn
Walter J. Rouse

Sandhills Community College
Raymond Stone, President

Dawson V. Carr
Avery Dennis

Reynold S.
  Davenport, Jr.
Fred Garrett

Surry Community College
Swanson Richards, President

Joseph B. Maye
Kathy Atkins Woodruff

William N. McCachren

Wake Technical Community College
Bruce I. Howell, President

Donald N. Chesson

Wilkes Community College
David E. Daniel, President

Blair M. Hancock
Brenda B. Moore

Elizabeth H.
  Klinkosum

Ohio

Cincinnati Technical College
Frederick B. Schlimm, President

Jerry A. Froehlich

Charles L. Jonas

Clark State Community College
Albert A. Salerno, President

D. Kay Frazier

Deloris Woodburn

Ohio (cont.)

Columbus State Community College
Harold M. Nestor, President

Lowell Gene Downey
Joseph Pezzano

Nancy Laughbaum
Charles Rinehart

Cuyahoga Community College
Nolen M. Ellison, Chancellor

James G. Banks
Harvey Kassebaum
Dorothy Merchant
Margaret W. Taylor
Donald A. Wheeler

David M. Humphreys
Mark Lewine
Dorothy C. Salem
John A. Venesile
Mary Jane Wheeler

Sinclair Community College
David H. Ponitz, President

Daniel Becker
Charles C. Williams, Jr.

Margaret L. Dotson

Oklahoma

Northern Oklahoma College
Edwin E. Vineyard, President

John Kuchera

Mary Perks

Oklahoma City Community College
Kenneth P. Walker, President

Joe D. Bush

Gus Pekara

Oregon

Chemeketa Community College
William Segura, President

Patricia L. Malone
Darlene Toole

Suzanne McLaughlin

Clackamas Community College
John S. Keyser, President

Thomas F. Richards
Marlene C. Tufts

James A. Streeter

Lane Community College
Jack Carter, Interim President

Tom Birkenhead
Betty James
Eilene Lepelley
Linda Riepe

Shirley Hewitt
Brenda Jennings
Jean Names Cross

Mt. Hood Community College
Paul E. Kreider, President

Gary Grimes
Lyle Mooney
Paul Sunset
Anna Marie Updegraff

Sally Jepson
Penny Slingerland
Anna Mae Tichy

Umpqua Community College
James M. Kraby, President

Ronald Alexander
Robert L. Johnson

Patrick Boyd

Pennsylvania

Butler County Community College
R. M. Sanderson, Interim President

Donald Drum
Wayne Shaulis

Charles Dunaway

Pennsylvania (cont.)

Community College of Allegheny County   John Lucarelli   John R. Starmack
Larry L. Whitworth, Acting President

Northampton County Area   Leonard R. Roberts   Pamela Tabery
  Community College
Robert A. Kopecek, President

Rhode Island

Community College of Rhode Island   Loren William Cheney
Edward J. Liston, President

South Carolina

Aiken Technical College   Tammy D. Hassell
Paul L. Blowers, President

Chesterfield-Marlboro Technical College   Richard Moorman   Zenda W. Rushing
Ronald W. Hampton, President   Diane Winburn

Greenville Technical College   Kevin J. Morris
Thomas E. Barton, Jr., President

Midlands Technical College   Kincheon H. Bailey, Jr.   Dee F. Bostick
James L. Hudgins, President   Alan L. Clayton   William R. Hames, Jr.
                                               C. Kay Harris   Charlotte D. Hixson
                                               James L. Lancaster   Beverly F. Lowry
                                               Leei Mao   William M. Oakland
                                               James R. Scott   Ronald J. Stockman
                                               Janice Stoudemire   Paul Taylor
                                               Mona L. Webb   Vinetta G. Witt

Orangeburg-Calhoun Technical College   Louis Boone   Mike Hammond
M. Rudy Groomes, President   Emily White

Piedmont Technical College   Katherine G. Adkins
Lex D. Walters, President

Sumter Area Technical College   Frankie Keels   Margaret Owens
Herbert C. Robbins, President   Roger Springs

Trident Technical College   Mary H. Dellamura   James A. Rehg
Charles W. Branch, President

Tennessee

Chattanooga State Technical Community College
Harry D. Wagner, President

Elizabeth Green
Patsy Littlejohn

Marilyn Green
Margaret Venable

Cleveland State Community College
James Ford, President

Renate Basham

Larry Speight

Dyersburg State Community College
Karen A. Bowyer, President

Billy Williams

Motlow State Community College
A. Frank Glass, President

Randall Bartley
Richard Gross
Billy Hix

Ruth Collins
Doyle Hasty
Vicky Young

Pellissippi State Technical Community College
J. L. Goins, President

Roger Crowe

William Hamlin, Jr.

Roane State Community College
Shirley Hoppe, Interim President

Susan A. Garner
Stephen Wheeler

Barbara M. Phillips

Walters State Community College
Jack E. Campbell, President

Anne Armstrong
Mary Lou Cook

Ruth Carpenter

Texas

Alvin Community College
A. Rodney Allbright, President

James Jay Corbett

Mary H. Knapp

Amarillo College
George Miller, President

Camille Cargill
Helen E. Lowe
Robert Wylie

Beverly Holt Fite
Willie M. Weaver

Austin Community College
Dan Angel, President

Yvonne Estes
Mary Leonard
Katherine Staples

Daniel Finley
Stephen B. Rodi
Hazel Ward

Brookhaven College
Patsy J. Fulton, President

Stephen William Link
Marilyn Sullivan

Marjorie J. Schuchat

College of the Mainland
Larry L. Stanley, President

Emmeline Dodd
William M. Tapp

Larry L. Smith

Collin County Community College District
John H. Anthony, President

Billie M. Cunningham
Tom Rodgers

Martha M. Ewing

XXV

Texas (cont.)

Eastfield College
Justus Sundermann, President

R. James Bennett
Robert G. Sharp

Diane M. Jordan

El Centro College
Wright L. Lassiter, Jr., President

Ralph Logan
Bette Neeley-Plog

Barbara V.
    Montgomery

El Paso County Community College District
Robert Shepack, President

Shirley Gilbert
Margaret R. Medina
Lucy Scarbrough
Charles Wise

Joe Martinez
Margaret Rodriguez
Sandra Tate

Galveston College
John E. Pickelman, President

Phillip Harris
John Rimar

Kelly Hejtmancik

Grayson County Junior College
Jim M. Williams, President

Millard D. Brent
Gerald W. Locke
Don H. Martin

Fred Caldwell
Sam G. Lusk
Ron Roberts

Houston Community College System
J. B. Whiteley, President

Anthony Chee
Jeffrey W. Lindemann

Carol Laman
R. Neal Tannahill

Howard County Junior College District
Bob E. Riley, President

Paul Ausmus

Mel Griffin

Laredo Junior College
Roger L. Worsley, President

Tom Mitchell

Lee College
Vivian B. Blevins, President

John C. Britt
Muriel H. Tyssen

Mary E. Gribble

Midland College
Jess H. Parrish, President

Julia Flaherty
Nancy Hart
Pamela Howell
Charles Klein
Joe Nye
Nancy Shaw
Warren Taylor

Celia Harris
Glenda Hicks
Clara King
Shea Nabi
Bob Peetz
Chloice Shofner
Jerry Tubb

Mountain View College
William H. Jordan, President

Jean W. Brown
Lew C. Sayers, Jr.

Larry Pool

North Lake College
James F. Horton, Jr., President

Carlos Gonzalez
D'Ann Madewell

Peter A. Lindstrom
Marilyn Mays

Texas (cont.)

Panola Junior College Gary McDaniel, President	John (Bill) W. O'Neal	
Paris Junior College Bobby R. Walters, President	Marilyn Fuller Pamela K. Hunt Betty Mills	E. C. Hancock Joan Mathis
Richland College Stephen Mittelstet, President	Harold Albertson Jana Flowers	John Barrett
San Antonio College Max Castillo, President	Rita J. Bordano Mary Ann DeArmond Johnnie L. Rosenauer	Robert T. Bryant Lewis M. Fox R. Barry Welch
San Jacinto College - South Parker Williams, President	Joseph J. Granata	Flora (Peggy) B. Hildreth
Southwest Texas Junior College Jimmy Goodson, President	John E. Heath	Mary Beth Monroe
Tarrant County Junior College - Northeast Campus Herman L. Crow, President	Elva Allie Gary Smith	Dolores Ingle-Sutter
Tarrant County Junior College - Northwest Campus Michael Saenz, President	Michael A. Cinatl Mollie A. Newcom	M. Lynne Hardin
Tarrant County Junior College - South Campus Charles L. McKinney, President	Jo Bagley Robert Platt	James B. Nichols
Temple Junior College Marvin R. Felder, President	Weldon Cannon Debra Foster	Henry Castillo
Texas Southmost College Juliet Garcia, President	Karen S. Chandler Irma S. Jones Walter Pierce	William C. Davis Wayne Moore Lucy Willis
Texas State Technical Institute - Amarillo Ron DeSpain, Campus President	Bill Banks	

Texas (cont.)

Tyler Junior College
Raymond M. Hawkins, President

Noami Byrum
Carroll M. Cassel
Linda J. Cross
J. D. Menasco
Larry M. Pilgrim
Victor Siller

Jamie L. Carter
David Crawford
Franklin Kimlicko
Judith Anne Parks
Jacque Shackelford
Linda Zeigler

Weatherford College
E. W. Mince, President

Shirley Chenault

Wharton County Junior College
Elbert C. Hutchins, President

Rhonda Armstrong

Jerry L. Long

Virginia

Central Virginia Community College
Johnnie E. Merritt, President

Thomas M. McGrath
Wayne Wiley

Thomas E. McKay

Piedmont Virginia Community College
James Perkins, Acting President

Jewell-Ann Parton

Wytheville Community College
William F. Snyder, President

Joseph M. Cockram
Karen S. Detweiler
Charlene T. Phillips

Betty V. Craft
John E. Matheny

Washington

Edmonds Community College
Thomas C. Nielsen, President

Rick Asher
Dick Mamolen

Marion Honsberger
Rod Schein

Grays Harbor College
Joseph A. Malik, President

Glen Clothier
Jeff Wagnitz

Richard Lane

Lower Columbia College
Vernon Pickett, President

Dorothy Crepin
Michael Strayer

Harvey Mashinter

Pierce College
Brent Knight, President

Mary K. Brown
Jan Halverson
Moses Pui-Chuen Lai
Clarke St. Dennis

F. Heath Cobb
Stephen Jaech
Nita Rutkosky

Seattle Community College District
Donald G. Phelps, Chancellor

Marcia Barton
Ray Gerring
Don Howard
George Iwasaki
George Lewis

Valerie Bystrom
Judy Gray
Cynthia Imanaka
Reuben Krogstad
Carol Thompson

Washington (cont.)

Walla Walla Community College Steven L. VanAusdle, President	Bill Piper	Jo Anne Rasmussen
Whatcom Community College Harold Heiner, President	Don McClary	Lillian McManus
Yakima Valley Community College V. Phillip Tullar, President	George L. Meshke	Judith K. Moore

West Virginia

Southern West Virginia Community College	Rose Brafford Charles D. (Donnie) Summers	Patricia (Peggy) McClure Harold Watkins
Gregory D. Adkins, President		
West Virginia Northern Community College Barbara Guthrie-Morse, President	Katherine J. Leisering Shirley A. Rychlicki	Ralph C. Lucki Audrey Secreto

Wisconsin

Blackhawk Technical College James Catania, District Director	Kay Carl Shirley Sweet	William Landvogt

Wyoming

Laramie County Community College Timothy G. Davies, President	Elizabeth Escobedo Mark Greer M. Anne Wolff	Sue Foy Ron Pulse

Preface

*Education is the point at which we decide whether we love the
world enough to assume responsibility for it and by the same
token to save it from that ruin, which, except for renewal, except
for the coming of the new and the young, would be inevitable.*

*And education, too, is where we decide whether we love our
children enough not to expel them from our world and leave them
to their own devices, nor to strike from their hands their choice of
undertaking something new, something unforeseen by us, but to
prepare them in advance for the task of renewing a common
world.*

Hannah Arendt

*F*ive years ago with the support of the Sid W. Richardson
Foundation of Fort Worth, Texas, we began what has become
a continuing goal to search for excellence in education. In the
first phase of our study, we produced *Profiling Excellence in America's
Schools*; we developed a framework for the study of public schools
using the ideas of Peters and Waterman (1982), who had successfully
examined excellence in the private sector. In a second phase of our
study, a single college—Miami-Dade Community College in
Florida—was highlighted as an example of excellence in public
education. In 1988 the third phase in our discovery of excellence in
the community college resulted in *Shared Vision: Transformational
Leadership in American Community Colleges*. This study of 256
outstanding community college CEOs yielded the first major picture
of exceptional leadership in the community college movement.

During the final stages of our college leadership study, we
began to talk about the idea of the *teacher as leader*. In July 1988 we
undertook an important and complex study of excellence in
community colleges—the excellence of teaching. We wrote to the
256 outstanding CEOs identified in *Shared Vision*, and then
supplemented this list with the 459 members of the National Institute
of Staff and Organizational Development (NISOD). We invited all
those community college presidents and CEOs to identify their

teachers who had been recognized for teaching excellence, either internally or by various external agencies across the United States and Canada. This process yielded 869 award-winning instructors, nominated by 251 CEOs of community, technical, or junior colleges in 39 states and six Canadian provinces.

Our attention to the issues involved in identifying and studying excellent teachers was heightened by what we perceived as a long-overdue need to research the very core of the community college—teaching and learning. The longer we talked, the more we began to see a plan evolve for a book that had a new slant on the role and importance of the teacher or college instructor. We envisioned a book about the teacher as leader who had a reciprocal relationship with students as followers, about the teacher as influencer who clarified students' paths to success, and about the teacher as motivator who empowered students to achieve their desires and accomplish their goals. We never looked at our study as becoming a "how-to" book, or a quantitative examination of products of teaching, or a meta-analysis of what research now exists. Rather, we wanted to redirect attention away from content and curriculum studies and toward the exemplary behaviors and competencies of teachers who are successful in the classroom. By doing so, we believe we are responding to the concerns emerging in higher education that must deal with the complexity of students' academic and interpersonal needs, that must be attentive to the growing cultural and demographic diversity representative of community college students, and that must respond to the challenges of a rapidly changing and highly technological workplace.

At the heart of the open-door college are the faculty and the students. These two essential ingredients form a relationship that ultimately determines to what extent the college is able to accomplish its mission. As human resource development organizations, open-door colleges exist to assist their students in becoming fully functional adults. Implicit in this charge is student recruiting, orienting, assessing, advising, placing, managing, tutoring, counseling, graduating, and job placing. Yet, all of these aspects are tangential to the central aspect of teaching and learning. Given the clear mission and dedication to teaching, one would expect that the research agenda for community colleges over the past three decades would have attempted to answer these questions: How does learning occur? How does this teaching-centered institution recruit, develop, evaluate, reward, and retain excellent teachers?

In 1988, a report was issued by the AACJC Commission on the Future of Community Colleges, *Building Communities: A Vision for a New Century*. In this report, we learned about the relationship of teaching and learning in the community college, and we were advised to strengthen learning and teaching:

> The community college should be the nation's premier teaching institution. Quality instruction should be the hallmark of the movement. We agree with Mortimer Alder's conclusion that 'all genuine learning is active, not passive. It involves the use of the mind, not just the memory. It is a process of discovery in which the student is the main agent, not the teacher.' Collaborative learning should be strengthened, quality instruction must be consistently rewarded, (and effective teachers should be grounded) in the scholarship of integrating, applying and presenting knowledge through effective teaching (pp. 25-26).

We believe that teacher as leader is a first step in the direction of focusing the strength and the energy of this movement toward teaching and its essential outcome—student learning. We feel like pioneers blazing a new trail and, like many who take risks, we are excited about our path's eventual destination. The nature of the educational research we have undertaken is exploratory and interpretative; it seeks to examine and learn from other disciplines and employ, modify, and make operational those theories and models that other researchers have used successfully to examine the concepts of effectiveness and excellence.

As with other studies, we have employed a core of research knowledge that focuses on explanation and also involves the use of description and improvement techniques. By describing, we look at the forms, structures, and relationships of various teaching behaviors through the use of instrumentation, measurement, and observation; here we have relied on the self-reporting of the award-winning instructors. And in order to examine self-reported data against other observed data, we requested that the teachers' CEOs and students provide us parallel information concerning the award-winning instructors. Improvement techniques, for the most part, are those that were analyzed by researchers and enacted in programs in the community colleges in the 1970s and 1980s. These included professional development programs and analyses of teaching methods and behaviors that improved student learning. Improvement studies are designed to develop knowledge about how teachers intervene in the lives of students in order to help them learn. In this area, much research exists that assists in identifying interventions that have a high probability of improving students' academic achievement. Walberg (1986) and his associates synthesized almost 3,000 such studies to identify interventions that improve student performance.

Teaching as Leading will provide an opportunity for teachers to analyze student needs, evaluate their teaching style, and plan strategies toward becoming situational teachers. Institutional strategies must be developed that provide powerful pre-service and in-service opportunities for community college teachers. This study and its various models will aid in this process. College faculty and administrators must revitalize professional development programs toward continuing the improvement efforts of teaching and learning, toward new recruitment of minority faculty to more accurately mirror our student population, toward examination of retrenchment problems among an aging faculty, toward instituting master teacher training and retraining programs for new teachers and new teaching skills. And institutions of higher education will have to refocus attention on the importance of a qualified cadre of teachers and instructors for the future and look to providing a fit between their graduates and providing a teaching core to meet the complex needs of the community college.

Teaching as Leading relies on explanation; if we are able to explain how exceptional teachers go about motivating students to learn, if we are able to explain how students say they are motivated by these teachers, and if we demonstrate how CEOs support this process, we will have increased knowledge about teaching and its relationship to learning. In this way, we can improve our ability to describe, predict, and control the essential aspects of teaching and learning with a high level of certainty and accuracy. Toward this end, college administrators must become much better at predicting which applicants can and will be successful in teaching the students who are attracted to the open-door college.

We believe that while our effort will be a contribution to a revitalized research agenda, others in this exciting movement will see fit to reorder priorities and make research in teaching and learning the top priority for the 1990s and beyond. We believe that the award-winning instructors identified in this study are the best in the United States and Canada. We also know that many teachers who read this book are laboring in the trenches without recognition. We believe that if every community college in the United States and Canada had chosen or had been given the opportunity to submit their best teachers—formally recognized or not—our findings would not have differed significantly from what we have presented here. If the AACJC Commission on the Future of Community Colleges is correct, then "community should be defined not only as a region to be served, but also as a climate to be created" (*Building Communities*, 1988).

We must begin by determining how to build a climate with teaching and learning as its core. Getting there will not be easy. If we continue our typical behavior concerning every new faculty hire, then the emphasis will continue to be on filling the empty line and not on selecting the best-qualified. Current emphasis on hiring that employs those similar to the present majority and neglects "others" does not focus on providing a match for the growing diversity among students. Unless changes occur, the assumption will be that teachers and students are not only at the bottom of the hierarchy, but at the end of the supply line. Without significant change, the focus will continue to be on the adversarial relationship between college management and teaching faculty. In this adversarial relationship teachers will not be seen as leaders who possess incredible influence over students, but as a faculty line, a consumer of precious resources, and as individuals who can be motivated through control and tolerated only because they provide an "employee" function.

The good news is that change is underway among the leading edge of the community colleges. Many CEOs are enlightened about teaching and learning and are asking the right questions. Many administrators are becoming educational leaders, and boards are developing policies that will allow for effective recruitment, selection, development, and reward of teachers. Many CEOs see the need to move the expanding mass toward a future where community colleges are premier teaching institutions and quality instruction is the hallmark of the movement. It is our hope that these practices will become normalized and formalized because teachers must be encouraged, supported, and empowered to do what they do best—motivate learners to become students in the most powerful way possible.

We trust that *Teaching as Leading* will be the first of many research efforts in the 1990s that are dedicated to the mission of accomplishing the dream of many in community colleges. That dream is appropriately expressed in *Building Communities* (1988): teaching and learning is central to all that we do. To do less than this not only destroys the dream, but denies the power that learning and education bring to the learner, the community, and the nation.

This book consists of 13 chapters. Chapter 1 provides a foundation for the concept of teacher as leader, with operational definitions of teaching and learning. Since motivation is a key aspect of teaching, motivation theories are explored in a teaching and learning context. The Porter-Lawler (1968) model of motivation is employed as a process for describing how motivation is linked to leadership and influence.

Chapter 2 employs an analysis of leadership theory in order to demonstrate the clear link between leaders and followers and the application of these ideas to the teaching and learning context. The chapter highlights the path-goal model (House and Mitchell, 1974) of leadership as the process for gathering behavioral information about teaching.

Chapter 3 presents the research paradigm. We believe that a major aspect of what takes place between access and the success of community college students is the individual and collective efforts of community college faculty. In studying the 869 award-winning instructors, we have collected over one million pieces of data about them. These data represent information from CEOs, the award-winning instructors, and their students. While we have described, predicted, made recommendations for improvement, and explained the behavior of the award-winning instructors, the study is exploratory in nature. We have not chosen a control group, and we do not know how the behavior of the award-winning instructors differ from the behavior of those not chosen to participate in the study. We will leave this task for others. What we have done is develop a paradigm of what the best do. We have described and analyzed not only what they do, but also how their students see them. Our chief aim was to be able to describe effective teaching behavior, predict what effective teachers do, make recommendations for improvement through self-evaluation, and explain how teachers were able to motivate students. We have sought to do this by employing several existing theories, by interpreting and adapting models specific to the teaching and learning process, and by developing our own teaching-learning framework that focuses on teaching styles and situational teaching.

Chapter 4 presents a profile of the award-winning instructors. Data presented in this chapter focuses on the biographical information provided by the faculty participants in the study. Aspects of experience, age, gender, and ethnicity are presented, as are teaching fields and disciplines of the participating teachers. Also, award-winning instructors were asked to provide institutional information—such as retention rates and institutional policies relating to student attendance, assessment, advisement, placement, and faculty development aspects.

Chapter 5 provides a framework for employing the path-goal leadership theory in explaining the interaction between teaching and learning. Three major propositions guide the application of path-goal theory to the teaching and learning context: first, the behavior of the teacher is acceptable and satisfying to students to the extent that students see such behavior as either an immediate source of satisfaction or as the means to a future pay-off; second, teacher behavior will increase student effort to the extent that such behavior makes satisfaction contingent on effective performance; and third, teaching behavior complements student efforts by providing coaching, guidance, support, and appropriate rewards. Six behavioral aspects of the teaching-learning path-goal framework are developed and explained in this chapter.

Chapter 6 introduces the Teaching as Leading Inventory (TALI). It was a research hypothesis that teaching behavior would vary across the six aspects of the path-goal model according to the motivation, experience, and temperament of the award-winning instructors in their interactions with students. Integrating the theories of Lewin and others, the idea of experiential learning was developed into an instrument capable of factoring the award-winning instructors into four teaching archetypes or styles. In accomplishing this task, Kolb's Learning Style Inventory served as a departure point for the development of the Teaching as Leading Inventory. Four teaching styles—Supporter, Theorist, Achiever, and Influencer—describe the dominant teaching behaviors of our participants. These styles incorporate the experiential aspects of Lewin and Kolb and support the leadership styles of House and Mitchell (1974) and Hersey-Blanchard (1982) emanating from path-goal research and the life-cycle leadership concepts.

Chapters 7 through 10 present the four teaching-as-leading styles developed from the Teaching as Leading Inventory. Although some overlap occurs, powerful evidence exists to support the four distinct styles of teaching. The authors believe that all four styles are appropriate in developing community college students. Each style has its strengths and weaknesses. In each adjacent chapter, complementary and opposite styles are discussed; our intent is that faculty will begin to see themselves as able to bring a large number of appropriate behaviors to their relationships with students in order to motivate and influence students to learn.

Chapter 11 is a summary of the four separate styles of teaching and moves the reader toward the idea that all teaching, especially the teaching of adults, should be predicated on assumptions of the developmental needs of students and their readiness to learn. A review of leadership theories supporting situational teaching is employed to demonstrate how the four teaching styles together present a holistic and contingent view of teaching.

Chapter 12 is dedicated to the future of community college teaching in the United States and Canada. Current professional development programs are highlighted in order to demonstrate the fact that the systematic selection, orientation, development, reward, and retention of excellent faculty is well developed at some colleges. If community colleges are expected to achieve the mission of student development, these practices must become integrated in the community colleges of the 1990s.

Chapter 13 makes the case for using the *A Nation at Risk, Involvement in Learning,* and *Building Communities* reports to help move the idea of teaching as leading to fruition in the community college. In this chapter, recommendations from these three major reports are discussed as strategies for making teaching and learning the central aspect of all community colleges.

In a study encompassing 869 award-winning instructors, over 3,000 students, and 251 CEOs, it is impossible to acknowledge every individual who has made significant contributions to this massive undertaking. However, we would like to thank all those who have assisted in making this book a reality. We have dedicated the book to those faculty who contributed their energy and effort toward our understanding of the central thesis of the book: teachers are, in fact, leaders in their relationships with students. This book is meant to celebrate! What remains is to recognize those who helped to put it all together.

Acknowledgments

First, we thank the many community college CEOs who provided us with the names of teachers who had been recognized internally or externally for excellent teaching. Often these visionary CEOs had programs in place for the recognition of excellent teaching and were also willing to describe the behavior of these teachers. Their inputs provided a major component of our study. Also, in this regard, we express our appreciation to the executive secretaries or administrative assistants who aided and assisted the CEOs in this important task.

Second, we thank the students who participated in the study. Even though the reader has not been able to see the total materials relating to a specific award-winning instructor, we have certainly been overwhelmed by the uniqueness and power of their descriptions. While faculty reported how they believed in their own behavior in motivating students, and while this view was supported in the CEOs' letters, it was the descriptions by the students that completed the story. The students often reported how the behavior of the instructor had changed their lives. For that single experience we owe a debt of gratitude to the 3,000 or more students who participated in the study.

We also owe a special debt of gratitude to Dr. Millicent Valek, vice-president of instruction at Arizona Western College. Mimi conducted research for her Community College Leadership Program dissertation by employing the path-goal leadership concept. Her investigations with the Great Teaching Seminar, held in Kerrville, Texas, in 1987, provided a foundation and pilot study for our research.

Joe Barwick, a student in the 1989 Community College Leadership Program (CCLP), provided tremendous assistance with the development of the Teaching as Leading Inventory (TALI) phase of the research. Joe also provided the drafts of the chapters reporting the teaching-as-leading styles.

Eli Eric Peña, Anita Janis, and John Rucker, doctoral candidates in the CCLP, provided the behavioral review analysis of the award-winning instructors and their students. They were ably assisted with this critical and time-consuming analysis by Jill Bailey-Duckworth and Kendall Karam. Charlotte Biggerstaff, a doctoral student in the CCLP program, also offered invaluable help early on; and Eli, after his internship at Miami-Dade Community College, returned to Austin in time to help us with the final phase of the book.

We owe special thanks to Don Matlock, professor at Southwest Texas State University, for his assistance in the development of a research model that allowed us to analyze multiple sources of data. We also express our appreciation to Bill Dirk and Jim Wiehe, graduate students in the Department of Educational Administration and Educational Psychology, respectively, for their detailed assistance with data analysis that resulted in many tables and charts in the research-oriented chapters.

Our two undergraduate student assistants were Alex Chaniotis and Vernon Weaver. Both made major contributions to the study by converting hand-written and taped field notes to readable copy. Unfortunately, Vernon became ill, necessitating the interruption of his education. We wish him a speedy recovery.

We acknowledge the sterling efforts of Suanne Roueche, director of the National Institute for Staff and Organizational Development. Suanne acted as editor, assisting in the development of a consistent writing style throughout the manuscript. With the help of Sheryl Fiedler, the latter stages of editing were integrated into the text. Libby Lord, administrative associate, and Reid Watson, administrative assistant, provided assistance in all phases of the project. For their excellent support, we are thankful. Lisa M. Gutierrez, a new member of the NISOD staff, also helped in pulling us to the finish line.

Susan Burneson, associate director of the National Institute for Staff and Organizational Development, assisted in the development of the award-winning instructors medallions. Ruth Thompson and a host of NISOD work-study students worked with Susan and Suanne in the preparation of the award-winning instructors ceremony and celebrations.

We are thankful for the resources made available through NISOD and the Sid W. Richardson Foundation to conduct this study. Without the significant support from these two entities, this study would not have been possible.

Finally, we extend our thanks to the American Association of Community and Junior Colleges (AACJC) and The Community College Press for publishing *Teaching as Leading*. From the beginning, President Dale Parnell and Executive Vice President Jim Gollattscheck saw the *Teaching as Leading* project as one of critical importance to AACJC—they have not wavered from that vision. Bonnie Gardner, editor of the *AACJC Journal*, Alison Anaya, and Susan Reneau of the AACJC staff have not only aided in the consistency and quality of the work, but have supported our efforts over 18 months of research. For them we are thankful.

We realize that we, on occasion, have referred to those about whom we have written as teachers, faculty, or instructors. We do not mean to differentiate among these terms. We also were not able to present most of the data that we have compiled; and if we have omitted information of crucial importance, especially to those who provided us with information, we apologize. In the final analysis, we are solely responsible for all that we have written and for what we have failed to write. As well, we are aware that the conclusions reached in this book do not necessarily reflect the views of AACJC or its Board of Directors.

George A. Baker III
John E. Roueche
Rosemary Gillett-Karam

Chapter 1

Teaching and Learning in the Community College

Identifying Exceptional Performance: The Teacher as Leader
Focusing on the Connection Between Teaching and Learning
Motivating the Learner
Motivational Variables that Influence Learning
Summary

There are three things that
men and women should honor;

They should honor their parents,
They should honor their history, and
They should honor education.

Chinese proverb

1

My role is one of motivator. That role is enhanced by my knowledge of subject matter and a love for what I do. My goal is to share what I know with my students in an energetic manner. I want to touch their lives—to teach them more about the world in which they live and more about themselves as valuable participants in that world.

Teresa M. Griffis
Mississippi Gulf Coast
Community College,
Perkinston, Mississippi

Although there seems to be general consensus around the belief that the focus of community colleges is on teaching, research has not focused on the dynamic relationship that exists between teaching and learning. Most authorities would agree that a vital link exists between the two, and some go so far as to suggest that teaching and learning are dependent on the sets of interactions that occur between the teacher and the student, who are involved in a reciprocal, interdependent relationship (Cohen and Brawer, 1989). Others stress the responsibility of teachers and assert that student learning is dependent on what takes place in the classroom; they contend that the time has come to speak and write boldly about what teachers can do to cause learning (Cross, 1989; Roueche and Baker, 1987).

The processes and products involved in the teaching-learning relationship deserve critical attention. We must pay heed to the signs that point to the dynamics of interrelationships in institutional settings—relationships of the institution and the community, the CEOs and faculty and students, the teachers and students. In fact,

3

we are aware specifically of a growing need to examine the mutuality
of the student-teacher relationship rather than continuing to treat
the student and teacher as independent and separate entities. We
must begin to ask questions concerning students' effects on teachers
and that of teachers on students. The following questions point to
the importance of shared relationships between teacher and student:

- To what extent do students shape classroom and teacher
  behavior, and to what extent do teachers shape classroom
  and student behavior?
- To what extent does teacher effectiveness (exemplary
  behaviors in the classroom) motivate, influence, and
  inspire students to pursue something beyond what is
  traditionally expected?
- Can teachers demonstrate flexibility and change in teaching environments that are atypical or exceptional; i.e., can
  teachers become situational leaders?
- How can we measure the role of the teacher as the leader
  in the classroom?
- Can teachers deal effectively and creatively with the ever-
  growing diversity and complexity of the contemporary
  and future classrooms?

This study attempts to answer these questions in the context
of examining the teacher as leader and by developing teaching-as-
leading styles that are situational and contingent on student readiness
and performance in the classroom.

IDENTIFYING EXCEPTIONAL PERFORMANCE:
THE TEACHER AS LEADER

The questions we raise may find answers by identifying
those teachers who by their reputations and recognition are
exceptional performers—by examining their competencies and
behaviors and by finding out what their students and administrators
have to say about them. Analyzing what is specific about teacher
behaviors and developing profiles for others to emulate and employ

underscores the contention that "in order to understand the best, we must study what the best do" (Peters and Waterman, 1982). What seems to be central to this process of examination are the concepts of influence and motivation, but only when these concepts are understood as part of dynamic teacher-student relationships. Elements that are essential to exceptional teaching and to motivated learning may be revealed by examining teacher-as-leader and student-as-follower relationships.

Research into the nature of this reciprocal relationship can lead to greater understanding of the explicit roles played by teacher and student who must work together to achieve mutual benefit. The purpose of our research is to examine the teacher-student relationship in order to define those competencies and behaviors that exceptional teachers employ to influence student values, attitudes, and behaviors and to measure their effect on their students. Our intent has been to discover the role of the teacher as leader and the student as follower as they interact to accomplish the dual goals of teaching and learning. By drawing on research that has focused on the practices of exemplary leaders—their vision and successes—and by choosing to look at the classroom experience as an extension of that concept, we are attempting to infuse new excitement and energy into the teaching-learning relationship.

To accomplish this goal, we examined relevant studies on teaching and learning and their interactive properties. In addition, we reviewed various theories of influence and motivation as they affect the ways in which successful teaching and learning are accomplished. We carefully examined the concept of leadership and its application to teaching and learning. In short, we have attempted to present these findings in such a way as to help the reader grasp the underlying structure of our overarching theme: that the teacher is clearly in the business of motivating students; that influence is an important tool of motivation; and that student readiness is the all-important contingency that must define the teacher's style of teaching. In the support of this unique presentation, we paraphrase an old adage: the key to being an effective teacher is leadership. Moreover, we are intrinsically curious about the dynamic process that occurs between teacher and student that results in successful behavior for both participants in the learning process. In Figure 1.1, we demonstrate motivational and performance relationships between the teacher and student:

Figure 1.1 **Teacher-Student Motivation and Performance**

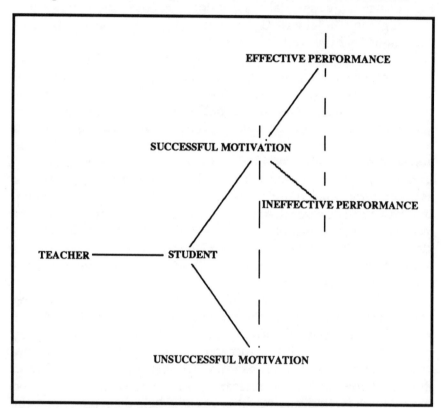

In this simple diagram, we are aware of the two outcomes of intended leadership: the leader in the role of the classroom teacher may direct the goal of the student, but the result of the teacher's behavior on the student may be either successful or unsuccessful. Teachers' performances in the teaching and learning situation are somewhat risky because students may not be motivated; even when students are motivated, their performance may still be ineffective. Hersey (1984) would suggest that long-term effectiveness is different from mere success; he would contend that success has to do with how well the job gets done (the percentage of students earning passing grades) and that effectiveness has to do with students' attitudes about performing their work (the independence and initiative students demonstrate about their work). For long-term effectiveness, teachers need to develop skills in dealing with their students by understanding their behavior, by understanding the dynamics of change on existing situations, and by accepting responsibility for influencing the behavior of students in accomplishing tasks and reaching goals.

We are evaluating teachers by considering their influence on students. Not only do teachers need to teach the curriculum, but they also need to build continuing cooperation among their students. We are interested in the teacher's responsibility for successful student behavior, and we are also concerned about the long-term effectiveness of student behavior. In the environment of the community college and considering the role of the teacher as leader, we are seeking to understand successful and effective behavior on the part of the teacher. And as history has demonstrated, the teacher is the crucial and pivotal reference in the classroom and learning experience. The teacher has been called the role modeler, the mentor, the purveyor of knowledge, and the one who takes students to the precipice of their own understanding—we choose another term for the teacher in his or her relationship to the student: it is the concept of the teacher as leader (Bass, 1985; Bennis and Nanus, 1985; Burns, 1978).

If, in fact, teachers are responsible for influencing the attitudes, values, beliefs, and behaviors of their students, and if they do so in such a fashion that learning indeed occurs, we contend that leading is taking place. We are convinced that it is vital that community college teachers be thought of as classroom leaders and that their selection, development, evaluation, and reward should proceed from this notion.

FOCUSING ON THE CONNECTION BETWEEN TEACHING AND LEARNING

When we began our study of the teacher as leader, we decided to examine the behavior of exceptional faculty who could be identified because they had won awards for exemplary teaching practices. We reasoned that the reputation for good teaching, whether demonstrated by a college, community, state, or national award, was an acceptable way to examine the behaviors and competencies of teachers in community colleges. Examining the competencies of instructors was only a part of our objective; we also wanted to look at the relationships among self-reported instructor behavior, nominations by college presidents or CEOs, and evaluations of instructor performance by students. One crucial factor that heightened our emphases on teaching and learning was the nature of the community college adult learner. Adult learners may be defined, according to Houle (1984), in the following categories: goal-oriented learners, who use learning to achieve specific objectives and select the institution or method that will best help them accomplish their purpose; activity-oriented learners, who participate in learning primarily for the sake of the activity itself; and learning-oriented learners, who pursue learning for its own sake and seem to possess a fundamental desire to know and grow through the learning process.

Cross (1981) contributes to our view of the adult learner; she finds that adult learners have more than one reason for engaging in learning, that they are motivated by the desire to apply knowledge or skills, that they develop individual patterns of learning, and that they enjoy learning and continue to engage in the process because of the pleasure they derive from it. Experiential learning theory, developed by Kolb (1984), looks at previous learning theories—including those of Lewin, Piaget, and Jung—to expand upon research concerning adult learners. Kolb's learning style inventory and concept of adult learning as "experiential learning" have made a significant impact on our understanding of learning and development in higher education. His ideas are more completely discussed in Chapter 7. For now, we seek conceptual clarity on the ideas of teaching and learning.

As in most studies of this type, we needed to understand the concepts of teaching and learning independently at first, acknowledging that there may not be a cause and effect relationship. According to Fenstermacher (1986), the perceived tight connection between teaching and learning has its origins in our misunderstanding of the use of the terms as a part of the fabric of our language. To illustrate, he described the relationship between the terms "racing" and "winning." The meaning of racing is, in many ways, dependent upon the meaning of winning; but the two terms do not have a causal link—i.e., one does not cause the other. Although the concept of racing would be meaningless in the absence of any concept of winning, one can race without winning. There is, then, a semantic relationship between the terms racing and winning such that the meaning of racing is dependent on the existence of winning. This is the relationship Fenstermacher calls ontological dependence.

If we employ this analogy to explain the complex relationship between teaching and learning, we can conclude that the meaning of teaching is dependent upon the existence of learning. Just because learning so often occurs after teaching is not sufficient reason to conclude that teaching, and only teaching, causes learning. Perhaps what is so confusing about the relationship between teaching and learning is researchers' emphases on the idea that variations in teaching yield variations in learning (Cross, 1971, 1976, 1981; Dressel, 1982; Hunter, 1982; McClelland, 1972). In these studies, we observe both conceptual and empirical relationships between teaching and learning, and we note that when teachers vary their teaching activity, there is an accompanying variance in what learners acquire. We must ask the question, therefore: Does this relationship mean that teaching causes learning? We think not.

If we examine the ways in which teaching and learning differ, we may begin to reveal the dependence of the concepts, while at the same time laying to rest the idea of causal linkage. For example, learning can occur when one is alone, perhaps when one is engaged in perceiving, analyzing, or problem-solving; teaching, on the other hand, most often occurs in the presence of at least one other person. Learning involves acquiring something; teaching implies giving something. According to Fenstermacher (1986), "no matter how we try to analyze the relationship, there is no parallel structure for doing so." The relationships between teaching and learning are probably best explained as the teacher's ability to improve, motivate, and influence a student's abilities and capacities to be a student. Walberg (1986) and Weinstein (1982) suggest that the teacher may have been more influential in improving the student's ability to play the role of student rather than specifically causing learning to occur. Along these same lines, it may be argued that:

> The concept of 'studenting' ... is far and away the more parallel concept to that of teaching. Without students, we would not have a concept of teaching; without teachers, we would not have the concept of students. Here is a balanced ontological dependent pair—coherently parallel to 'looking' and 'finding,' 'racing' and 'winning.' A central task of teaching is to enable the student to perform the tasks of learning (Fenstermacher, 1986, p. 39).

Thus, in their parallel, dependent roles, teachers explain, describe, define, refer, correct, influence, and support, while students recite, practice, seek assistance, review, check, research, and develop material. In this view, the key teaching task is to support and improve the learner's desire to "student." According to Weinstein and Mayer (1986), whether and how much the learner "learns" from being a student is largely a function of how the learner learns. We erroneously assume that the task of teaching is to produce achieved learning, rather than to enable the student to perform the task of learning (Fenstermacher, 1986; Weinstein and Mayer, 1986). The research on teaching and learning has usually focused on the idea of the production of learning. This study centers on the teacher's role in enabling the student to learn.

The central goal, or task, of teaching is to teach the learner how to learn. Rather than simply conveying or imparting content to the student, the role of the teacher is to instruct the learner in the skills necessary to acquire the content. In this view, teacher goals include instructing the learner on the procedures and demands of the studenting role, selecting curriculum, designing materials appropriate for the level of the learner, maximizing learner access and opportunities to these materials, monitoring student progress, and serving as a primary source of knowledge and skill (Biddle and Anderson, 1986; Walberg, 1986). And, in our view, the teacher's leadership ability—which adds motivational, intellectual, and interpersonal dimensions to their teaching goals—guide the teacher toward his or her central role of teaching the learner how to learn.

What is unique about this view of teaching is the shift in emphasis from demonstrated acquisition of content by the student to the teacher's provision of activities that properly develop the student. We seek to shift attention away from the view of teaching that sees learning as merely the acquisition of knowledge, and to the idea of learning as the use of knowledge with teacher as enabler. Thus, while the teacher does not bear responsibility for the achievement of learning, he or she can be held accountable for the orchestration of activities necessary to master the tasks assigned. In other words, to the extent that the learner is uncertain of the way to use or apply his/her knowledge, the teacher must shoulder the blame. If the learner lacks the "studenting" skills necessary for performance, or if the teacher fails to motivate the student to mastery, the teacher must accept a share of responsibility for student failure. When this failure occurs, we argue that the teacher, whom we place in a role of motivator and influencer, has not provided effective leadership in the classroom.

Thus, we are arguing that while learning is dependent on the mastery and use of cognitive skills, we see the role of the teacher as a vital one in influencing the values and attitudes of the student. We focus attention on the role of the teacher as a motivator and influencer, a leader in the classroom who engages and arouses students' needs, who clarifies paths and expectations, who reduces barriers to success, and who increases pay-offs and satisfaction. We are, therefore, defining teaching as a dynamic and interpersonal relationship in which knowledge and skills are conveyed through mutually held goals and are delivered through the processes of motivation and influence.

The teacher does not convey or impart content. Rather, the teacher instructs, motivates, influences, and enables the student to acquire content from the teacher, the text, or any other source; and as students become skilled at acquiring content, they learn. The teacher as leader is held accountable for the activities that are consistent with being a student. As with any leadership position, the teacher as leader has an obligation to the follower; and the student, as the follower, has an obligation to the teacher.

MOTIVATING THE LEARNER

Although teaching and learning may differ in some important ways, teachers can and do motivate learners to learn. In turn, some evidence exists that learners also motivate teachers to teach (Brophy and Good, 1986; Wittrock, 1986). Naylor, Pritchard, and Ilgen (1981) describe motivation as an allocative process in which an individual distributes the personal resources of time and energy to acts in order to maximize their effect. These "acts" are behaviors characterized by direction and degree of commitment that, in the teaching and learning context, refer to the time and effort that teachers and learners are willing to devote to the learning task. In other words, learning opportunities are maximized when both the teacher and the learner allocate sufficient time and energy to the process of learning and the instructor seeks ways to move the learner along the path toward his or her goals. Vroom (1964) suggests that motivation can best be understood in its relation to performance. Performance is expressed as a function of ability and motivation. Motivation, when defined as a predisposition to act in a specific goal-directed manner, is an extremely powerful concept, used to explain what takes place in the teaching and learning context. The concept also explains why it is important for teachers and learners to be goal-directed in their behavior.

MOTIVATIONAL VARIABLES THAT INFLUENCE LEARNING

While empirical studies examine motivation from multiple perspectives, the conceptual framework suggested by Porter and Lawler (1968) integrates these perspectives. It brings together the content theories of Herzberg (1968), Maslow (1954), and McClelland (1978), which focus on what motivates people to perform, and the process theories of expectancy, equity, and attribution, which explain reward control behaviors (House and Mitchell, 1974; Vroom, 1964).

With regard to teaching and learning, Porter and Lawler (1968) argue that student and faculty satisfaction is an effect rather than a cause of performance. In other words, the ability to perform leads to satisfaction. Different performance determines different rewards, which in turn produce variations in teacher/learner satisfaction. This model, which is described below and reproduced in Figure 1.2, can help us better comprehend the relationships between motivation, performance, and satisfaction. An explanation of each of the nine features of the model is discussed and related to examples of teacher behavior, drawn from the 869 award-winning instructors and their more than 3,000 students who participated in our study.

Figure 1.2 **The Porter and Lawler Model Relating to Teaching and Learning**

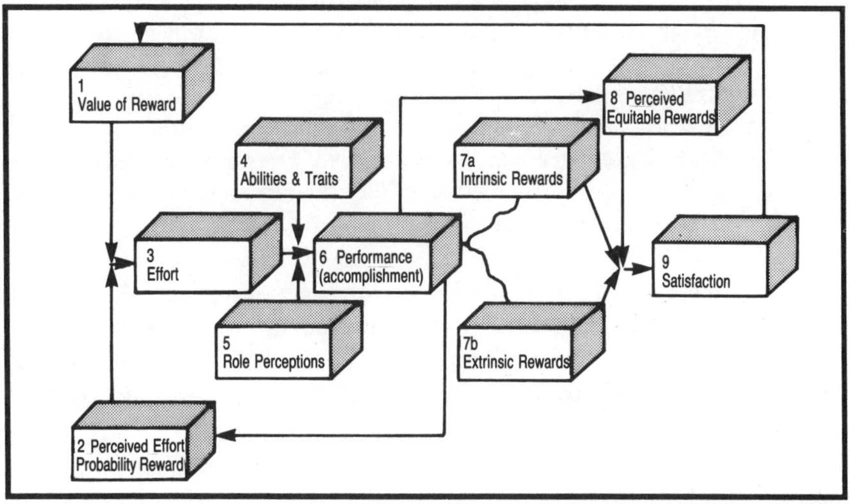

Reproduced by permission,
Porter and Lawler, 1968

Value of reward: Students and teachers desire various rewards from the teaching and learning process, assigning them a kind of valence measure that varies with the individual and the situation. For example, a student might want the learning process to lead to a course grade, a degree, or a job, while a teacher might seek job security, recognition, advancement, or evidence of achievement. For example, the following student speaks of the motivation of her instructor, Janice Udrys (Schoolcraft College, Livonia, Michigan), who has inspired her to want to be a math instructor.

> *From the first day of class my instructor gave me the motivation to become a good math student. My expectations have been met, and I have decided to go as far as possible in mathematics. I have become aware of the growing need for mathematics instructors; and because of my class experiences, I have decided to make the study of advanced mathematics my own goal.*

Peter Adams's (Essex Community College, Baltimore County, Maryland) motivational ability is illustrated in his ability to act as a coach in the classroom. He states:

> *I begin to feel like a coach, helping them to write better, instead of a judge, continually pointing out their shortcomings; and they begin to feel a power over their writing that most of them have never before experienced. They come to me having been trained to see revisions as punishment, something they have to do if they write a really bad paper; after a semester in my 'revision workshop,' they have a new vision of revision: they see it as a powerful tool they can use to improve their writing.*

Perceived effort/reward relationship: This variable in the motivation process refers to teacher and learner expectations that a given amount of reward depends upon a given amount of effort. For example, if students are placed in a class that demands a high level of ability, and students perceive their ability to be less than adequate, they would envision a low effort-to-reward correlation. In the example that follows, Janice Udrys talks about a student who had a low effort-to-reward probability.

> *I have most success in teaching nontraditional students; i.e., the 'older' students who have had some time between high school and their return to education. However, I was very unsuccessful with one particular lady ... it became evident to me that the problem was not comprehending mathematical concepts but a psychological attitude that it's too hard and she won't get it, no matter what.*

Effort: The amount of energy an individual exerts to achieve a specific outcome is also important in the complex motivation model. For example, student effort might be the amount of energy expended to prepare for a test, while teacher effort could refer to energy spent preparing a lesson. If either effort led to success, the individual would most likely associate effort with performance, often a faulty assumption. On the other hand, if the effort did not lead to success, the performer might erroneously assume that failure implies that not enough energy was expended, rather than looking at other intervening variables, such as ability. Generally, the amount of energy expended depends on interaction between the value of the reward and the perceived effort-to-reward probability. It is important to remember that effort refers to the energy expended to accomplish a task, not to an analysis of success or failure. The following remarks demonstrate Peter Adams's awareness of the differences between his enthusiasm and the students' readiness for learning:

> The most unsuccessful teaching experiences often occur when I am most well-prepared: I come into class with too much to say and my ideas too fixed....I realize that I have no idea what my students are thinking or even if they are thinking. I 'deaden' them. They are not about to venture on stage to follow my 'act.' The problem was the way I approached a class I was well-prepared for. I was so excited about what I knew, I felt I had to beat the class over the head with it. What I need to learn to do is to hold back on my 'stuff,' however wonderful I think it is, so that it doesn't overpower the students.

Abilities and traits: According to the model, effort does not lead directly to performance but is mediated by individual abilities, aptitudes, and role perceptions. Intellectual ability is clearly central to teaching and learning. Intelligence, defined as a complex of cognitive skills and problem-solving abilities important to learning and transfer, is education's most important product as well as its most important raw material (Corno and Snow, 1986). Traits or distinctive qualities, like appearance, personality, and intelligence, have been the subject of extensive behavioral research (Yukl, 1989) and are more recently being developed into competencies (Klemp, 1977). The Porter and Lawler (1968) model considers them relatively independent of the situation but interacting with it. Students are often uncertain and unmotivated to succeed even though they show up for college; often it is a critical teacher like Jack Sterret (Brunswick College, Brunswick, Georgia) who points the way:

> *I told her college was the only way out she had—she needed to succeed at something at this point in her life. The next test she did better: I was determined she would make it. If she missed class I called her at home. She passed the course and signed up for the next class I taught and did better. She plans to finish a four-year degree and open a dress shop in Brunswick. I learned again how much the work we do influences people's lives, hopefully in a positive manner. Sometimes one word from a teacher can make a student try harder, or cause a student to drop out of school.*

Role perceptions: These are the kinds of activities people believe are necessary to perform a task successfully. Mintzberg (1979) contends that teachers engage in two basic sets of activities: one, they categorize student needs into contingency teaching situations through intuitive diagnosis; and two, they apply, execute, and evaluate the process. In other words, teachers take on roles that are expected of them and assume that their behavior will be rewarded. Role perceptions of teachers are inherent in the way both teachers and administrators define the job of teaching and the kind of effort teachers believe is essential to effective performance. Benjamin Streets (Blue Ridge Technical College, Flat Rock, North Carolina) talks about his high, but incrementally earned, expectations and his students' reactions to those expectations:

> *I feel that through my enthusiasm and excitement about learning, my students are motivated to learn and develop more of their potential. They know that I care about each of them as individuals and I demand a lot of them. I believe that if your demands are high, yet reasonable, you get a lot back. One of my students last year said, 'This isn't Harvard, you know!' I took that statement as a real compliment. I believe in lots of praise and encouraging words. They are freely given when earned. Finally, I believe that success is a matter of degrees, but it is success, nonetheless.*

Performance: The interaction of the value of rewards and the expected effort-to-reward relationship creates expectations around performance. This performance depends not only on the amount of effort exerted, but also on abilities and role perceptions. In other words, although teachers and students may exert considerable effort, if ability is lacking or the path to successful teaching or learning is unclear, performance may fall short of expectations. Rewards for achievement and performance are demonstrated by Richard Lyons (Jefferson Community College, Louisville, Kentucky) when he talks about his relationships with his students:

> *Being honest and sincere with my students is important. I try to build mutual trust and to create in students a feeling that I will not let them down. I do see myself as an enabler. Sometimes students tell me they did not think they could do as well as they did in my class. When they found out they could learn and learn well, they were encouraged. They felt rewarded for achievement. Their reward comes in enhanced self-esteem when work done produces a positive outcome, an achievement. I do not give up on them until after long trials at different methods; then we meet together and decide on alternative goals...students must learn that one failure is not a debilitating experience in life and that having alternatives turns failures into successes.*

Rewards: Porter and Lawler define rewards as those things people desire. They may be either extrinsic (administered by others) or intrinsic (administered by the individual). Extrinsic organizational rewards for teachers include climate, salary, benefits, status, and job security, while for students they may include classroom climate, grades, and supportive teaching. Intrinsic rewards for both teachers and students, on the other hand, generally result from achievement, self-recognition, responsibility, personal growth, and even the teaching and learning process itself. While Herzberg (1976) suggests that intrinsic rewards are the real motivators, Porter and Lawler consider both types important. Figure 1.2 illustrates that research shows intrinsic rewards to be more likely to produce higher teaching and learning satisfaction. A student talks about her satisfaction and encouragement, even after her own retirement and "advanced age":

> *After a career as a teacher and then three years of semi-retirement, I felt the need to find a productive outlet for my energy and*

interests. Other cultures and world geography have always fascinated me, so I called the community college and spoke with the travel and tourism instructor, Ben Streets. He wisely suggested that we meet. Ben's intelligence, enthusiasm, and relaxed manner convinced me that I should become involved in the program. Three months later my interest and joy in learning had increased, and my appreciation for Ben as a teacher and human being had soared. However, I became concerned about the feasibility of class at my age. Ben immediately turned to me, and with a sincere and convincing manner, allayed my concerns. Ben's ideas were certainly encouraging, but what really impressed me was his sensitivity and the vitality of his response. I was already convinced of his expertise as a teacher. In addition, I felt privileged to witness Ben's dedication to motivating the young adults in the program in their difficult task of learning career skills while coping with jobs, personal stresses, and other demands.

Mary Jean Fletcher (Jefferson Community College, Louisville, Kentucky) offered us insights into her view of the intrinsic rewards of teachers, as they relate to their students:

I realize that a teacher never can tell where her influence stops. Teaching is effective only when learning takes place. I must place the responsibility of thinking on the students. I must create a relaxed and comfortable atmosphere which is conductive to learning. I must instill within students a positive attitude and confidence. I must emphasize accomplishments rather than failures. I must exercise patience with all students....My approach to teaching is to get the students involved. My students are not only able to solve math problems, but should be capable of making their own decisions in solving other problems which they encounter in everyday life.

Perceived equitable reward: This refers to the amount of reward that teachers and learners believe they should receive as a result of a given level of performance. Individuals have an intuitive notion about how much reward should be forthcoming for successful performance. Learners assign the greatest value to grades, recognition, and the development of job-related skills in the short term, and education-related rewards, like a degree or diploma, in the long term (Brown, 1987). Notions about rewards are based on perceptions of their relations to expectations, task demands, and individual contribution. Generally, ideas about perceived equitable reward reflect what teachers and learners believe should be granted for high performance on a particular job or task. A student in Mary Jean Fletcher's class reflects this idea:

> *The teacher and learning process in Ms. Fletcher's class has been an inspiration and a great asset to me. It also has been an enjoyable and interesting experience in learning. I will always value and treasure every moment of knowledge I gained in hopes of successfully obtaining my goals. I am sincerely appreciative and thankful for having the opportunity of knowing and experiencing the teaching of this fine instructor. She has been dedicated, motivating, understanding, and most of all patient in her efforts. She continues to advocate the luxury and importance of an education. She provides assurance and positive attitude to her students, which creates an eagerness and desire from the students. Ms. Fletcher has a unique talent for teaching, and because of that it has helped me to build confidence and self-esteem and has given me much motivation in wanting to advance further in my efforts of pursuing a degree. This good, old-fashioned teaching has inspired a lot of students, and hopefully will continue for more to come. Ms. Fletcher is a hard-working dedicated teacher who sincerely shows concern and happiness for and to her students. If she could be spread over the nation in all schools and classrooms, then students would become more eager and motivated to learning and staying in school. This society today needs a lot more teachers like her to bring about a positive change among students with low self-esteem and motivation.*

Satisfaction: This concept refers to an attitude or an individual's internal state. To the degree that an individual's sense of perceived equitable rewards exceeds actual rewards, a person will be dissatisfied. For example, if a teacher awards grades that are unrelated to actual student achievement, learner dissatisfaction and reduced motivation are likely to follow. Or, if faculty were rewarded commensurate with performance, the satisfaction of high performers would likely increase. Brenda Moore (Wilkes Community College, Wilkesboro, North Carolina) knows about satisfaction as an essential element of her teaching style. She spoke of her student:

> As I stopped to help Sandy, I put my arm respectfully and lovingly around her shoulder and leaned down to help her. That day she stayed after class to tell me with tears in her eyes, 'after being in school 13 years, you are the first teacher who has ever touched me.' She needed a 'hands-on' approach to demonstrate my caring—in the long run this proved to be a marvelous motivator.

SUMMARY

If the focus of the community college is on teaching, then teaching is an issue and an area in need of examination and understanding. Since it is virtually impossible to discuss teaching without its concomitant relationships to learning and to the student, we have examined those relationships. We attempted to identify the dynamics of the interrelationships between teaching and learning, first by examining the concept of leadership as it applies to teaching, and then by a more deliberate discussion and definition of the concept of learning. We hold that teachers are accountable to students' learning and have an obligation to guide learners toward mutually held goals that develop and instruct the student. We believe that the teacher influences and motivates the student to learn how to learn.

The Porter and Lawler model of motivation is important to this study of teachers as leaders because the model focuses on what motivates teachers to teach and, perhaps more importantly, what motivates students to learn. The theories of Maslow, Herzberg, and McClelland help us understand this interactive process by identifying the different rewards that both teachers and learners seek. In addition, this dynamic model of motivation helps us understand how rewards control behavior. This aspect of motivation becomes extremely important when we attempt to link student and teacher behavior to the path-goal theory of leadership. We may review the process by which student motivation occurs. The necessary motivation to learn occurs when students' behavior reflects the expectation that some expended effort on their part (stemming from their abilities, their performance, and their "studenting") will result in a reward or rewards.

Perceptions of equity or inequity interact with the reward actually received to determine the student's level of satisfaction, which in turn provides the motivation to engage in subsequent behavior. Effort may not automatically or easily convert to successful performance. The student's pre-learning, readiness to learn, aptitudes, and role perceptions interact to send the student a message that results in motivation that leads to accomplishment. We are reminded that a student must possess a minimum level of ability and an appropriate understanding of performance in order to succeed. In most cases, performance is determined when a grade is awarded by the teacher. If students receive grades they do not expect or deserve, and do not receive grades they expect or deserve, motivation in subsequent learning situations will surely decline. The basic principle of motivation in teaching and learning can be expressed by the following formula: student and faculty performance is a function of the collective ability of both parties, multiplied by the strength of shared motivation. According to this principle, no teaching or learning task can be performed successfully unless the student or teacher has the necessary ability (e.g., intelligence, verbal or spatial skills, dexterity, and understanding) to do so.

In the next chapter we turn to the concepts of leadership and influence to further examine the dynamic factors of the teaching and learning relationship.

Chapter 2

The Teacher as Leader

> *Education is not merely the shaping of values,*
> *the imparting of facts or the teaching of skills;*
> *it is the total teaching and learning process*
> *operating in the schools, conducted by both*
> *teachers and learners, engaging the total*
> *environment, and involving influence over*
> *persons' selves and their opportunities and*
> *destinies, not simply their minds.*
>
> James MacGregor Burns

2

Do we know ourselves? Do we believe in the value of education? Do we understand the learning process? Are we comfortable being educators? Do we think highly of our role in society? If we answer 'no' to these questions, we will not likely motivate students to continue the lifelong learning process.

Boyd Smith
Newfoundland and Labrador
Institute of Fisheries and
Marine Technology
St. Johns, Newfoundland, Canada

My goals, for every student I teach, are to understand human needs, to listen to others, and to respond in a manner that gives people information, compassion, and direction when it is needed. In order for me to teach those goals, I need to understand myself. To 'do' or accomplish those goals, students should come to understand themselves.

Robin Woods
Johnson County
Community College
Overland Park, Kansas

*M*otivation is a critical process that, when successfully used by teachers and students, allows for a broadening of their skills and a deepening of their commitments to goals. Both partners in the teaching and learning process must be motivated to achieve at high levels; that is, they must be predisposed to act in a specific, goal-directed manner. Motivation is directly related to performance, and influence is a precursor of motivation. Influence accounts for increased effort, when the person influenced perceives that such effort will lead to rewards and these rewards are directly related to effort. In this way, teachers influence learners and vice versa.

THE NATURE OF THE LEADERSHIP PROCESS

Leaders, in the popular sense, are people who draw other people to them. They are people whom others want to follow and who command the trust and loyalty of others. Their tasks, their goals, and their teaching are dependent on their perception of their influence within the classroom and among their students. Teachers plan and organize instruction, controlling what, how, and when something is taught—they are hired to provide a service and are generally given the authority, responsibility, and accountability to provide information, to increase skills, and to influence students to learn.

Stogdill (1974) set the stage for defining leadership as the process of influencing the activities of an organized group toward goal achievement and goal attainment. We see the teacher in the role of providing leadership to students, who are then influenced to learn to learn and to consider learning as a lifelong process. In our study, we have defined leadership in teaching as the process of influencing groups of students to achieve learning.

This definition implies two important concepts. First, leadership in teaching is a relationship between two or more people, in which influence and power are unevenly distributed; instructors, by the nature of their role, have been given authority to exert influence on learners. Second, such leadership carries with it an obligation to the followers; students must consent to being influenced in an environment that is not threatening to them. In accepting the teacher as leader, students relinquish some of their freedom to make decisions on how or if they will achieve their goals. Often students fall short of success because they find it hard to commit to this relationship. Conversely, if teachers do not see this decision-making role as necessary to effective teaching, both leaders and followers will suffer. We are interested in the concept of leadership as influence and the interrelationships between the leader and the follower. Leadership in teaching is clearly linked to effective student performance, and the literature reveals widely differing concepts of leadership that have consequences for how the variable is operationalized in the teaching and learning process. We will review some of the ideas that are particularly relevant to our study.

THEORETICAL APPROACHES TO LEADERSHIP

Although leadership has been extensively studied from numerous theoretical perspectives, the vast majority of these studies have examined effectiveness (Yukl, 1989). In other words, how effective is the leader in his or her role, and more importantly, how do we measure that effectiveness? In our study, we define effectiveness in terms of how well the teacher is able to influence students toward accomplishing shared goals. We have found that students allude to this issue of effectiveness by reporting that certain teachers have played a major role in changing their lives. A student of Ann Rose, Miami-Dade Community College, Miami, Florida, states:

> To say that Ms. Rose changed my life is to say it all. . . one day
> I believed nothing was more important than my ability to provide
> the next meal for my children and myself (I am a single mother),
> and then, on another day, I began to see value in what I was doing
> for myself and for my future. I realized that Ms. Rose never saw
> me just as a student, but as a fellow human being who brought
> something into her life just as she shared and passed on to me her
> gifts of knowledge and critical thinking. It really is too simple to
> say Ms. Rose is just a teacher; she is, rather, a 'woman for all
> seasons.'

Such leadership, as it applies to teaching and learning, has its origins in theory related to leader traits and behavior, factors within the situation, and forms of power and influence. Research on leader effectiveness in the twentieth century has generally proceeded from four distinct approaches: trait, behavior, situational, and power-influence approaches. Examining these distinct approaches to leadership will add to the understanding of the concept of the teacher as leader.

The Trait Approach. Studies of leadership traits and characteristics dominated research during the first half of the twentieth century (Yukl, 1989). Theories were based on the historical antecedent of the "great man" as "natural" leader and assumed leaders had traits that set them apart from others. Leadership was examined in the general context of participation and interaction within a group, and leader effectiveness was measured by accomplishment of a group task or goal. Had studies of teaching as leading been accomplished during this period, measures of student learning would have been the key research variable.

Stogdill's (1948) review of studies on individual characteristics, such as physical traits, personality, abilities, and aptitudes, led him to conclude that leaders differed from non-leaders to some extent. While traits such as intelligence, dependability, persistence, and initiative were found to be relevant to leader effectiveness, Stogdill noted that their relative importance varied depending on situational factors. Explanations based on trait theory were not generalizable to another population or to other leaders. Research of this type was found in studies that focused on measurable characteristics of teachers.

For example, in a study of student evaluation of instruction instruments dating between 1960 and the present time, researchers found that over one-half of the items in the student evaluation instruments measured teaching traits (Pate, 1990). Hillway (1958) reported that no comparisons could be made between earlier studies of successful community college teachers' characteristics (Koos, 1949) and his own study of teacher traits. In another study, Blocker, Plummer, and Richardson (1965) also used teacher traits to measure concurrence of teachers' role perceptions to the community college mission. Their findings were disappointing; teaching values and traits did not match with the values and mission statements of their community colleges. A serendipitous finding of their study was, of course, that teacher traits are not consistent indicators of leadership roles or effectiveness in job performance. This finding supports the criticism meted out to studies of leadership based exclusively on the trait approach.

Research about leadership traits reveals that no innate, genetically determined set of universal leadership characteristics either exists or can be determined in formulating a general basis for leadership theory (Stogdill, 1974; Yukl, 1989). Rather, research has noted that the traits that set leaders apart from followers vary from situation to situation (Cutherbertson, 1982). These ideas have led researchers to conclude that leadership should be conceived of as a set of observable behaviors, rather than a set of personal unobservable traits (Jago, 1982).

Don Bailey (Westark Community College, Fort Smith, Arkansas) speaks of both roles and traits as behaviors when he discusses his educational philosophy:

> *I am a motivator, a listener, a learning resource, a coach, a communicator, an overseer, and a human being. For each of my roles as a teacher, I am aware of students' needs, their competencies, their opportunities, and their individuality. I am also a human being who behaves toward students out of a sensitive and caring nature—I care who students are.*

The Behavior Approach. If trait research sought to identify who leaders are, then behavior research attempted to identify what they do. Early behavior research identified two distinct types of leader action: one aimed at accomplishing organizationally relevant tasks, and the other met the human needs of individuals. Although researchers labeled these behaviors in different ways, they could generally be classified into one of the two categories: organizational task or individual relationships (Blake and Mouton, 1964; Likert, 1967; Hersey and Blanchard, 1982). These concepts were present in early research on community college teachers. In these studies, the concept of organizational task invariably meant both curriculum and instruction aspects were present, and the concept of individual relationships focused almost exclusively on the developmental needs of students (Cohen, 1968; Cohen and Brawer, 1977; Cross, 1976; Hillway, 1958; Monroe, 1972; Roueche, 1972).

Likert (1967) saw the behaviors characterized by close supervision of students and specification of curriculum procedures as task-centered behaviors and those characterized by an emphasis on meeting the socio-emotional needs of students and sharing decision making as people-centered behaviors. He cautioned that although task-centered leadership behaviors resulted in higher production in the short run, they were also associated with greater attrition, absenteeism, and negative attitudes toward work and the organization. Likert argued that people-centered leader behavior seemed to be more effective in producing long-term success, although both types of behavior were necessary to achieve effectiveness. Steven Schada (Oakton Community College, Des Plaines, Illinois) spoke of his student-centered approach to teaching:

> The students are the reason I teach, why I often succeed at teaching, and why I totally enjoy teaching. I want to be the teacher who makes a positive difference in the lives of students. And as I continue to teach effectively, I will make a difference, and the rewards will be incalculable.

One of Sharon Whitehead's (Somerset Community College, Somerset, Kentucky) students also discusses what this student-centered strategy means to her:

> One night before an exam, I learned that I had lost track of my American Literature book. I tried to find a friend or classmate that might have a book I could use. I had no luck in finding such a person until I thought about calling Mrs. Whitehead. I called her and told her my situation, and she said she would run down to the college to get her book for me to use to study for the exam. I told her thanks, but that I wouldn't be home because I had to work. It made no difference to Mrs. Whitehead. She insisted that she bring the book to me at work. This event really inspired me. To think that a teacher cared so much as to bring me her own book to study because I had lost mine was uplifting. It changed the way I felt about teachers...they really do care.

Halpin (1955) and the Ohio State University studies also identified two key independent leadership factors that reflect the task and people dichotomy: initiating structure and consideration:

> In a teaching-learning context, initiating structure refers to the teacher's behavior in delineating the relationship between himself or herself and the students, and in

endeavoring to establish well-defined patterns of curriculum, patterns of communication, and ways causing student learning...consideration refers to teaching behaviors indicative of friendship, mutual trust, respect, and warmth in the relationship between the teacher and members of the group (p. 18).

Among the contributions of this research was the development of a leadership construct that depicted leader behaviors occurring along two distinct axes rather than a single continuum. This model consisted of four quadrants, each of which represented certain combinations of behaviors associated with either initiating structure or consideration. The measurement and categorization of leadership style was of particular importance here; a consistent pattern of behaviors was recognized. Halpin concluded that the successful leader is one who contributes to both goal achievement and group maintenance and makes extensive use of both types of behavior. This research orientation sought to identify a "best" leadership style. The Hersey-Blanchard life cycle theory, a key aspect of this study, is based on this model.

The Situational/Contingency Approach. Implicit in both the trait and behavior approaches was a belief that the mystery of leadership could be revealed by isolating certain personality characteristics or actions. However, as later research demonstrated, emphasis on traits and patterns of behavior was inadequate to explain or predict leader effectiveness, primarily because it excluded the importance of the situation on the behavior of leaders. The teaching and learning context seems especially suitable to the situational or contingency approach to the study of leadership. Tannenbaum and Schmidt (1958) explained that leadership behavior that is related to decision making often varies according to situational factors.

If we adapt their discussion to the teaching and learning context, we would suggest that teachers should behave in ways that make sense in any given situation. Three sets of forces (or expectancies) can be considered: those within the teacher, including personality, value system, confidence in others, leadership inclinations, and feelings of security in the face of uncertainty; those within students, such as needs for independence, readiness to accept responsibility for decisions, tolerance for ambiguity, identification with the course context and curriculum goals, knowledge and expertise to solve problems; and finally those within the general situation in which leadership will be exercised, including organizational climate and culture, the nature of the instructional program, and time constraints.

Ideas about the importance of adaptive leader behavior have been supported by many theories on the effect of situational variables on leader effectiveness. Two in particular have direct bearing on our study: the path-goal theory and the life cycle theory. Path-goal theory was developed by House and Mitchell (1974) and examines the effects of leader behavior on follower attitudes and expectations about job satisfaction, leader acceptance, and effort-performance-reward relationships. Effectiveness is determined by the extent to which leader behavior increases follower motivation to perform, satisfaction with the job, and acceptance of the leader.

Path-Goal Concept: Building on the basic two-factor distinctions of task- and relationship-oriented behavior suggested by the Ohio State studies, House and Mitchell (1974) identified four types of leadership behavior: directive, which provides high structure for task accomplishment; supportive, which emphasizes socio-emotional support for group needs; participative, which emphasizes high follower input into the decision making process; and achievement-oriented, which emphasizes high achievement and expectations for followers.

We note that our reseach concurs with these types of leadership behavior; and inasmuch as the path-goal leadership theory guided our study, our teaching-as-leading styles (discussed in Chapter 6) were somewhat patterned on House and Mitchell's (1974) behavior types. However, in addition to identifying four behavior types, House and Mitchell (1974) developed a theoretical framework for determining which type is likely to be effective under given conditions. The researchers also identified two types of contingency variables that influence leader effectiveness: characteristics of subordinates and environmental pressures with which followers must cope in order to accomplish their goals and achieve satisfaction.

The characteristics-of-subordinates variable focuses on the student's perception of the teacher's ability to meet the student's needs as a determinant for acceptance of teacher-as-leader behavior. House and Mitchell (1974) suggest that student characteristics are the primary determinant of perception and subsequent acceptance of teacher behavior. The second type of contingency variable is the environmental factor, which is beyond the control of the student but still impacts satisfaction or performance. Such factors include the nature of the task, the formal authority system of the organization, and the primary work group (House and Mitchell, 1974). The interaction of personal characteristics of students and environmental pressures produces the contingencies that moderate the effects of given teacher leadership styles—directive, supportive, achievement-oriented, and participative styles.

Directive leadership is most effective when there is a need to reduce role ambiguity for the follower, a process that increases follower satisfaction and acceptance of the leader. As the teacher clarifies role expectations, the effort-to-performance relationship is strengthened, and motivation to perform increases. Jerry Long (Wharton County Junior College, Wharton, Texas) was responsible for a demonstrable change in the life of one of his students, who said:

> *Mr. Long had more faith and understanding in my abilities than I did, and his ability to motivate me was demonstrated when I won first place in the Lincoln-Douglass debate at the regional speech tournament—once he made me aware of my role and talents, the rest was easy.*

Supportive teacher leader behavior, on the other hand, is likely to be effective when the task is frustrating, unpleasant, boring, or stressful, because such behavior would provide the student with a source of intrinsic satisfaction for compliance. Libby Holt (Florida Community College, Jacksonville, Florida) is a math teacher whose students think highly about her ability to take a "difficult and boring" course and make it understandable; her students said, "She made me choose math as my college major," and "She has inspired me to think about becoming a math teacher."

Achievement-oriented behavior is appropriate for increasing

the learner's motivation to perform when the learner is faced with an unstructured or ambiguous task. Mary Beth Monroe (Southwest Texas Junior College, Uvalde, Texas) says:

> *All the while I am teaching, I need to be training my students to think for themselves, to teach themselves, and to prepare themselves for meeting the unknown challenges of the world.*

Participative leadership is recommended when students have a high need for autonomy and achievement because of increased intrinsic rewards associated with meaningful involvement in decision making. Again, based on characteristics of learners, participative teaching can be the most effective way of reducing role ambiguity for the student. James Ford (Community College of Aurora, Aurora, Colorado) thinks of himself as an enabler; he says:

> *I bring expertise to the classroom, but so do my students. By creating an atmosphere of mutual learning, I believe that students discover their raw talent and potentiality for thinking, learning, and growing. They may come to be taught by an 'expert,' but, hopefully, they will go away with confidence in themselves as learners and, even, as teachers.*

The Life Cycle Theory: Another situational theory of leadership, developed by Hersey and Blanchard (1982), is referred to as the life cycle theory. Since this model focuses on the development of followers, it is most appropriate for the teaching and learning context. Essentially, the theory suggests that a relationship exists among task behavior, relationship behavior, and other situational variables that may be plotted curvilinearly on a graph to demonstrate four leading styles: telling, selling, participating, and delegating.

Built upon a framework that accepts task behavior and relationship behavior as explanations for leader behavior, the life cycle theory suggests that teacher effectiveness is further moderated by a critical situational variable—follower maturity. Guided by Hersey and Blanchard (1982), we contend that effective leadership will result from the interplay of three factors: (1) the amount of guidance and direction teachers give to the students; (2) the amount of socio-emotional support a teacher provides; and (3) the readiness or maturity level that students exhibit in performance of their tasks, functions, or activities. Hersey and Blanchard's use of task direction and socio-emotional support behaviors are essentially the same as those identified in the Ohio State studies, but maturity as a situational variable warrants further explanation. Maturity is defined within the constraints of the task to be performed; it involves a readiness factor in relationship to task performance; it is situation-specific. Hersey and Blanchard describe maturity of followers as "the ability and willingness to take responsibility for directing their own behavior ... considered only in relation to a specific task to be performed" (p. 151). Hersey and Blanchard also address the problem faced by teachers in community colleges where maturity or readiness to learn often varies significantly within a group of learners.

> In addition to assessing the level of maturity of individuals within a group, a leader must assess the maturity level of the group as a group, particularly if the group interacts frequently together in the same work area, as happens with students in the classroom. Thus, a teacher may find that a class as a group may be at one level of maturity in a particular area, but a student within that group may be at a different level. When the teacher is one-on-one with that student, he or she will probably need to behave very differently than when working with the class as a group. In reality, the teacher may find a number of students at various maturity levels (p. 151).

The teacher's diagnosis of the maturity level of students in a specific teaching situation may demonstrate that teacher behavior should vary depending upon what is required for successful group performance. Thus, a class of students characterized by a low maturity level is capable of less self-direction and requires that the teacher emphasize task behavior. As the group matures in its ability and willingness, however, teacher behavior should be adjusted appropriately. A group characterized by above-average maturity (i.e., having the ability and willingness to accomplish the task) requires little direction or socio-emotional support from the leader. As with the House and Mitchell concept of path-goal theory, the

Hersey and Blanchard concept of the life cycle model of leadership has import to the concept of teacher as leader supported by this study. In the following figure, the House and Mitchell, Hersey and Blanchard, and our own leadership styles are compared:

Figure 2.1: **Leadership Behaviors and Styles**

House & Mitchell	Hersey & Blanchard	Baker, Roueche & Gillett-Karam
Directive	Telling	Theorist
Supportive	Selling	Supporter
Participative	Participating	Influencer
Achievement	Delegating	Achiever

The life cycle model of leadership rejects the idea that there is one "best" way to lead, although it forcefully prescribes a particular leadership style for a given situation. It expects that teachers should be able to accurately assess their own behavior and the maturity of their learners relative to a specific task, so that they can adapt behavior accordingly.

As noted earlier, situational leadership theories seek to account for variables within a situation that impact and moderate leader effectiveness. Generally built on earlier research into the task or relationship orientation of leaders, these theories attempt to isolate key situational variables that bear upon leader behavior. Most focus on the student in the teacher-and-student relationship. By considering the importance of student acceptance of the teacher and by examining student needs, maturity, abilities, personality, and peer interactions, these theories have helped clarify the relational nature of leadership and the importance of leader behavior that adapts to needs of learners. Equally important is the examination of the situation in terms of its complex environment factors, including the nature of the task, the teacher's position power and authority, and the many diverse forces operating both inside and outside the classroom and the community college.

The Power and Influence Approach—Burns and Transformational Leadership. The concept of a power and influence approach to leadership theory is perhaps best explained in the ideas of James MacGregor Burns, whose 1978 book, *Leadership*, has become a focus of modern studies of leadership. Burns states:

> We recognize, I believe, that leadership is interpersonal, that leaders cannot be seen in isolation from followers, that the linkage between the two embraces the dynamics of wants and needs and other motivations, that leadership is largely a teaching process beginning with the parental nurturing of children, that creative leadership is closely related to conflict and crisis or at least to debate and dialogue, and that—above all—transforming leadership carries grave but not always recognized moral implications (p. 18).

Burns (1978) looks at leadership in terms of the mutual goals held by both the leader and the follower. He defines leadership as the tapping of existing and potential motive and power bases of followers by leaders for the purpose of achieving change. Burns believes that the leader-follower relationship is the interaction of individuals who function with the same purpose in mind and pursue common goals, but who operate with varying degrees of motivation and power. Leadership over human beings is exercised when persons with certain motives and purposes mobilize in competition or conflict with others, using institutional, political, psychological, and other resources so as to arouse, engage, and satisfy the motives of followers (p. 18).

Burns identifies two basic types of leadership: transactional leadership and transformational leadership. Transactional leadership is the routine exchange of one thing for another between leader and follower. For Burns this is exchange theory limited to short-lived relationships in which sellers and buyers cannot repeat the identical exchange; they are constantly moving on to new types and levels of transactional gratifications. Routine transactions, such as the relationship between giving a test and receiving a grade, or between making an assignment and having students carry it out, are examples of transactional leadership. Bass (1985) indicates that transactional leadership is based on contingent reinforcement between leader and follower of the need to attain a specific goal. Objectives are developed to reach the goal, and both parties understand and expect a reward for successful completion of the task or punishment for noncompletion. Transactional leadership is one of exchange, a positive or negative pay-off from the leader to the follower for a task completed or not. Once the exchange is complete, there is no further need to interact unless another process of contingent reward is introduced (pp. 11-13).

Transformational leadership is unique and has more distinguishable behaviors associated with its conceptualization. It builds on the human need for meaning, it creates institutional purpose, it involves vision and judgment, it involves values and the shaping of values in others, and it requires of the leader and the follower the ability to transcend their own limited views and perform beyond what is normally expected. Transformational leaders seek to arouse and satisfy higher needs in the follower, to engage the full person of the follower. These leaders attempt to elevate the follower from a lower to a higher level of need according to Maslow's (1954) hierarchy of needs. Burns (1978) and Bass (1985) indicate that Maslow's needs are overlapping and interdependent; each need does not have to be satisfied before moving to a higher level. Therefore, Burns examined patterns in the origins and socialization of leaders that helped to explain why they are great leaders. He looked to biology, psychology, and sociology to explain the forces that affect children's and adolescent's behaviors that later become the building blocks for leaders' actions. Then by adding the philosophical dimension to his other inquiry, Burns pointed out that "power is legitimate only when it releases human potential previously locked in ungratified needs and crushed expectations" (p. 18). Burns's transformational leader is a moral leader who cherishes values, ideas, and knowledge. He explains:

> Transformational leadership is the relationship of mutual stimulation between leader and follower which engenders conversion of followers into leaders and may convert leaders into moral agents. Moral leadership ties the leader

to the follower on the basis of mutual needs, aspirations, and values. It allows the follower to choose among leaders, and it ensures that leaders take responsibility for their commitments. Moral leadership emerges from and always returns to the fundamental wants and needs, aspirations, and values of the followers (p. 434).

The central process that involves the leader and the follower is one of conflict and choice among motives and values and the ability of the transforming leader to achieve change (dialectical change coming out of conflict and choice between follower and leader) in the direction of "higher" values. Finally, it is important to Burns that leadership can be taught. Burns says,

Ultimately education and leadership shade into each other to become almost inseparable, but only when both are defined as the reciprocal raising of levels of motivation rather than indoctrination or coercion can they be understood as a unit worthy of learning and sharing (p. 448).

In Figure 2.2, the essential elements of the leader and follower relationship are categorized by teacher attributes and student responses. A dynamic that involves continuous growth for both the follower and the leader is an essential feature of the model. Teacher attributes are those characteristics of moral leadership that arouse appropriate responses and actions among students. These responses ultimately transform students toward personal autonomy and independence in learning and teaching. The model incorporates ideas of the major thinkers in leadership theory and develops a conceptual structure for behavior and response between teacher and student.

Figure 2.2: **Transformational Leadership Model**

DYNAMICS OF CHANGE:	Encourages INTELLECTUAL STIMULATION
	Allows CONFLICT AND CHOICE MOTIVES AND VALUES
	Demands REVITALIZATION AND RENEWAL

TEACHER ATTRIBUTES	STUDENTS' RESPONSES
Creates Teaching-Learning Purpose, Mission & Culture	Understands Purpose, Mission & Culture
Arouses, Engages & Satisfies Needs	Brings Commitment to the Teacher
Has Vision & Sense of Future Direction	Identifies with Teacher's "Vision"
Inspires, Influences & Motivates	Gains Insights and Conceptual Clarity
Ties to Student by Mutual Needs, Aspirations & Goals	Shares Goals with Teacher
Values People over Things	Believes He/She Makes a Difference
Has High Tolerance for Change not Ambiguity	Has Choice to Follow Teacher
Demonstrates Sound Judgment, Values & Morality	Moves Toward "Higher" Values
Has Commitment to Intellectual & Personal Development	Is Empowered & Educated to Lead
Makes the Student the Leader	Converts to Become Leader/Teacher

Gillett-Karam, 1988

The transformational leader as college president was the subject of *Shared Vision: Transformational Leadership in American Community Colleges* (Roueche, Baker, and Rose, 1989). In that study, the attributes of presidential leadership were defined as vision, influence, people orientation, motivation, and values. We compared the findings of the theoretical framework from this study to the leadership behaviors exhibited by the award-winning instructors of our study; we found that where college presidents and CEOs score highest on the factors of vision and influence, college teachers and instructors score highest on the factors of motivation, influence, and people orientation. (These findings will be discussed in Chapter 3.)

CONCLUSION

The modern community college, like the contemporary corporate marketplace, responds to socio-economic-political challenges. Where the corporations must face rapid technological advances, stiff foreign competition, revolutions in management-labor relations, and changing consumer tastes, the community college must face unstable student enrollments, alarming attrition rates, shrinking economic resources, encroaching governmental controls, astounding levels of adult illiteracy, increasing average student ages, rising pressures placed on curricula by expanding and changing technologies, rapidly changing demographics, the challenges of student diversity, and an impending faculty shortage. These problems have forced the community college to re-examine its mission and direction for the future, and thus to ask the question: How can the community college meet the challenges of an environment that demands quality and excellence? Researchers (Bennis and Nanus, 1985; Kanter, 1983; Peters, 1987; Peters and Waterman, 1982) have led us to understand not only the importance of quality and service, flexibility and continuous innovation, and improvement of our institutions, but they have cautioned us that without capable leadership we will not survive these ever-present challenges of an expanding society.

We have been forced to examine and re-examine leadership in higher education. The Carnegie Foundation for the Advancement of Teaching (1980) saw presidential leadership as the central question facing higher education; and the Association of Governing Boards of Universities and Colleges Commission determined that colleges and universities are in desperate need of leadership (Kerr, 1984). Principal works by researchers of the community college (Fisher, 1984; Fisher, Tack, and Wheeler, 1988; Roueche, Baker, and Rose, 1989; and Vaughan, 1986) have reiterated this need for leadership.

Because the emphasis of leadership and followership is on collective purpose and change, the factors that are stressed are those that unite and differentiate leaders and followers. Leaders may modify their leadership in recognition of followers' preferences (a teacher in the classroom may find that a single teaching style is limiting), or in order to anticipate followers' responses (the flow of lecture-discussion might change direction often and quickly); or to harmonize the actions of both the leader and follower with common motives, values, and goals (the classroom climate should be conducive to this harmony). Najam Saeed (Somerset Community College, Somerset, Kentucky) talks about communication as a vital clue for common interests of the teacher and his or her students:

> *I try to remain aware always of the tendency to impose or force my students to live with 'my' standards. Rather I seek the*

> *students' levels and responses as an indicator of the proper level from which to proceed. There is a sense of communication which is ever-present in the classroom between me and my students: we respect our common rights to teach and learn, we examine difficulties, and we design a solution when necessary to overcome barriers.*

Leadership of this type occurs in the day-to-day pursuit of collective goals through the mutual tapping of leaders' and followers' motivational bases and in the achievement of needed change. We are assuming that the teaching and leading cycle is continuous and situational, and that exemplary teachers reach out to their students to profit from mutually shared goals. Teaching is what excellence is all about.

Bonnie Giraldi (Cecil Community College, North East, Maryland) talked about a first-semester student who wrote the following on an evaluation of her: "Mrs. Giraldi thinks I can do better work than I really can. I do it so she doesn't know that I'm not as good as she thinks I am." Several semesters later, the same student wrote, "I have excellent skills and know that I am well trained for the work force. I can't wait to prove myself." Giraldi continues: "By believing in my students, they come to believe in themselves. What better role can I have?"

Chapter 3

Teaching as Leading:
Toward an Integrated Research Design

The scholar who studies teaching
should view results in terms of relationships:
teaching as an influence on learning,
the meaning of teaching in the context of a curriculum,
and the role of the faculty member as teacher.

Robert Menges and
B. Claude Mathis, 1988

3

$\mathcal{F}$rom its inception, the community college has been known for its commitment to and fundamental belief in teaching. Two-year colleges point with pride to their reputations as "teaching institutions." Although there are limited data to support the fact that dedicated and resourceful teachers, instructors, and professors of the community college have much training in "how" to teach, good teaching is part and parcel of their attachment to the culture of the community college. Excellent teaching is probably more related to motivation and experience than to formal preparation in the teaching profession. Obviously, some of the dedication of teachers to this profession stems from the teachers' identity with the mission of the community college as a social institution dedicated to providing quality education on an egalitarian basis. Community colleges in the United States and their counterparts in Canada have offered continuing opportunities for higher education to a student population whose major characteristic is diversity. The community colleges have a commitment to diversity; their educational goals are linked to the democratic principles of allowing open access regardless of background, status, or handicap. This ideal represents the community college's greatest virtue, but it also carries with it great responsibilities and challenges.

While the message of the community college has been egalitarian, the reality of higher education thinking has always leaned toward an elite- or merit-oriented selection of students. We preach and promote "open-door" admissions and "access" to higher

45

education for everyone, but we have learned by hard experience that our open door is in fact a revolving door for many, and that access to opportunity is often access to failure (Roueche, Baker, and Brownell, 1971; Roueche and Baker, 1976, 1983, 1984). Although our critics are severe in their exposure of our problems, the community colleges retain that determined and energetic spirit of North Americans who excel at solving problems. We have had many examples of successful experiences and programs that have brought the community college closer and closer to its goals. We refuse to dilute our dream of what the community college "ought to be," and in that refusal our ambitions, insights, and visions drive us to achieve a better environment to meet our commitment to the goals of maximum human development for the people.

There is a culture that has grown up around the conceptualization and operationalization of the community college. That cultural identity separates the community college from the senior college and suggests that although its purposes and mission grow out of a need to educate all of the people, the community college as an institution represents a dynamism that is best understood by its adaptability and flexibility to uncover and meet the needs of its participants. If modern institutions, as the contemporary sages suggest, must thrive on chaos and paradox, it seems that the community colleges have a head start on many organizations. We have been existing on chaos and paradox for almost half a century. From that chaos, however, have come new opportunities and new challenges to the educational practices of our society. To a great extent those opportunities and challenges have been the "vision" that drives our leaders. In the community college, that leadership has come from legislative leaders, founding fathers, presidents and CEOs, and essentially from the teachers who have the day-to-day contact, confrontation, and involvement with students.

IDENTIFYING THE RESEARCH ISSUES

Identification and definition of competencies and behaviors associated with effective teaching are essential to the unique mission of the community college. No college can exist without students, and students would not be in college if they did not have some perception of the benefit of education. Colleges are being called upon to prepare students for immediate employment and to develop students' coping skills for survival in an increasingly complex world (Cohen and Brawer, 1989; Roueche and Snow, 1977). A critical challenge for higher education focuses on understanding the importance of not only what to teach but how to teach. As teachers, we must do more than examine content and curriculum, and we must do more than study student scores and placement potential. When we say we must make appropriate choices about how to teach, we must remember the community college ethos and culture; we must find revitalization and renewal in our focus on our students, in our ability to motivate them, and in our ability to "draw from" our students their own dedication and love for learning. The future demands this from us. And so say the researchers:

- If students of community colleges are often unmotivated (Roueche and Snow, 1977), then we
  need to examine how those who do motivate their
  students accomplish this critical goal (Roueche and
  Baker, 1987).
- If community college students are "nontraditional"
  students, we need to examine those programs which
  make them as successful as the traditional students in
  higher education (Cross, 1978).
- If the community college is focused on "empowering
  students" and ensuring the adult learner the "right
  to learn," then access must be deliverable (*Building
  Communities*,1988).

A major aspect of what takes place to distinguish between access and success, and access and failure, is the collective and individual efforts of community college faculty. To say that the teaching and learning dimension of community colleges is under-researched is to say that the universe in which we live is under-researched. This study represents one step in a journey toward a goal for major research efforts as a part of the agenda for community college research into the 1990s and beyond.

QUALITATIVE AND QUANTITATIVE RESEARCH
METHODOLOGIES: AN INTEGRATED APPROACH

Our research—while descriptive, predictive, and improvement-oriented—is primarily exploratory in nature; it is an effort to raise questions about the roles of teaching and learning that have not been previously asked, much less been answered, in the environment of the open-door college. These questions, as they relate to teaching and learning in the community college, do not, therefore, fit into well-recognized theories or constructs. Moreover, we have noted in our attempt to relate theoretical emphases to our study that the prevailing view of methodological research is one of the "shifting" paradigm. If one examines, for example, the body of organizational theory research, one finds that the rational, logical positivism model of the 1930s and 1940s has been replaced in the 1980s by a nonrational model. While organizational theory has evolved, educational theory has not: one research principle, or model, or paradigm in education, shared by and uniting all research, does not exist. Menges and Mathis (1988) speak to the problems encountered when attempting to discover unified research in higher education:

> Research in higher education seems fragmentary; the literature is often unwieldy; it needs middle-range theoretical constructs to unify themes emerging from the individual pieces. Many of these research reports, summaries of studies, commentaries, and personal opinions seem to be independent of scholarship in other areas. The study of higher education has not yet diversified organizationally in ways characteristic of more mature fields of study. More investigation is needed to find the best balance between effectiveness and efficiency in maintaining and improving quality in educational programs (p. 361).

Moreover, Menges and Mathis refer to the various resources and methods available to the educational researcher:

> Methods appropriate for investigating these issues

(teaching and learning, assumptions faculty make about processes of teaching and learning) are not the methods typically used by laboratory investigators. Methods must fit the natural environment of academic workplaces and study places. Research procedures must be sufficiently flexible to accommodate frames of reference possibly quite different from those initially held by researchers. Data should be collected from dialogue, since inquiry is itself an interactive teaching-learning encounter. Discussion of results from such research may well be more elaborative than reductive, and conclusions are likely to be more suggestive than definitive (p. 366).

We are proposing, therefore, that as educational researchers we are in the midst of a conceptual shift in research methodology, and that current research and researchers point to a view of the research that is integrative. This shift in research is noted by many and, in particular, by the U.S. Department of Education, which has announced a set of new research priorities for the nation's 19 educational research centers. Our own exploratory construct employed in this research uses both qualitative and quantitative forms of research. We see the benefits of using naturalistic or qualitative inquiry as an observational, interpretative methodology to describe the award-winning instructors who participated in this study; and we can also see the benefits of employing some quantitative, process/product-oriented research to provide content analysis of the large numbers of cases we studied. In the final analysis, however, what we have done is to quantify qualitative data. We did this by triangulating our research. A description of our research methodology follows.

QUALITATIVE RESEARCH

Employing qualitative methods in the research on teaching has been around for only a short period; usually this approach is thought of as participant observational research, and it is probably best known in the ethnographic studies of anthropologists who were interested in examinations of the *ethnoi*, or "others" (Wittrock, 1986). Interpretative research and its guiding theory developed out of interest in the lives and perspectives of people in society who had no previous voice. Pestalozzi is one of these heroes of research on teaching, whose innovations in pedagogy were directly related to a shift in the intelligentsia's view of the "other." In this case, Pestalozzi, in his concern for social reform, infused interest in and attention to the educability of the poor, or those children who were previously considered unteachable. Pestalozzi's achievement was monumental—he found that children could learn regardless of their social status or class; and "Gertrude," as the wise influencer, offered an intergenerational model for the exemplary classroom teacher (Wittrock, 1986).

But it was only after World War II that American researchers began to turn their attention to issues of education as they could be observed in practice (Erickson, 1986). Practitioners at Teachers College, Columbia University, were influenced by the work of anthropologist Margaret Mead and began to compile ethnographic research on medical students. Later, the Council of Anthropology and Education evolved out of the interest in research methods applied to the teaching framework. Another organization, the National Institute of Education (NIE), concentrated on the ethnographic study of education (Erickson, 1986). The research of the NIE is oriented to the common needs and demands that grow out of the public school tradition; it continues to be a higher education research arm that focuses attention on observational studies. The NIE report, *Involvement in Learning* (1984), confronts the issues of excellence in higher education and sees the importance of student-teacher dynamics.

Cazden (1986), who wrote of the historical consequence of the NIE, points out that the contemporary research methods on teaching are divided between the process-product tradition (the rational method) and the descriptive tradition (the qualitative method). Coding responses to behaviors may provide an example of the differences in the approaches. In the process-product tradition, the independent variables to which learning outcomes are related include frequencies of categories such as the concept of "classroom talk," in which coding methods measure the number of times that teachers give students praise (Flanders, 1970). We learn from these studies a precise quantifiable concept that links teaching to learning.

In the descriptive system, coding systems are not relevant until it becomes clear, in the course of the research, which categories of behavior are meaningful to the participants themselves. These "interpretative methods," using participant observations, are most appropriate when one needs to know the specific structure of occurrences, the meaning-perspectives of particular actors in particular settings, the location of naturally occurring points of contrast that are observable, and the identification of specific causal links (Erickson, 1986). Qualitative studies can answer the following questions:

- Given a specific social setting of the community college, what is happening?
- What do the actions of the groups (administrators, teachers, and students) involved mean to themselves?
- How do occurrences relate to social institutions (higher education) and learned cultural experiences (conduct, climate, reciprocity)?
- How does the specific setting (classroom experience, the teacher-student relationship) relate to other internal and external settings?

There are patterns in our actions as we perform them; we can specify them and find commonalities in them. From these patterns we may employ, observe, examine, and relate the behaviors of the group to the individual and local instance. The interpretative point of view leads to research questions of a fundamentally different sort from those posed by standard research: we are less interested in asking what teacher behaviors are positively correlated with student gains on test scores than in how the effective teacher enhances motivation and builds interpersonal relationships (the "how" questions integrate task-oriented skills and human skills).

In a purely naturalistic (qualitative) inquiry, direct observational fieldwork is the most common research technique; in some cases, however, substitutions for direct observation, including the use of archival and historical documents or content analysis of organizational documents or communications have been successfully employed. Walberg (1986) reports that some qualitative researchers have successfully attempted generalization in their collection and analyses of multiple cases or multiple studies of individual cases. The strength of their work may be combined with quantitative findings. Light and Pillemer (1982) illustrate the combined approach and suggest quantifying qualitative information, presenting quantitative studies in narrative fashion, and tallying statistical and descriptive evidence. Polit and Hungler (1987) also point out qualitative approaches that seek quantification. They believe to do so is to develop a system that is consistent with the aims of research and is faithful to the message conveyed in the qualitative materials. When the researcher converts the narrative information to a numerical system and subjects the data to quantitative analysis through statistical procedures, the system is known as content analysis. This analysis involves coding, counting, and rating of the strengths of the concepts under scrutiny. It is often useful, moreover, to quantify qualitative data as a means to deal with the volume of research data that is produced in such studies. This was an appropriate path for our research, which had thousands of participants and a million pieces of data.

We believe that an understanding of human behaviors, problems, and characteristics is best advanced by the judicious use of both qualitative and quantitative data. Goodwin and Goodwin (1984) contend that adherence to one form of research does not preclude the use of another; adherence to one paradigm does not preclude the use of methodologies from the other. They recommend that, in some cases, both types of methods should be included in the same study. Jick (1979) would agree; his contribution to using both qualitative and quantitative research sources for studies is called the triangulation methodology. He argues that qualitative and quantitative studies should be viewed as complementary rather than as rivals. Triangulation is defined as the combination of methodologies in the study of the same phenomenon; the metaphor of triangulation is from navigation and military strategy that use multiple reference points to locate an object's exact position (Denzin, 1978; Smith, J.K., 1983). Since multiple viewpoints allow for greater accuracy, organizational researchers can improve the accuracy of their judgments by collecting different kinds of data bearing on the same phenomenon.

Thus, the effectiveness of the teacher-leader can be studied by interviewing teachers, observing their behavior, and evaluating their performance records; or the views of effectiveness of the teacher-leader by the participant, by their students, and by their administrator might be compared and analyzed for validation to ensure the particularity of the described competency. Triangulation can test reliability and offer convergent validation; but it also can capture a more complete, holistic, and contextual portrayal of the concepts studied. Thus, triangulation may be used not only to examine phenomenon from multiple perspectives, but also to enrich our understanding by allowing for new or deeper dimensions to emerge. Qualitative data and analysis function as the glue that cements the interpretation of multi-method results: qualitative data are used as the critical counterpoint to quantitative methods. The analysis benefits from the perceptions drawn from personal experiences and observations and is enriched because of it. Cronbach (1975) would say the convergent approach utilizes qualitative methods to illuminate behavior in contexts where situational factors play a prominent role.

In our study we attempted to gain insights into teacher behavior by having them describe their actions. Students also provided descriptions and evaluations of their teachers, and we asked presidents to describe the behaviors of teachers that led to their selection as award-winning instructors.

THE STUDY: TEACHING AS LEADING

Our chief objective in this study was to view the teacher as influencer and motivator in the classroom. We wanted to discover, among award-winning instructors in community colleges in the United States and Canada, those competencies and behaviors that made them successful in motivating learners to learn. Following the procedure and methodologies used by Flanagan (1954), Evans (1970), McClelland (1978), House and Mitchell (1974), Klemp (1977, 1979), Hersey and Blanchard (1978), Burns (1978), Peters and Waterman (1982), Kolb (1984), and Roueche, Baker, and Rose (1988, 1989), we developed an interpretative and convergent approach to investigate teaching as leading.

We began by agreeing with the model developed by Peters

and Waterman (1982); they found that self-generated quality control in the marketplace was more effective in explaining corporate success than inspector-generated quality control. They pointed to wrong-headed analysis, overly complex analysis, and imprecise analysis of rational models as concepts that concentrated on costs and product development but seriously neglected quality and value. In their research they identified, studied, and learned from outstanding and successful institutions and leaders what was valuable about their institutions and themselves. The underlying premises of such research methodology are to identify the best, to study the best, and to learn from what the best do that make them successful. We are aided in our understanding of the factors of superior performance in any role by identifying and studying persons who perform best in that role. The researcher, then, may choose to study the elements of superior performance not by asking what the actor thinks is important, but by studying what excellent people actually do when they are engaged in the performance of their jobs.

Klemp (1977) has also attempted to identify the characteristics that are tied to effective performance. His empirical approach, which is similar to that of Peters and Waterman, consists of three steps: identify individuals who are successful; find out what they do that makes them successful; and examine how and why they are doing what they do. Interestingly enough, one of the most consistent findings is that the amount of knowledge one acquires of a content area is generally unrelated to superior performance in an occupation and is often unrelated even to marginally acceptable performance. Klemp found three factors of success critical to effective performance—cognitive, interpersonal, and motivational. Cognitive skills, or information-processing and conceptualization skills, allow syntheses of information from previous analysis and inductive thought. Teachers who use cognitive skills see thematic consistencies in diverse information, have the ability to understand many sides of controversy and have the ability to learn from experience. Interpersonal skills are sometimes referred to as communication skills but include the teacher's use of empathy, listening, and positive regard for others. Finally, the important skill of motivation rounds out the final factor of success and efficacy; this factor exists at two levels—influencing self and influencing others. What is critical about these skills is that they can be taught, and what is relevant for us about these ideas is that they are transferable to our own view of the teacher as leader. Although we assume the cognitive skills of teachers and infer that their degrees and their teaching awards pay homage to those skills, we are mostly interested in identifying, studying, and learning about their interpersonal and motivational skills. We believe that once we know how and why they are such successful performers, we will be able to demystify the great teacher as an innate function and to bring illumination to the idea that being a great teacher involves a set of behaviors that can be learned. In order to unlock the key to the successful performers we must understand the concept of competencies.

TEACHING COMPETENCIES

Competence is seen as a cause of effective performance, not a synonym for it. We can say that the competence of a person may be judged by his or her performance (Klemp, 1979). Confusion between competencies and measurements of knowledge, skills, and personality traits (test scores, college grades, career competencies scores) often results in the invalid conclusion that competencies and measurements are similar. That is not so. McClelland (1972) found that once a person enters a given occupation, none of the measures that have a high correlation with competencies can quantifiably, reliably predict that person's performance on the job. Thus, his message is that if competencies are to be measured, then definitions and operational intent must be assigned to those competencies. Thus, a competency can be defined as a generic knowledge, skill, trait, self-image, or motive of a person that is causally related to effective behavior referenced to external performance (Klemp, 1979, p. 42). In Figure 3.1, we demonstrate Klemp's idea:

Figure 3.1: **Competencies and Performance**

Competencies' Causal Link to Performance		
Knowledge		
Skill		Effective Behavior
Trait	>>>>> Linked to >>>>>	and
Self-Image		Job Performance
Motivation		

Adapted from Klemp, 1979

Although a competency may be inferred from behavior, the two are not equivalent. Competencies should be thought of as the processes that allow results or outcomes to occur. The causal link between competencies and effective performance means, therefore, that the development of a competency should lead to increased effectiveness. Also, competencies are only as useful as the performance criteria to which they lead: if the teacher's primary goal for her student is success in class, the competencies that should be emphasized are those linked to that criteria; and on the other hand, if a teacher's goal is to make a change in his students' lives, then we must search for external criteria that transcend aspects of classroom performance.

Job function analyses identify job requirements that are sometimes labelled as the criteria for those skills or characteristics that "cause" job performance. This approach can benefit the researcher in the search for relevant competencies, but it focuses on the job function as the determinant of competency rather than on the person who performs the job well. If we consider the job of the classroom teacher, we might note such tasks as class preparation and course development, attendance, testing, and grading. The competencies that relate to these tasks include knowledge of subject matter, skills in writing and recordkeeping, and a proven college degree in subject matter. Yet when we asked students what makes a difference between one teacher and another, students used the following words to describe their best teachers: concerned, caring, student-oriented, bright, energetic, influencing, and enthusiastic.

The competencies that underlie the observable aspects of performance are different and more complex than those that relate to the functions of a job. But these competencies are usually tied to broader work and life outcomes, and to some extent the actual identification of competencies is an inferential process. Thus, a research design must be developed to aid in our understanding (and testing) of competencies related to effective teaching.

Exemplary Teachers. The competencies of the exemplary classroom teachers may provide us with functional clustering of individual competencies that tend to occur in situations where effective performance is demonstrated. Identifiable behaviors of exemplary community college teachers, distinguished from "average teachers," which have been reported by various researchers (Easton, 1984; Guskey and Easton, 1983; Hirst and Bailey, 1983; Roueche and Baker, 1987; Schneider, Klemp, and Kastendiek, 1981) are summarized here:

- Exemplary teachers see themselves as facilitators of a student's own active learning rather than as experts transmitting information; in a word, they are student-centered.
- Exemplary teachers look for and commend their students for enhanced self-esteem, realization of new possibilities, and signs of having gained new perspectives; they see value in learning.
- Exemplary teachers understand that adult learners are unique and that experiential learning is a part of adult learning theory.
- Exemplary teachers understand students' needs, concerns, and interests and integrate them in their teaching; they assume a directive and influential role in facilitating learning.
- Exemplary teachers create situations through a variety of strategies to keep students actively involved in the learning process.
- Exemplary teachers are actively involved as leaders in the classroom through motivational, interpersonal, and cognitive skills.

Exemplary teachers have definable characteristics that are demonstrated as a combination of behaviors and attitudes. They have a high commitment to teaching and learning and receive energy and satisfaction from student success. They view their role as one of leadership with the end goal being students' willingness to take responsibility for their own learning (Valek, 1988). Contingency theory, or situational leadership, views leadership in terms of the varying degrees of interaction among group members and the effects of their motivation, satisfaction, and expectations; leadership is seen as the effort of one group member to change the motivation or behavior of the other members. A member becomes a leader when others perceive him or her as having the ability to reinforce the behavior of others and when the motivational functions of the leader are to increase the number and kinds of rewards available to followers (Bass, 1985; Evans, 1970; Hersey and Blanchard, 1982; House, 1971; House and Mitchell, 1974).

Theory Review. Path-goal theory (see Chapter 2) predicts effectiveness based on leaders' influence on subordinates' motivation, ability to perform effectively, and satisfaction. This theory is central to our study of teacher as leader. This theory allows parallels to be drawn between the behaviors (competencies) of effective leaders and effective teachers. The effective teacher as leader motivates and influences students to value outcomes for which the teacher can provide pathways to attainment. By examining how the leader in the classroom influences students' perceptions of work goals, personal goals, and paths to goal attainment, we can better understand the practices of exemplary teachers.

A leader's success is dependent on matching leadership style to a particular situation. Leadership situations must be dependent, therefore, on the nature of the group being led and the nature of the job itself. We have found that it is necessary to look at different situations to realize what is required from the leader-follower relationship. Moreover, we realize that most leadership situations call for some kind of blend between task-oriented leadership and people-oriented leadership. Hersey (1984) and Hersey and Blanchard (1982), in the life cycle theory of leadership, tell us that the one most important factor in determining leadership effectiveness is the point of maturity that followers have achieved in their lives; thus, teachers' effectiveness as leaders are dependent on a blend of different degrees of task leadership and people leadership based on students' maturity.

We now recognize that both the work of leaders and their style of leading vary with the situation. We also are aware of the totality of organizational alignment, which maintains a balance between internal resources and external environment. Organizations must adapt to changing demands to survive, and they must understand the development and shaping of their culture. Leadership is necessary to both maintain that balance and to meet the demands of imparting culture. Leadership has a moral obligation to followers— beyond the give-and-take of the immediate transaction—and demands that the leader and the follower go beyond the narrow limits of imparting facts, measuring production, and balancing finances; they must be willing to transform their experiences, to envision and dream the goals to be realized. Transformational leaders (Bass, 1985; Bennis and Nanus, 1985; Burns, 1978) are those who have the vision and rationality to focus on the whole, to share a sense of meaning, to stimulate and arouse, and to facilitate belief and trust in a shared vision (Roueche, Baker, and Rose, 1989). The integration of the leader who goes beyond the ordinary has been incorporated into our research methodologies.

The teacher as leader, as an element of our study, does not negate the role of the teacher-student-leading-learning construct. Most observers would agree that a crucial part of teaching has to do with learning. We have previously noted the relationship between teaching and learning. Moreover, the community college setting and mission of open access for all people are vital links to the teaching and learning milieu. Many community college students are unique to the higher education environment; we have learned that we cannot employ the same teaching and learning relationships that we find in high school or in the university. We believe that a key aspect of adult learning is the experiential approach. Kolb (1984)— drawing on the learning theories of Dewey, Piaget, and Erikson and the psychological theories of Lewin, Rogers, and Jung—saw experience as the source of learning and development. He maintains that learning is a social process based on cultivated experiences in which separate learning styles can be distinguished based on personality type, educational specialization, professional career, current job, and adaptive competencies. "Learning from experience,"

Kolb maintains, "is the basis for human development" (p. xi). This developmental perspective forms the basis for applications of experiential learning in educational settings for the adult learner. The structure of the learning theory provides a basis for application to the teaching as leading concept.

RESEARCH STAGES

The teaching as leading research project involved a series of inquiries and actions designed and implemented to support and demonstrate the general questions that we wanted to answer in our study:

- What are the relationships between teaching and learning?
- How can we define and understand the importance of changing our emphases in teaching from what to teach to how to teach learners?
- What do exemplary teachers do in the classroom that motivates learners to learn?
- What are the behaviors, competencies, and strengths of exceptional teachers in relationship to the influencing process developed by path-goal, life cycle, and experiential learning theories?
- How do students and administrators give support and evaluate the job their teachers are doing?
- To what extent do teachers vary in levels of leadership competencies (developed through analyses of path-goal theory—teacher leadership qualities questionnaire)?
- To what extent can we analyze and report teaching styles by application of the Teaching as Leading Inventory?

The intent of this research was to examine the complex phenomenon of teaching, focusing specifically on the influencing process as practiced by effective teachers in the community college setting. The steps in the teaching as leading research project were:

- to measure and integrate research and theories of teaching, learning, and leadership
- to identify community college teachers who had been acknowledged by their own institutions (administrations and students) as "award-winning instructors;" in other words, to identify, study, and learn from the best
- to gather demographic data on exceptional community college teachers, including biographical information, background and work experience data, and institutional information
- to analyze the unique (not the average) skills, behaviors, and characteristics (competencies) of these effective faculty members
- to interpret and analyze instructors' self-reported data and critical incident explanations of successful and unsuccessful experiences and teaching philosophies
- to interpret and analyze college administrators' attitudes and explanations of teaching as they recommended the exemplary teachers of their institutions
- to analyze and examine student responses to faculty in the areas of leadership, factors of success, and critical incidents
- to develop a model that captures in precise behavioral indicators the skills, abilities, and characteristics that were common to these teachers
- to categorize the skills, abilities, and characteristics of excellent teachers into four (situational) teaching styles: Supporter, Theorist, Achiever, and Influencer.

The research structure is depicted in Figure 3.2. In this figure, the data sources, the research documents, and the participants are displayed.

Figure 3.2: **Research Structure**

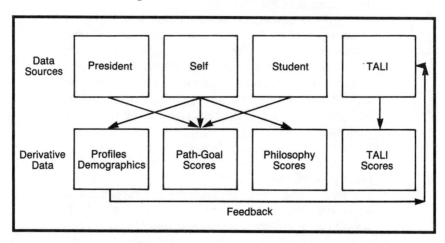

IDENTIFYING AWARD-WINNING INSTRUCTORS

Community colleges throughout the United States and Canada participated in this study. Letters of inquiry and nomination went to all the college consortia included in the National Institute for Staff and Organizational Development (NISOD), which numbers more than 500 members, and to the colleges of the 256 CEOs who participated in a previous study on transformational leadership in the American community college. (Many of the colleges whose presidents or CEOs were part of the *Shared Vision* study also belonged to NISOD.) Nominations were sought from about 600 community colleges.

CEOs were asked to submit the names of faculty who had received formal recognition or awards for teaching excellence (national, regional, state, or local awards) during a three-year period prior to the request. The CEOs were also asked to write a nomination letter for those faculty; information was solicited in this nomination format—spotlighted in the Roueche and Baker (1987) study, *Access and Excellence*—which developed a "teaching for success" structure based on Klemp's three factors of success: motivation, interpersonal skills, and intellectual skills. Those concepts and their explanation are repeated in Figure 3.3:

Figure 3.3: **Teaching for Success**

Motivational	Interpersonal	Intellectual
Commitment	Objectivity	Individualized
Goal Orientation	Active Listening	Teaching Strategies
Integrated Perception	Rapport	Knowledge
Acts Positively	Empathy	Innovation
Rewards Orientation		

Roueche and Baker, 1987

The CEOs' letters of recommendation, q.v., President Evaluation Instrument (Appendix 1), were analyzed according to several dimensions of leadership: transformational leadership, teaching for success, selection process, teaching field, and path-goal theory. We hoped to raise very basic questions about institutional support when we examined the recommendations of the college CEOs: to what extent does college leadership—the CEOs—support teaching and teaching activities? To what extent does college leadership observe those behavioral competencies that exemplary teachers reveal? We received recommendations from 251 college presidents or CEOs who nominated 869 instructors. Unfortunately, we also received many letters from CEOs or other officials who said that they had not recognized effective teachers in the past or did not have teachers who met the award criteria.

After we received the nominations of teachers from the North American and Canadian colleges, we wrote to the nominees to solicit their participation in the study. Their awards and honors as exceptional teachers were the basis of their inclusion in the study. We did not impose other criteria for their selection to the study. The nominees immediately became the instructors whom we intended to celebrate; they became our award-winning instructors. Later, when we began to analyze our data, we discovered that many of the award-winning instructors did not meet the test of at least three student evaluations. Thus, while 869 teachers are recognized in the dedication, we found that in order to analyze data, certain rigorous standards had to be maintained for data collection: each nominee had to have his or her CEO's letter of recommendation, his or her own questionnaire for all the items, and at least three student responses reporting faculty evaluations. Because of this process, the original number of awardees was reduced to 635; and eventually, because of reports that contained data errors, the final statistical analysis was conducted on 435 teachers. The college, the CEO who was the incumbent at the time, and the award-winning faculty are listed in the Dedication of this book.

The award-winning instructors were sent a four-page questionnaire (Appendix 2); we asked essential questions concerning biographical information, work experience information, institutional information, teaching information, and time-use information. The critical incident technique (CIT), developed by Flanagan (1954), provides the researcher with an effective and well-tested method for analyzing the behavior of leaders. It is an empirically based method for determining needed abilities for a particular task in order to establish standards or to make inferences. Elements of incidents (observable human activity sufficiently complete as to permit inferences and predictions about the person performing) and the incident's critical quality (occurring in a situation where the purpose or intent of the act seems fairly clear to the observer, and where its consequences are sufficiently definite to leave any doubt of its effects) are categorized by relationships, and frequencies of categories indicate those most often observed in comparable situations (Flanagan, 1954, p. 327). The CIT limits its reporting to those behaviors that make a significant contribution to the study; the technique is competency-based, focusing on actions, behaviors, and accomplishments in job-related activities and characteristics and qualities associated with effective performance of activities.

Flanders found that the technique was extremely useful in determining whether individuals possessed essential competencies for solving problems and whether they could apply the range of skills needed to accomplish tasks (1982, p. 12). A variation of the CIT is the Behavioral Events Interview Technique (BEIT) of McClelland (1982). This technique asks respondents to talk about high and low points in their job experience; the goal of the interview is to identify the competencies to do various jobs well. Similar patterns of identifying recurrent themes and tracking (using an empirical coding technique) are used in the BEIT. Klemp reports that by performing a content analysis (from coding the BEIT), a profile of competencies involved in effective job performance may be identified (1980). These two interviewing techniques have been used effectively in the field of educational research by Klemp, Huff, and Gentile (1980); Schneider, Klemp, and Kastendiek (1981); Huff, Lake, and Schaalman (1982); and Roueche, Baker, and Rose (1989). We adapted the use of these methodologies in order to formulate the questions we asked the award-winning instructors; faculty were asked to respond to the following questions :

> (1) Describe an incident or situation in your teaching experience in which you felt highly successful in motivating students to learn. What was the situation? What happened? What did you do? What was the student response? What was the overall outcome? What did you learn from the experience?
>
> (2) Describe an incident or situation in your teaching experience in which you felt you were unsuccessful in motivating your students to learn. Describe that situation. What happened? What did you do? What was the student response? What was the overall outcome? What did you learn from the experience?
>
> (3) As fully as you care to, explain your personal philosophy of the role of the teacher in enabling student learning.

We concluded the faculty portion of the questionnaire by asking the instructors to write a list of adjectives or words they would use to describe excellent teachers. Included with the teacher's questionnaire was a Student Evaluation Questionnaire (Appendix 3). We asked that a student facilitator be named and that the instrument be distributed in the manner of an evaluation: the instructor was asked to leave the room, and the students completed the form anonymously. The students responded to questions based on the path-goal model and checked words (adjectives) that "best" described their instructor, along the lines of the Klemp (1980) and Kolb (1984) formats. Then the students were asked to describe a situation in which their instructor was successful in motivating them to learn; this description was designed to mirror the instructor's description of a situation in which he/she motivated students. Finally, we asked for biographical data from students including gender, ethnicity, number of semesters in college, and reasons for taking the course.

Later, in May 1989, at the Eleventh Annual NISOD Conference, we asked the award-winning instructors to complete the Teaching as Leading Inventory (TALI). This was the final element of our extensive data collection. Almost 400 of the original 869 instructors were able to complete the TALI, developed by Baker (1989) along the lines of Kolb's Learning Styles Inventory. A compact form of the TALI is included in Chapter 6, so that readers might identify their own teaching style.

SUMMARY

In their discussion of the existing research efforts in higher education, Menges and Mathis note that "literature on teaching, learning, curriculum, and faculty development leaves an indelible impression of enormous diversity, even of fragmentation." They believe, as do we, that each element of higher education—teaching, learning, the curriculum, and the faculty—must be seen as "interacting elements in the broader universe of higher education" (1988, p.361). Our research goals reflect this attitude, and our aim has been to present an integrated approach to the concepts of teaching and learning in community colleges. In the following chapters, we present the data analysis of our findings.

Chapter 4

Profiling Characteristics of Award-Winning Instructors

Award-Winning Instructors' Biographical Data
Age, Gender, and Ethnicity
Educational Background
Degrees
Teaching Fields
Disciplines
Institutional Information
Attrition and Retention
Attendance, Assessment, Advisement, Placement,
and Faculty Development
Time Use Information
Student Characteristics
Gender, Age, and Ethnicity
Course Information
Conclusion

*Arouse in the other person
an eager want; then satisfy it.*

Burns, 1978

4

*T*he role of the community college instructor is not one in which traditional practices have had much meaning, primarily because of the nature of the changes community colleges introduced into higher education. The "people's colleges" promised students that opportunities would be available in higher education for all the people. The educational system that the community college introduced was one in which the principle of democracy was applied — the adult population was "enfranchised" to learn. The new community college student had requirements unique to the traditional higher education milieu; the instructors of the community colleges were called upon to provide a vanguard that would explore and test new procedures and alternatives to meet students' special needs, while at the same time guiding them to the traditional goals of higher education. In order to do this, to pave new pathways for higher education for the people, we maintain that community college instructors have played a special role that should be celebrated and reported. We have defined their role as one of leadership.

The ability of the teacher to raise students' motivation levels toward greater responsiveness to learning was a principle that guided this study of exceptional college teachers. Our goal was to examine the behaviors of award-winning instructors as they reported, discussed, and explained their experiences as motivators and influencers. We identified competencies that characterize exemplary job performance. But we were also curious about who these excellent performers were, their backgrounds and biographies, their working environment, their use of time—and who their students were. We sent questionnaires to the 869 award-winning instructors who were nominated for our study, and we asked the instructors to allow their students to evaluate them. Those data are presented here.

AWARD-WINNING INSTRUCTORS' BIOGRAPHICAL DATA

The faculty profile of the participants revealed that time and experience were critical to our outstanding faculty; not only was the average faculty member 47 years old, but faculty on average had at least 16 years of college teaching experience and another four years' experience teaching in other institutions, for an average total of 20 years' teaching experience. In an earlier study of exemplary community college teachers (Valek, 1988), similar characteristics were revealed; she reported an average age of 46, 12 years' community college teaching experience, and 10 years of other teaching experience. Cohen and Brawer (1987) found that the average age of community college faculty increased from 42.4 years to 45.7 years between 1975 and 1983, and their average teaching experience went from 6.8 years to 11.2 years. We may surmise, therefore, that although there existed a cohort of teaching faculty who remained about the same age, there were fewer incoming, young teachers entering this teaching field during those years—in other words, faculty just got older. The biographical data representing age of the award-winning faculty are not significantly different from the ages of faculty in other studies; however, the number of years of teaching experience differs considerably among the award-winning instructors. We found a direct correlation between number of years of teaching and exemplary teaching practices: the greater the number of years of teaching, the more likely the faculty member would be perceived as excellent and the greater the number of awards that likely had been won.

Age, Gender, and Ethnicity. Although the youngest award-winning faculty member was 29 and the oldest faculty member participating in the study was 74, the majority (85 percent) were between the ages of 38 and 59. Cohen and Brawer (1987) also report teachers' ages and teaching experience. Their data is interesting in that they compare data from 1975 to that gathered in 1983. In 1977, Cohen and Brawer found that one-third of the faculty whom they studied (humanities faculty in the California community colleges) were between the ages of 25 and 35; by 1983 this proportion decreased from 33 to 15 percent. The age range between 36 and 50 remained the same, 43 and 44 percent, but the 51 to over-60 category increased from 24 to 32 percent. Cohen and Brawer reported that 20 percent of the liberal arts faculty at the Los Angeles Community College District were 61 and older. Given that faculty are becoming older, Cohen and Brawer also noted that the number of years in teaching is on the increase. In 1975, 86 percent of the faculty they studied had taught between one and 10 years; by 1983, that number fell to 46 percent, as the number of teaching years between 11 and 20 years increased from 15 to 48 percent. The number of faculty teaching over 20 years increased from 2 to 6 percent. These data are revealing: those faculty whom Cohen and Brawer singled out in the Los Angeles Community College District are likely retired today; and if faculty maintain present trends, a cohort of aging faculty is likely to become a predictor of future faculty shortages. We will address the issue of faculty age and impending faculty shortages in Chapter 13.

Fifty-four percent of the award-winning instructors were male, and 46 percent were female. Cohen and Brawer (1987) reported that two-thirds of the instructors they studied were male, and one-third were female. Most award-winning instructors (88 percent) were Anglo; ethnic groups represented only 12 percent of the total population. These groups included Asian (6 percent), Black (4 percent), and Hispanic (2 percent). For all colleges and universities, however, 90 percent of the faculty are Anglo; 4 percent are Black, 4 percent are Asian, less than 2 percent are Hispanic, and less than 1 percent are American Indian (Equal Opportunities Commission Report, 1985); this figure remained relatively stable between 1975 and 1985.

Although we found little variation among award-winning faculty members' ethnicity, we did determine that an age difference existed among the various groups. Hispanics, at age 42, were the youngest award winners. Blacks and women were also younger than the average age of the whole group—45 and 46 years old respectively. But we also found that Hispanics had less teaching experience than did the group as a whole; however, these differences were not statistically significant. Regardless of ethnicity, the award-winning instructors had more experience teaching than did other community college teachers (Cohen and Brawer, 1989; Valek, 1988). Interestingly, members of ethnic minorities had more doctorates than did Anglos, albeit they represented a smaller percentage of the total award-winning instructor population. Hispanics held the largest percentage of doctorates, followed by Asians, then Blacks, and finally Anglos. Table 4.1 demonstrates the relationships between ethnicity and other teaching factors.

Table 4.1: **Ethnicity and Teaching Factors**

Ethnicity	Age	College Teaching	Other Teaching	Doctorate
Anglo	47	16 years	4 years	26.2%
Asian	47	16 years	4 years	39.1%
Hispanic	42	9 years	4 years	42.6%
Black	45	15 years	4 years	30 %
Gender				
Male	47	17 years	4 years	26.7%
Female	46	15 years	4 years	28.6%

In only one situation—one in which the instructor reported rank (instructor, assistant professor, associate professor, professor, department head, division head)—did we see a significant difference in terms of teaching experience: division chairs reported both the longest experience teaching at the community college level—20 years—and had the greatest number of years of experience in "other teaching years"—more than 10 years. Division chairs, who represented about one-eighth of the award-winning instructors, have teaching experience of well over 30 years.

Finally, in all other analyses of data, including presidents' ratings of their faculty, students' ratings of their instructors, scales measuring motivation (McClelland, Maslow), leadership (Roueche, Baker, and Rose, 1989), and teaching-learning path-goal attributes, we did not find any differences based on the gender variable. And in only one case, the manner in which students' described and evaluated their faculty by rating them according to a list of motivational, cognitive, or interpersonal adjectives, did we find a difference based on the sex of the instructor. Students reported a significant difference in their perceptions and evaluations of female instructors compared to male instructors: female instructors were described with more attributes than their male counterparts. Students ascribed greater weight to those attributes they used to describe their female instructors.

Educational Background. We asked for and examined educational information about the award-winning instructors and their families. Faculty members' mothers had, on the average, 11.7 years of education; their fathers had 11.5 years of education. Thirty-one percent of their mothers were high school graduates, and 12 percent were college graduates. Twenty-four percent of their fathers completed high school, and another 7 percent were college graduates. About 10 percent of the fathers had graduate degrees or college work beyond the undergraduate level; only 3 percent of the mothers had graduate degrees. In actual numbers, however, about one of every 100 instructors' parents held graduate degrees.

Degrees. The two tables below present educational background and earned degrees of the award-winning instructors. College majors are reported according to the fields most often represented; all the teaching fields of the award-winning instructors are presented in Table 4.4. The participants themselves provided the following characteristics about their education:

Table 4.2: **Award-Winning Instructors' Degrees**

Degrees	Majors	Percentages (Faculty Holding Degree) *
AA	Nursing, English, Sciences, Math	14.8
BA/BS	English, Math, Business, Biology, History	98.3
MA/MS	English, Education, Math, Business, History, Biology	89.0
Ph. D.	English, History, Education	27.8

* An assumption is made that instructors holding higher degrees also hold other degrees.

Award-winning faculty are well-educated; the vast majority have master's degrees, and more than one-fourth hold Ph.D.'s. Other studies also report degrees and preparation—Ottinger (1987), Cohen and Brawer (1987), El-Khawas (1988), and American Association of Community and Junior Colleges (1988). Although only Ottinger cites data parallel to our own, the differences between her data and ours reflect her interest in the highest degree held by the community college instructor. In both the Cohen and Brawer (1987) and the AACJC (1988) reports of faculty education, only the doctorate is reported; furthermore, in the AACJC report, the doctorate is broken down by gender. Findings from these studies are provided in Table 4.3.

Table 4.3: **Faculty Degrees in Other Studies**

Highest Degree Held by Community College Faculty - Other Studies			
	Associate's	Bachelor's	Master's	Ph.D.
Ottinger, 1987	5%	10%	63%	22%
Cohen and Brawer, 1987			Ph. D.s in Liberal Arts:	25%
AACJC, 1988			Ph.D.s: Males	27%
			Females	13%

Teaching Fields. By grouping the separate disciplines, we found that the social sciences' disciplines had the greatest numerical representation, followed by vocational-technical, humanities, sciences, English, business, math, nursing-health, developmental and adult education, and general education. This table represents the majority of teaching fields reported by award-winning instructors. Although we first grouped faculty by their disciplines and found that, according to their actual numbers, they followed the categories listed below, the actual discipline or instructor named most often by students did not follow this categorical pattern.

Table 4.4: **Teaching Fields**

Award-Winning Teachers' Teaching Fields by Category		
Social Sciences	**Vocational Technical**	**Humanities**
History	Engineering	Languages
Social Sciences	Computer Sciences	Speech
Psychology	Criminal Justice	Art & Drama
American Studies	Home Economics	Journalism
Government	Aeronautics	Music
Sociology	Automotive	Humanities
Economics	Agriculture	Philosophy
Geography	Electronics	
	Drafting	
Sciences	Fire Sciences	**English**
	Industrial Modeling	
Biology	Hotel Hospitality	English
Microbiology	Secretarial Sciences	
Physical Sciences	Paralegal	
Natural Sciences	Early Childhood	
Chemistry		
Physics		
Marine Studies		
Business	**Math**	**Nursing-Health**
Business Administration	Mathematics	Nursing
General Business		Physical Development
Management		& Health
Accounting		Health Care
		Radiology Technology
Developmental & Adult Education		**General Education**
Developmental Education		Curriculum & Instruction
Adult Education		Physical Education

Disciplines. The teachers who were most often named as award-winning instructors were those who taught English, math, biology, business, history, nursing, developmental education, social sciences, art, psychology, computer information systems, criminal justice and paralegal, and vocational-technical courses. English teachers in our study and in one previous (Valek, 1988) were the largest single discipline to be nominated as award-winning instructors, accounting for 11 percent of all nominated teachers. Biology and math teachers each accounted for 8 percent of all nominated instructors. Teachers from two business fields, general business and management, accounted for 6 and 4 percent of the nominees. The table below reports several combined instructional fields and the percentages of awardees in those fields.

Table 4.5: **Award-Winning Instructors and Teaching Discipline**

Discipline Fields of Instructors	Percentages of Awardees
English and Humanities	27
Math and Sciences	22
Social Sciences	16
Vocational Technical	10
Business	10
Nursing	8
Education	7

The most prevalent faculty titles of award-winning instructors were instructor and professor; 45 percent of all faculty from the United States and Canada indicated they were instructors, and 24 percent said their title was professor. An additional 6 percent had titles of assistant professor, and 7 percent were associate professors. About one-fifth of the award-winning instructors had administrative duties as well as their teaching responsibilities: 6 percent were department heads and 12 percent were division chairs. On the average, although instructors had 20 years' college teaching experience, they have been in their present position for about 12 years.

INSTITUTIONAL INFORMATION

On the average, faculty conduct between four and five classes per week and teach approximately 120 students; in this statistic, award-winning instructors look exactly like the general population of community college instructors (Cohen and Brawer, 1989). What is different about these instructors is the lower rate at which their students become attrition statistics: excellent teachers tend to retain more of their students than does the general teaching population. The average attrition rate for exemplary instructors is 14.6 percent; for the general population of students that number is more regularly defined from one-third to one-half of the student population (Astin,1975; Bean, 1986; Riesman,1980; Roueche and Baker, 1983; Tinto,1987). This finding was critical to our study and underscores another study of successful teachers by Guskey and Easton (1983), in which high levels of student achievement and low attrition rates were reported. If we consider that one of the community college's most significant problems is its high attrition rate and that this issue has been central to a large portion of research about the community college, then our findings are critical.

A brief review of the research around the concept of student attrition follows. We intend to demonstrate, from these sources, that the exemplary classroom teacher is, undeniably, a critical element in the retention of students; and, perhaps, the instructor is the single most important ingredient in student retention in the classroom and in the college experience. In Table 4.6 we demonstrate researchers' reported percentages of student attrition in community colleges.

Table 4.6: **Attrition Figures as Reported by Other Researchers**

Sources	Percentages
Roueche and Baker, 1983	25 to 40
Reisman, 1980	50
Bean, 1986	45
Tinto, 1982	45
Heverly, 1987	33

Attrition and Retention. Roueche and Baker (1983) warn us of the "revolving door of attrition." From the 1970s through the 1980s researchers report this indisputable problem of retaining students in community colleges (Astin, 1975; Noel, 1985). Various reasons attempt to explain this high rate of non-completion, including personal reasons, transfers, and academic dismissals. Willett (1983) relates attrition to the open-door policy; Astin (1978) discusses lower ability, lower socioeconomic status, and personal characteristics as the major reasons for high attrition rates; Herndon (1984) points to academic reasons (including rank in high school, grade point average, tests of aptitude and ability), demographic and personal characteristics (such as gender, age, ethnicity, socioeconomic status, place of residence, types and amounts of financial aid, marital status, and number of children), and motivational reasons for non-persisters; and finally, A. Smith (1983) expresses concern with counseling, advising, and quality of instruction as significant for lessening high rates of attrition.

Gates and Creamer (1984) focus on institutional characteristics that are critical to solving the retention problem in community colleges; they believe that by merely addressing student characteristics we cannot adequately address the problem of retention. Programs, policies, organizational patterns, and interactive climate are also necessary for student success. The challenge here is for the institution to carry the student forward by reinforcing the necessary skills for goal attainment and accomplishment. Kramer (1985) explains the issue succinctly when he points out that student goals and institutional goals must be congruent for student persistence to occur. Institution-fit models (Tinto, 1987) and social integration models (Neumann, 1984) are essential elements for increasing student retention. Villela (1986) points out that education cannot be separated from the providers; he supports the idea that crowded classes and instruction by television may seriously impair students' persistence, especially at the freshman level. He suggests that faculty should counter this tendency by attempting to be aware of student satisfaction, as well as by maintaining quality, enthusiasm, and personal contact. Pascarella (1986) offers another institutionally intervening variable for student success—orientation. Student orientation is seen as a means to understand institutional expectations for increased goal attainment and development of higher levels of social integration skills. Tinto (1982) focuses on faculty stewardship of new students as an institutional response to retention. Losak (1986) noted that, for community college students, the academic success rate increased as basic skills increased. In the Miami-Dade model, Roueche and Baker (1987) reported that the challenge for the community college is to carry the student forward by reinforcing the necessary skills to accomplish goals. Matlock (1988) found that strategies that appear to increase retention are those that provide social support or those that combine social support with academic strengthening.

Obviously, we have seen institutional response to the particular needs of the open-door college. In the last 10 to 15 years, community colleges have developed and instituted programs to support the needs of the unique community college student. Beginning in the late 1960s, Roueche (1968) drew attention to community college students as a cohort that should be studied. From a series of research issues and a number of researchers (Cross, 1976, 1978, 1989; Roueche, 1972; Roueche and Roueche, 1977; Roueche and Snow, 1977), we have learned about the special needs of the community college student and have been guided in our thinking about the responses that colleges as institutions had to make to meet the needs of the community college student. In *College Responses to Low-Achieving Students: A National Study,* Roueche, Baker, and Roueche (1984) examined some of the results of previous decades of research. Most of the colleges surveyed had instituted remedial and developmental programs as an integral part of their curricula. In a subsequent study by Roueche and Baker (1987), Miami-Dade Community College's programs were highlighted as an exemplary model for student achievement. Basic skills and language deficiencies, in a culturally and economically diverse educational setting, became the rallying point for institutional change. For all the years of frustration over the concept of access in the community college, a prototype was discovered in the successful practices instituted by the Miami-Dade Community College system (McCabe, 1988).

It is the intention of this study to add our voice to those we have mentioned here, and by example, to point out that what the exceptional faculty member does in his or her classroom is a key to student retention and success; it is our contention that the efforts of master teachers, reflected through the teaching-learning path-goal framework and the teaching-as-leading styles (as reported in Chapters 5 and 6), will have significant value in promoting retention in the community college. We would postulate that good teachers do make a difference when they motivate and influence their students toward greater satisfaction and understanding of their educational goals. Further, we can add that a large percentage (about 75 percent) of the institutions for which they work have programs in place to aid in retention. A discussion of these programs follows.

Attendance, Assessment, Advisement, Placement, and Faculty Development. No matter how we attempt to slice the pie or describe the component parts of the educational imperative of the modern community college, one irrefutable fact must be acknowledged: levels of readiness in an open-door institution can be expected to be varied; and the institution, if it is to meet its commitment to egalitarian education for all the people, must respond to the varied needs of its student body. In fact, much of what we know of the culture and environment of the community college is integrally involved in the continuing struggle to provide a quality education for inadequately prepared students. How do colleges accomplish this seemingly impossible task? How successful are they in doing so?

These two questions guided us to ask our award-winning instructors about the internal policies of their institutions. We were curious about the institutional programs that addressed this issue; moreover, we assumed that because of the emphases in the 1970s and the 1980s on the development of institutional practices to meet the needs of the nontraditional community college student, we could ascertain a relationship between exemplary teaching and the institutional programs that support teaching.

Access and Excellence: The Open Door College provides illumination into both the historical antecedents of this dilemma of access and the process by which community colleges began to respond and find workable solutions for student success without destroying or diminishing the innovative concept of open-door admissions. Roueche and Baker (1987) draw our attention to the societal reforms of the 1960s and 1970s, which had a direct and immediate impact on education and the need for educational reform. As the civil rights movement gained momentum, minority students began to turn more and more to educational channels for access into the system that had begun to open for them. It is not surprising, therefore, that students, including minorities, who had fought for the expansion of their rights, included educational rights—as well as political rights—in their struggle to change the values and practices of the society in which they were living. It was a true social revolution. Community colleges were founded on the premise of providing access for populations who previously had little opportunity to attend higher educational institutions. In the early 1960s it was the community college, and not the senior colleges and universities, that immediately opened its doors to Blacks and Hispanics. Dr. Bob McCabe, president of Miami-Dade Community College, said: "When Miami-Dade opened its doors in 1960, it was the only college within 250 miles of Miami that would accept Black students" (1984).

Students focused on admissions standards, prerequisite courses, and minimum competencies as obstacles to higher education; and as colleges began to respond to student demands, college policies were dramatically affected. To allow a wider variety of students into college, standards had to be relaxed, and admissions policies were virtually eliminated. But this very practice contained its own new direction for learning: opening colleges to everyone meant that diversity and differences among students would be the rule rather than the practice, and institutions had to accommodate the needs of their students.

In our examination of the characteristics of institutions at which the award-winning instructors taught (almost 300 community colleges throughout the United States and Canada), we looked at faculty reports on whether the institution had policies or programs that included attendance, assessment, advisement, placement, and faculty development. In Table 4.7 faculty response and rating of these programs appear; percentages refer to the actual number of faculty reporting the particular program, and the effectiveness rating refers to the numerical score assigned to responses of excellent, good, fair, and poor (4, 3, 2,1 rating system).

Table 4.7: **Institutional Programs**

Institutional Policies	Percentages	Effectiveness*
Attendance	61	Good/Fair (2.56)
Assessment	84	Good (2.97)
Advisement	89.3	Good (2.86)
Placement	72.8	Good (2.88)
Faculty Development	82.6	Good (2.75)
Faculty Development Program		
Includes:	Percentages	Effectiveness*
Selection of Faculty	67.9	
Evaluation of Faculty	44.2	
Development of Faculty	22.5	(overall rating): 2.75
Promotion/Tenure of Faculty	70.3	
Merit Rewards for Faculty	73.1	*(Scale 4-1)

Faculty members on the whole reported that two-thirds or more institutions had set guidelines for policies that aid in student retention and student development, and they rated the effectiveness of these programs as "good." Almost all the colleges had advisement and assessment programs in place, and three-fourths had a placement policy. Although only about 60 percent of the institutions had an attendance policy, the faculty were in agreement that attendance was critical in the classroom and that student attendance in class was a necessity for student success. About three-quarters of the colleges of the award-winning instructors had assessment, advisement, and placement policies in place. Examples of these programs and policies will be discussed in Chapter 13.

Although most of the instructors (83 percent) reported an institutional policy for faculty development, a curious pattern emerged. Only 22.5 percent of the instructors reported that the faculty development office concentrated on the development of faculty, and 44 percent reported that faculty evaluation was a program of the faculty development office. We can surmise that colleges that may have a faculty development office may not use the programs effectively, or the programs that should be included may not exist or may not be included there. Faculty development is sometimes seen as outside the purview of the college operation; faculty as professionals tend to think of development as professional or academic development and gear that development toward other institutions or professional organizations (Mintzberg, 1979). In most cases in the community college, "faculty development" refers to orientation sessions for new faculty or for part-time faculty; regular, full-time faculty are not consistently involved in programs of faculty development.

We found, for example, when our first inquiry went out to community colleges throughout the United States and Canada to name their award-winning instructors, that most of the colleges we contacted did not have a faculty award system in place. We take particular note of these situations and offer the suggestion that faculty development and faculty celebration of excellent teaching should be an integral part of institutional response to all faculty members in the community college. We cite effective programs that are working in Chapter 13.

In almost seven out of 10 colleges, selection, promotion and tenure, and merit reward for faculty emanates from the faculty development office. We are cognizant of a problem in these aspects of faculty development, too. In a system that should be focused on the continuous development of faculty—on renewal, on recognizing new teaching and learning theories, on preventing burn-out, on expanding and enhancing methodologies, on providing innovations for faculty who may be mired "in doing it their way only"—we find little coordination and complement to developmental practices. For example, to suggest that hiring and selection be a part of the faculty development office—without a concomitant evaluation structure tied to that procedure—is somewhat perplexing. Essential questions that involve the faculty development office should include these:

- What are the programs offered by the faculty development office?
- How do programs reflect on the reciprocal relationships between institutional goals and the goals of teaching and learning?

- How do programs meet the demands of expansion, curtailment of programs or courses, financial exigencies, and the like?
- What attention is paid to selection, hiring, and evaluation of faculty?
- How are trends, new practices, new discoveries, and new programs integrated into the information and knowledge of existing faculty?
- To what extent is the faculty development program involved in celebrating teaching effectiveness, in providing for master teachers as teachers of teachers, in celebration of good teaching, and in merit and other rewards for teachers?

TIME USE INFORMATION

Faculty reported that they spent an average of 16.7 hours weekly in the classroom. In terms of preparation time, each faculty member spent another 15 hours per week. Faculty held 10 office hours per week and reported another 6.1 hours per week spent with students. In all, faculty members spent an average of almost 48 hours per week in the classroom and with their students. In these data too, signposts of exemplary teaching are revealed: award-winning instructors spend more time with their students, and they appear to spend more time on their job. Valek's (1988) study found that students' single most reported and observed behavior of their instructors was the availability of their instructors outside of class time to help them when they were experiencing difficulties; next they ranked clear explanation; and then they valued "providing additional help." Interestingly, it was "the instructor is available out of class when needed" factor that most caught the attention of instructors' supervisors in the Valek study (1988, p.110). Providing time and experience to students in the community college is a critical factor in eliminating, or at least limiting, frustrating barriers to learning success. This concept figures prominently in the discussion of the teaching-learning path-goal framework in Chapter 5.

STUDENT CHARACTERISTICS

We have a profile of the students who participated in the study. We asked the award-winning instructors to randomly choose five to seven students from their classes to evaluate them; the students returned their questionnaires directly to us. The questionnaire asked the students to rate their instructor's motivational, cognitive, and interpersonal skills; to describe their instructor according to a set of adjectives we provided; and to write about a situation in which their instructor was successful in motivating them to learn. We also asked students about their personal characteristics—including gender, age, and ethnicity. They provided information about the number of semesters in college and the reasons they were taking the course.

Gender, Age, and Ethnicity. Sixty-three percent of the students participating in our research were female and 37 percent were male. Their average age was 28. Of the students, 77.5 percent were Anglo, 7 percent Hispanic, 8 percent Black, and 7.5 percent Asian. Almost one-fourth of the students who responded (and indicated their ethnicity) were members of ethnic minorities. (El-Khawas, 1988, reminds us that less than 21 percent of the community college students are reported by their colleges as members of ethnic minorities: Hispanics, 6 percent; American Indian, less than 1 percent; Asian, 3.5 percent; and Black, 10 percent). Student characteristics in our study are provided in Figures 4.8 and 4.9.

Figure 4.8:

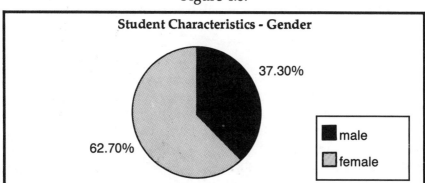

Figure 4.9:

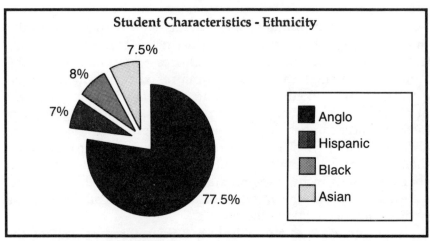

Course Information. Students on average reported that they had been in college between four and five semesters and that they were enrolled in their present course primarily because they wanted to complete a degree or improve their present skills. Almost half of the students indicated that they would transfer to another college or university, and about one-fourth of them were enrolled in the course in order to get a new job. Although the question was worded negatively, "I have no specific educational goal at this time," students clearly denied the concept—less than 5 percent of the students did not have specific educational goals, and the indication was that the vast majority had them. Those goals and students' perceptions of their instructors will be discussed in Chapter 5.

CONCLUSION

The award-winning instructors were mature and highly educated; their long teaching experience was primarily in community colleges and focused on the development of their students. They reported extremely low student attrition rates, forcing our attention on research about attrition and retention that examines both student and institutional characteristics responsible for the abnormally high attrition rates among community college students. It appears that the experiences and practices of exemplary instructors are found to be a critical factor in student retention.

Assessment, advisement, and placement are institutional practices that, for the most part, are in place in those colleges where award-winning instructors teach. And although three out of five colleges report attendance policies for students, nearly all the instructors further emphasized the importance of attendance in their classes. According to Roueche and Baker (1986), the single factor that related highly to student success in the public school and that emerged again and again was the issue of attendance.

We found that although most colleges had a faculty development office, that office did not focus on the development of the college faculty or even on faculty evaluation. Selection, promotion, and merit rewards for faculty were the more likely reasons for a faculty development office to exist than for training or "development" of faculty. The celebration of good teaching and the institutionalization of faculty awards for excellence in teaching also appeared to be the exception rather than the rule at community colleges.

Exemplary teachers spent almost 50 hours a week on the job, and much of that time was spent in office hours and in additional hours per week for meeting students and providing "extra" help. Clearly, the instructors in this study were focused on meeting student needs and on performance that exceeded the usual time faculty spend attending to college business.

Female students outnumbered the male students in our study almost two to one, and about one-fifth of the students we studied were members of ethnic minority groups. We found that the majority of the students were interested in completing their degrees, in improving their skills, and in transferring to another college. They all appeared to have educational goals. With that finding, we turn to the concept of the teaching-learning path-goal framework, which reports the views of both faculty and students.

Chapter 5

Award-Winning Instructors:
Seeking the Path to the Goal

———

A Framework for Teaching and Learning
Explaining the Teaching-Learning Path-Goal Framework
Engaging the Desire to Learn
Increasing Opportunities for Success
Offering Guidance and Direction
Empowering Students
Eliminating Obstacles
Motivating for Increased Satisfaction
Award-Winning Instructors and the Teaching-Learning
Path-Goal Framework
Successful Behaviors
Unsuccessful Behaviors
Philosophy of Teaching
Conclusion

*A comparison of results achieved
to goals intended determines
our effectiveness.*

Ewell

5

*A*s we examined the critical incidents the award-winning instructors reported, we began to see patterns emerge that engaged the teacher and the student in a common pursuit. We learned that the interdependent relationship between teacher and student concentrates initially on finding mutual paths to attain the educational goals that best suit both of their needs. Although we expect that by their training, teachers have the necessary abilities and professionalism to perform their jobs, we also know, by experience that students may or may not bring sufficient skills to the college environment to fully partake in shared learning experiences. We note that community college education must be understood within a particular framework that celebrates the uniqueness of the history and experiences of the community college. The following concepts have guided our history and experiences as a unique institution of higher education:

- the college environment is one that upholds the standards and expectations of higher education;
- the community college's mission emphasizes providing educational opportunity through the open door;
- the community college recognizes student diversity, both culturally and educationally; and
- the community college's central focus is as a teaching institution.

With these concepts in mind, we took the next step in our research: we developed a framework for examining the behaviors and competencies of exemplary teachers along the lines of a teaching-learning path-goal model. We begin with the premise of two actors, the teacher and the student, who come to the classroom with varying and different goals and needs. The driving dynamic in this situation became the ability of the instructor to motivate and influence the student to accept, to find satisfaction with, and to demonstrate by performance, a common path toward educational success. Defining the terms "teaching-learning path-goal" is critical: The teaching-learning concept refers to the relationship between teachers and students in the learning experience; the concept of the path implies both direction and a dynamic, bringing to mind the journey that individuals must take to achieve their potential; and finally, the term goal is intrinsically tied to the concept of path—the path points the way to the goal, and the goal is the achievement of educational objectives. In the graphic demonstration below, goals are illustrated as separate and individual; then, as they are dynamically challenged by the motivating and influencing abilities of the teacher as leader, a single, unified path of common educational goals emerges: this is the path-to-goal concept.

Figure 5.1 - **Achieving a Path Towards the Goal**

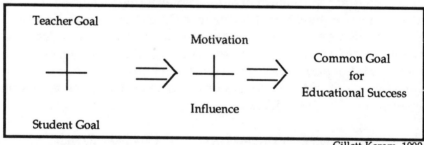

Gillett-Karam, 1990

A FRAMEWORK FOR TEACHING AND LEARNING

Recognizing that teachers function as leaders in the classroom allows us to apply the theoretical framework that House (1971) proposed in his motivational theory of leadership. This application allows us to predict and understand how leader (teacher) behavior influences follower (student) motivation. The implication for teachers as leaders is that students are motivated by teacher behavior to the extent that this behavior influences goal paths and goal attractiveness.

Two general propositions of path-goal theory (House and Mitchell, 1974) help explain teacher-as-leader behavior and its implications for the motivation of students. First, teacher behavior is acceptable and satisfying to students to the extent that students see teacher behavior as either an immediate source of satisfaction or as instrumental to future satisfaction. Second, leader behavior will be motivational (increase effort) to the extent that such behavior makes satisfaction of student needs contingent on effective performance and that such behavior complements the environment of students by providing the coaching, guidance, support, and rewards necessary for effective performance.

These two propositions suggest that the leader's strategic functions are to enhance students' motivation to perform, satisfaction with the job, and acceptance of the teacher as leader. More specifically, House and Mitchell (1974) formulated six positions for leader behavior that strategically increase their likelihood of follower satisfaction and success. We have adapted these ideas to form a teaching-learning path-goal framework; they include the following:

- recognizing and engaging students' desire to learn;
- increasing the opportunities for quality educational performance and success in college;
- offering positive guidance and direction toward goals through coaching;
- working to eliminate or at least reduce obstacles to learning;
- motivating students toward increased satisfaction for and development of learning skills; and
- helping to clarify learning goals and empowering students to achieve active learning contingent on effective performance.

This framework provides the basis of the coding methodology we employed to examine the incidents award-winning instructors reported. Research (Easton, 1984; Guskey and Easton, 1983; Hirst and Bailey, 1983; Roueche and Baker, 1987; Schneider, Klemp, and Kastendiek, 1981; Valek, 1988) supports the notion that especially effective teachers' performance and behavior mirror the strategic functions suggested by the path-goal theory of leadership (House and Mitchell, 1974); moreover, from our examination of the research and teacher behaviors, we developed the teaching-learning path-goal concept as a framework to explain exemplary teaching behavior. Then, by taking the concept one step further and adding the ideas of Burns (1978), we postulated that leadership behaviors are primarily teaching behaviors, since the obligation of the effective leader, through teaching, is to make, produce, and develop the follower into the leader.

Teachers will probably always take into consideration the needs, readiness, aptitude, capabilities, and desires of their students; this is an environmental "given" in the teaching-learning milieu. Burns (1978), Bass (1985), and McClelland (1978) would argue that the relationship of the leader to the follower, or the teacher to the student, is dependent on the behaviors and attributes of the leader and the responses of the follower. For example, although each new semester begins with heightened awareness of course requirements, expectations of the college environment, goals and aspirations for successful teaching, and desires to succeed on the student's part, it is the particular coordination of those diverse elements into a defined structure that makes teaching the heart of the college experience. We contend, given the scope of demands from either external or internal actors, that none of this coordination need be mysterious or impossible to manage.

Rather, we believe that the exemplary practices and behaviors of teachers as leaders in the classroom constantly give definition to and challenge the dynamics of the classroom and teaching. Exemplary teachers do not expect or want static states in their classrooms; they are teachers who understand contingencies and the dynamics of change. They are situational teachers who respond to demands in the environment, in their classes, in the individual student, and in their courses. Teachers as leaders have high tolerance for change as they influence and motivate students to realize their potential. They exhibit characteristics that tie their students to them by mutual aspirations and student goals. More importantly, students find that they can transcend their immediate problems and needs, because they bring commitment to their exceptional teacher, because they identify with the vision and dream of their teacher, because their teacher heightens their imagination and gives them new insights, and because they become more productive and increase their ability to apply what they learn to their lives.

Influence and motivation are, foremost, tools of the effective teacher as leader. What comes to mind here is the notion of the sculptor whose talent and genius recognizes the beauty of a finished form in a solid block of marble. So, too, does the teacher recognize in the classroom the potential for clear thinking and higher levels of student accomplishment and performance. But to accomplish this potential, teachers must hone their own skills and tools. These tools are not the hammer and chisel of the sculptor, but rather the interpersonal and motivational skills that influence the development of learners. The demystification of these instructional competencies by excellent teachers indicates that others may employ these skills. We know, for example, that motivation enhances learning and achievement. Wlodkowski (1985) reported that if students are matched according to ability, opportunity, and conditions to achieve, the motivated person will surpass the unmotivated person in performance and outcome. We also know that teacher influence on students enhances student performance and outcome (Klemp, 1982).

The concept of influence is really not an unusual one—people spend a great deal of time trying to influence other people, whether in the classroom, the workplace or in the home. Influence is especially important when one person has some responsibility for the work or effort of another or others. Instructors want learners to feel positive toward learning and to feel motivated to expend the effort it takes to accomplish learning. Effective teachers do more than theorize about what it takes to help students develop a positive attitude toward learning: they purposely clarify the consequences, change the conditions, and influence the involvement in the learning task. The teacher as leader is a pathfinder who recognizes in students, semester after semester and course by course, the potential that will lead them to the path of their own understanding through shared interaction. Their path-goal orientation will be discussed according to the functions of leadership exhibited by the teacher.

EXPLAINING THE TEACHING-LEARNING PATH-GOAL FRAMEWORK

The path-to-goal concept is a tool for examining the relationship between instructor and student. Teacher behaviors, guided by motivation and influence, recognize and engage student desires to learn, offer guidance and direction through coaching, help clarify learning goal paths, work to limit learning obstacles, increase opportunities for educational success, and empower students toward active learning. These concepts are illuminated from the rich data derived from the award-winning instructors' narratives of successful and unsuccessful experiences in which they "motivated students to learn," and from reports of their philosophies of teaching. Student contributions expand the self-reported information of the award-winning instructors; they evaluated their instructors by commenting on experiences in which their instructors "motivated them to learn."

Recognizing and Engaging Students' Desire to Learn. Teachers can and do recognize and arouse students' needs for outcomes over which they have some control, such as students' need to successfully master a skill, complete a course, develop self-confidence, and understand the relationship between their present task and their future goals. In short, the exemplary instructor both recognizes and engages students' desires to learn, is interested in identifying students' educational goals in relationship to the particular course, and is concerned about students' paths to educational success. Often the teacher must initially recognize limitations that prevent students from articulating their goals or verbalizing their needs in a class. And although assessment and diagnostic testing may aid in the teacher's understanding of the cognitive accomplishments of students, recognizing and arousing students' desires to learn is a skill that an excellent teacher employs to draw from students their own educational identity. This instructor skill or competency is one that purports to accomplish the very core of the educational experience—it seeks to "draw out" from the student that which is latent or hidden and to initiate the process of education for the student.

This attribute of the teacher as leader suggests that the instructor ably aids students in recognizing and clarifying their own goals in relation to instructional goals, and that the teacher as leader is a diagnostician, an enabler, a counselor, and a communicator. But perhaps most of all the teacher is an influencer and a motivator, an individual who tries and succeeds at drawing out students' attitudes about learning. By recognizing what students bring into the classroom and by tying their attitudes and abilities to the particular course, the teacher as leader arouses, engages, and satisfies students' needs. The teacher, in fact, forms ties and bonds with students by identifying students' personal and instructional needs and, by integrating those needs into the course. We do not subscribe to the idea that any knowledge is "given" to the student, but rather we believe that teacher and learners share in the responsibility of gaining knowledge and becoming effective in their job performance. These features of the student-teacher relationship are revealed in the competencies that instructors report about themselves in relation to the strategic function of recognizing and engaging students' desire to learn:

- diagnosing student needs at the beginning of the course;
- clearly communicating the goal and purpose of instruction through well-organized course syllabi;
- providing a forum for student input to course goals, objectives, personal expectation, and needs; and
- being aware of the total student—including abilities, course readiness and skill preparation, problems, needs, individuality, personality, and maturity.

Increasing Opportunities for Quality Educational Performance and Success. Teacher behavior increases students' personal pay-offs for work and goal attainment. Exemplary teachers know the inherent value of aiding students in recognizing and facilitating their own educational goals. This is the process of recognizing, redirecting, and changing the focus away from the external agent who causes learning to occur, and toward the internal agent, or the student gaining responsibility for his or her own learning. That students must take responsibility for their own learning is the subject of a great body of educational research. Roueche and Mink (1980) maintain that the locus of control, or the stimulus for learning, may originate externally or internally, and that there is a danger of students and learners becoming dependent on an external source for their own learning. The learner, they maintain, should be able to relinquish the external motivator and employ an internal locus of control over learning and environment (Roueche, 1982). In another study, Roueche and Mink (1980) found that student achievement directly related to college success in developing greater responsibility and self-direction: hence, the concept of "internality." But in order for the student to function with increased internality, the teacher must be the provider of increased opportunities for success. For example, in their examination of environmental factors that promote or impede student success in college, Roueche and Mink (1976) found that teacher expectations figure prominently in overall student success. Rosenthal and Jacobson (1968) dubbed this concept the "Pygmalion effect," in which less-knowing persons perform to the level expected of them by authorities; this concept demonstrates the effect of expectations on performance.

According to Schneider, Klemp and Kastendiek (1981), effective teachers are characterized by leading their students to enhanced self-esteem and to recognizing signs of new perspectives. Essentially, students come to understand the value of the particular course they are taking, the value of their education, their individual responsibility for learning, and the value of lifelong learning. The instructor attempts to influence student values toward learning as a function of their own behavior; the teacher as leader in the classroom helps students realize and clarify their attitudes and beliefs about their own education and about the value of education in general. Generally, instructors speak of their cultural values and commitment to providing quality higher education learning; and specifically, instructors' philosophies mirror the mission of the community college of increasing the opportunities for a greater, more diverse population of students to obtain a higher education. The teacher has an internalized educational philosophy that leads students to fully understand and value education. In summary, the teacher who increases student opportunities for quality educational performance and success does so by:

- operating from a clearly defined educational philosophy;
- viewing learning as a valuable activity in and of itself;

- relating course content and value to real-life situations;
- viewing his/her own role as a facilitator of learning;
- expressing high expectations of student performance;
- helping students learn to learn;
- encouraging belief in students' self-worth;
- caring about students;
- gaining a sense of satisfaction from student achievement;
- allowing students to take responsibility for their own learning.

Offering Positive Orientation, Guidance, and Direction Through Coaching. One of the primary functions of the effective teacher is to clarify the path-to-goal attainment; most often, this is demonstrated through clear, concise course structure and communications of expectations around the course (Easton, 1984; Roueche and Baker, 1987). It is also demonstrated as a willingness to take a highly directive role as the facilitator of student learning (Omaha Boy, 1985; Schneider, Klemp, and Kastendiek, 1981). The teacher offers a positive learning environment, making the teaching-learning path-to-goal attainment easier to travel by coaching and directing; i.e., the teacher coaches, explains assignments, tutors, supports students in their efforts, and verbalizes confidence in students' abilities. Given their expertise, cognitive abilities, professionalism, and successful experiences, teachers can make short work of guiding students toward goal attainment by:

- demonstrating well-defined class organization;
- identifying course expectations and communicating them clearly;
- matching needs of students with a structured plan for growth and improvement;
- encouraging students' efforts through consistent and appropriate feedback;
- reaffirming through repetition the goals, objectives, and value of the course and learning; and
- identifying and affirming students' responsibilities.

Using Effective Performance as an Expectation by Which to Empower Students. The teacher as leader plays an important role in clarifying expectancies, or facilitating the expectations for effective student performance. The more the instructor is able to clarify, the more likely students are able to become active agents in their own learning—this is the process of empowering students. It is the role to which teachers as leaders are building from the very onset of their relation to students: it is the path that transforms the follower into the leader, and it is best demonstrated through the strategies teachers employ to help students recognize their possibilities. This is accomplished by holding students accountable for their best learning interests and by setting and verbalizing high standards (Roueche and Baker, 1987; Schneider, Klemp, and Kastendiek, 1981). The teacher helps students clarify expectations regarding their performance. The teacher helps students recognize possibilities; take responsibility for outcomes; realize that success in the course is dependent on doing the assigned work, attending class, participating, and seeking help when needed. Cross (1976) explains that instruction must be tied to increasing students' responsibility for their own learning; she maintains that success is achievable if some basic principles are followed: the learner must be active rather than passive; the goals of learning must be clearly stated to the learner; small learning units must be sequential; feedback and evaluation must be made essential parts of learning and course revision; and provision must be made for different rates of learning. The instructor empowers the student by:

- setting and upholding standards of behavior;
- being able to model expected behavior;
- reviewing and clarifying student expectations regarding outcomes and performance leading to outcomes;
- making students aware of consequences of their actions;
- providing appropriate feedback, both positive and negative, regarding student performance; and
- accepting and empowering students regarding their active involvement in the teaching-learning process.

Working to Limit and/or Eliminate Learning Obstacles. The limitation or reduction of frustrating learning obstacles involve the teacher as leader's recognition of individual student needs and an effort to understand and accommodate those needs. Effective teachers select materials that students can read and understand, as well as acknowledge their students' frustrations in learning (Hirst and Bailey, 1983). They tend to adjust course work to accommodate student needs (Roueche and Baker, 1987), which may involve the integration of information about individual students into diagnostic theories that yield prescriptions for action (Schneider, Klemp, and Kastendiek, 1981). The teacher reduces barriers by accommodating student needs for additional assistance, by negotiating learning activities, and by encouraging the formation of peer-learning networks. In short, the teacher works to eliminate or reduce learning obstacles by:

- assessing problem situations and individualizing approaches taken to resolve them;
- listening to students with an open and accepting attitude before responding;
- exploring alternatives with students for changing unacceptable situations;
- developing and/or modifying curriculum to meet student needs;
- maintaining supportive interpersonal communication with students;
- being sensitive to student perceptions;
- maintaining a supportive classroom atmosphere;
- meeting with students outside of the classroom;
- providing additional help for students;
- encouraging student use of support and resource services; and
- using peer and or other tutoring.

Motivating Students to Increased Satisfaction for and Development of Learning Skills. The teacher-as-leader increases the opportunities for personal satisfaction contingent on effective performance. This is accomplished by recognizing the experiences and successes that students bring into the classroom as adult learners and through the interpersonal relationships that teachers establish with students. Good teachers recognize their students as individuals and acknowledge their own life experiences; they value students as adult learners. Teachers must encourage, promote, and shape the pre-existing skills into the practical learning skills necessary to accomplish educational objectives (Weinstein, 1982). The exemplary instructor accomplishes this by motivating students to reach for greater, more refined learning skills: rather than merely understanding factually, students come to understand analytically; rather than succeeding only in "Business Math," they find they can do algebra and calculus. Motivating students to reach for higher goals is the moral act of the teacher as leader: the teacher recognizes student abilities not yet uncovered, encourages enthusiasm for learning and for moving to higher challenges, and thus changes the student's behavior. Consistently, effective teachers are distinguished by the strong degree of personal interest in and attention to their students (Easton, 1984; Guskey and Easton, 1983; Hirst and Bailey, 1983; Roueche and Baker, 1987; Schneider, Klemp, and Kastendiek, 1981). Motivating students to increase their satisfaction for and development of learning skills is accomplished by:

- motivating students to be totally involved in the learning process;
- considering students' adult and experiential learning and soliciting contributions from students;
- capitalizing on students' experiences by incorporating them tangibly into classroom teaching;
- promoting trust and respect between student and teacher, and among students;
- encouraging independent thinking;
- viewing student maturation as a desirable goal of education; and
- encouraging risk-taking (see Table 5.2).

Table 5.2: **Teaching-Leading Path-Goal Framework**

Theme	Attributes
Recognizes and Engages Student's Desire to Learn	Diagnoses student needs Communicates goal & purpose of instruction Provides for student input Aware of total student
Increases Opportunities for Quality Educational Performance and Success	Has educational philosophy Sees learning as valuable activity Relates course to experiences Is a facilitator of learning Maintains high expectations from student Helps student learning process Encourages belief in student self-worth Cares about student Finds satisfaction in student achievement Allows student to take responsibility for learning
Offers Positive Orientation, Guidance, and Direction Through Coaching	Demonstrates well-defined course organization Identifies and communicates expectations Matches student needs with plan Encourages student effort with feedback Repeats goals and objectives of course and learning Identifies and affirms student responsibilities
Uses Effective Performance as an Expectation by Which to Empower Student	Sets and upholds standards of behavior Models expected behavior Clarifies expectations and performance for outcomes Teaches student consequences of actions Provides appropriate feedback Accepts and empowers student
Works to Limit or Eliminate Learning Obstacles	Assesses and resolves problems individually Listens with open, receptive attitude Explores alternatives for change Develops and modifies curriculum to meet needs Maintains supportive communication Sensitive to student perceptions Maintains supportive classroom environment Meets with student outside of classroom Provides extra help Encourages use of support and resource services Uses peer and other tutoring
Motivates Student to Increased Satisfaction for and Development of Learning Skills	Motivates student toward greater involvement Considers student to be adult Capitalizes on student experience Promotes trust and respect Encourages independent thinking Encourages maturation as a goal of education Encourages risk-taking

Baker, Roueche, and Gillett-Karam, 1990

AWARD-WINNING INSTRUCTORS AND THE TEACHING-LEARNING PATH-GOAL FRAMEWORK

The faculty who chose to participate in the study responded to questions asking them to discuss both successful and unsuccessful teaching experiences. We also asked the award-winning instructors to discuss their philosophy of teaching. Our respondents wrote rich scenarios of their experiences and philosophies.

Successful motivating experiences: in a discussion about a class in developmental studies, Ruth Hatcher (Washtenaw Community College, Ann Arbor, Michigan) talked about the challenges of teaching adult learners:

> *More important than learning skills to basic adult learners are (1) a sense of comfort and confidence and (2) a sense that English is not just a 'classroom subject,' but a way of evaluating all of their experiences. Our classroom became a place where it was safe to make mistakes, safe to ask questions, and safe to speak up. I was challenged to make writing real. A lesson planned to define denotation and connotation became a linguistic analysis of different words for different drugs, which became a paper assignment describing effects of different addictive drugs. Or an assignment based on the essay 'Why I Want a Wife' became an assignment on 'Why I Don't Want a Husband.' It was only after the class had reached the 'comfort zone' and was allowed to explore their lives' problems in their writing, that I could begin to mention subject-verb agreement. And when I did mention subject-verb agreement it was easily accepted. Although the effects of the use of the comfort zone or the sense of family in the classroom are not always quantifiable, their relevance is always demonstrable in the success of my students.*

Unsuccessful experiences: Jerry Long (Wharton County Junior College, Wharton, Texas) is a speech and English teacher who has had many successful experiences with students, but he remembers one unsuccessful experience with a student:

> *I learned, perhaps too abruptly, that teachers must be ever listening for the cry out of personal anguish from students. One*

of my students used his arrogance and ego statements to conceal his goals from us and perhaps even from himself. Later, I discovered that he had a set of standards of excellence he had set for himself, and when he realized he was not achieving them and that he was not getting any help from me, he decided to quit trying. Had I recognized that his arrogance was only a cover-up for his far-reaching goals—had I listened more carefully—I might have helped him. I didn't and I am sorry for it.

Philosophy of teaching: in the description by Opal Conley (Ashland Community College, Ashland, Kentucky) we are treated to a description of her commitment not only to teaching and students but also to the values of egalitarianism in the community college. She says:

To me, education is a human and a humanizing endeavor. The best and the brightest, I aim to challenge; but I do not neglect the underachievers, for I recognize that they need me the most. I do not think of myself as a teacher, but as a learner with the students. Students need reason to learn; they need to know why they must pore over materials that are difficult to understand. By making information relevant to their experiences and to their proposed careers, many students develop an insatiable appetite that makes every moment I spend in the classroom a challenge and a pleasure. My door is always open, and I have found no better way to utilize my time than devoting it to students; they are not hesitant in seeking assistance—for that I am grateful.

Using these descriptions and coding them according to the major themes and attributes of the teaching-learning path-goal model (Table 5.2), we learned about the characteristics of exemplary instructors as they employ their award-winning behaviors. We found critical characteristics affecting all the behaviors of instructors who participated in our research. These characteristics were the overarching themes of exemplary teachers (the factors that were demonstrated consistently and covariantly in our analyses, whether we employed the Statistical Packages for the Social Sciences [SPSS] or factor analyses). They included the following concepts about the award-winning teachers:

- their dedication to the principles of the community college mission of providing opportunities for student success, regardless of the level of readiness or special needs of nontraditional college students;
- their belief that good teaching and good teachers do make a difference to student success, and their demonstrated willingness to do whatever was necessary to accomplish this; and
- their creativity factor in which motivation and influence were employed as the essential dynamic used to facilitate learning, regardless of the situation or contingency.

Successful Behaviors. The principal finding from the self-reported descriptions of the award-winning instructors was their commitment to teaching and to students. A six-part emerging pattern characterized instructors' successful motivational behaviors: first, faculty provided a clear goal direction and matched their curriculum to course and content goals:

> She carefully breaks down what needs to be mastered into organized units that are clear, concise, and sequential so that the students can reach the required standards. She creates a caring climate in the classroom that is non-threatening to the student's relationship with the teacher and with other students (President Jess Parrish talks about Shea Lynn Nabi, Midland College, Midland, Texas).

> She makes clear the operating rules of her class in a syllabus and through discussion at the start of each quarter (President Nolen M. Ellison explains Margaret W. Taylor's clear standards for student direction, Cuyahoga Community College, Cleveland, Ohio).

Second, instructors tended to be highly directive early on, providing guidance and appropriate coaching in a very positive manner:

> Mr. Chinen has the ability to build a positive self-concept in his students. He has a special rapport with his students

and makes them use their potential to the fullest. He allows
students to make mistakes, to learn to correct mistakes, and to
learn from that experience (President John Morton, Kapiolani
Community College, Honolulu, Hawaii, emphasizes Robert
S. Chinen's positive reinforcement of students' needs).

Third, instructors were well aware of individual student's needs
and accommodated the individual differences among their students:

Charlie is a true role model for educators. He makes every effort
to individualize the teaching/learning process. He is an educator
who supports unique assistance for every student. He has a very
inquisitive mind and has always been involved in projects that
enable us to better understand the teaching/learning process
(President David Ponitz talks about Charles Williams,
Sinclair Community College, Dayton, Ohio).

Fourth, award-winning instructors were focused on providing
regular and helpful feedback for their students:

Mr. Churchill gives students the tools to learn for themselves and
nurtures student growth through setting up circumstances in
which students can experience success. He is an active listener
who communicates to students that what they think is valuable
and worthwhile. He provides effective feedback, oral and written,
and structures his materials so that there is a variety of ways in
which a student's success can be measured (President David A.
Vardy explains Edgar Churchill's helpfulness to students,
Newfoundland and Labrador Institute of Fisheries and
Marine Technology, St. John's, Newfoundland).

Fifth, faculty reported that they held high expectations for their
students, but they did not relinquish their caring attitude and/or
their concern for their students:

The keys to her teaching success in mathematics are her high
standards and her commitment to student achievement. She
relieves their mathematics anxiety by her supportive, positive
approach to learning that clearly defines achievable expectations

(President Robert W. Ramsey talks about the classroom standards set by Edith Goodman, Camden County College, Blackwood, New Jersey).

Finally, faculty were willing to relinquish their own control over the classroom environment and their students and could empower their students toward active learning and a sense of responsibility for learning to learn:

> *Because she is a true teacher, she has the ability to implement innovative designs and, more importantly, motivate students to ongoing success* (President Larry D. Carter sees Cynthia Barnes as a teacher who allows students to take the initiative for their own learning, Community College of Aurora, Aurora, Illinois).

> *Betsy Klinokosum exemplifies a strong commitment to keep current with the demands of a rapidly changing world. She encourages students' initiatives and independence. Her success is manifested in student achievement* (President David E. Daniel discusses Betsy Klinkosum's ability to empower students, Wilkes Community College, Wilkesboro, North Carolina).

Perhaps none of these findings would have been considered so significant if award-winning instructors' students and college presidents had not corroborated their instructors' behaviors. We asked students to evaluate their instructors, by rating how they felt about their instructor, by responding to a series of adjectives they would use to describe their instructors, and by writing a critical incident in which they described their instructors' abilities to motivate them. On the whole, instructor responses were confirmed by students' evaluations. Students' successful motivating incidents were coded similarly to those of their instructors and revealed a pattern parallel to that of their instructors' self reports. Students used the same pattern of path-to-goal behaviors as did their instructors, and they gave similar weights to their instructors' behaviors with one exception—they were somewhat less confident in expressing their own ability to take over the responsibility for learning. (However, students were doing the evaluations early in the semester and were still pursuing their paths to independence.)

Students and faculty both aggregated the themes of the teaching-learning path-goal framework: engaging students' desire to learn and offering guidance and direction; increasing motivation and satisfaction and working to limit learning obstacles; and increasing opportunities for educational success and empowering students toward self-directed learning. Students' principal concept was their focus on their instructors' teaching abilities—this concept was much more important to them than the course they were taking or the value of the content. Students spoke about their instructors by using such terms as helpful, motivating, positive, committed, interesting, dependable, humorous, confident, enthusiastic, competent, energetic, and intelligent. They also indicated that their instructors listened to them, that they considered them leaders, and that they were successful and creative teachers. Students rated the importance of feedback; they were highly interested in helpful and informative feedback and, in fact, valued this more than their instructor's recognition of their individual differences or needs. Like their instructors, students placed emphasis on the importance of their instructor's concern for them and the relationship between this concern and their own ability to increase their self-worth and self-esteem. And although students knew their instructors held high expectations for them, they expressed some reluctance to operate on their own and to take over responsibility for their own learning. In Table 5.3, faculty and student reports of teaching behaviors are compared. The numbers represent the percentages of faculty and students who reported the particular behavior.

Table 5.3: **Concurrence Among Instructors and Students**

Award-Winning Instructors and Students' Concurrence: Path-Goal Framework					
Instructors	95.0	94.5	92.8	92.0	83.9	83.4
Students	90.7	93.4	88.2	90.4	84.6	69.5
(1)	(2)	(3)	(4)	(5)	(6)

(1) engages desire to learn	(2) offers guidance and direction	(3) motivates learning
(4) limits learning obstacles	(5) increases successful opportunities	(6) empowers students

Although we were somewhat surprised at the difference between faculty perception of the level of readiness for student independence and the students' perceptions that they were ready to take responsibility for their own learning, we were able to use this discrepancy to predict the teacher archetype to be applied in the teaching life cycle (explained in Chapter 7).

Unsuccessful Behavior. Faculty reported a different pattern of behaviors when they discussed their unsuccessful experiences with motivating students to learn. While successful instructor behavior concentrated on understanding students' desire to learn or on offering diagnoses and direction, unsuccessful behavior patterns demonstrated instructor need to reduce frustrating barriers and to intensify exploration for alternatives for change. Only after they had a grasp on the obstacles that hindered the teaching-learning goal path did instructors become highly directive, use their coaching, and personally recommit themselves to their students' successes. They attended to individual student needs and recommunicated the goal and purpose of instruction. They saw the importance of modelling expected behavior and teaching students the consequences of their actions before they allowed them independence; they solicited their students' contributions and resources.

In reporting the situations in which they were unsuccessful in motivating their students to learn, instructors were aware of their own inability to eliminate or reduce learning barriers that stand in the way of successful student performance. Although they reported feeling less able to motivate their students, they described stronger affiliation with their students as they were able to relate to and empathize with their feelings of frustration. Faculty emphasized the importance of immediately assessing problem situations that reward students, encouraging their perceptions of their self-worth, affirming their capabilities, and then working diligently to develop and communicate new goals to meet the demands of the new situation.

By comparing reports of successful and unsuccessful motivation, one cannot fail to note the importance of contingency-based behavior. Given the theoretical basis of our teaching-learning path-goal framework, we found that the patterns of behavior were adaptable and dependent on contingency situations. And although we theoretically knew to expect leader behavior to be contingency-based, we were encouraged to find that our analyses of self-reported and student-reported data—based on actual experiences—confirmed the theory. Compatibility of goals and working toward mutual achievement of goals categorized the pattern of successful behaviors; recognition that problems existed and immediate attention to solutions were the guiding behaviors of teachers as they reported unsuccessful experiences. The final phase of our inquiry into teaching behaviors pitted teachers' philosophical premises of teaching against their actual experiences and teaching practices. We assumed that by asking teachers to give us their philosophy of teaching we would find what teachers believe their behaviors should be.

Philosophy of Teaching. Not surprisingly, the exceptional teachers demonstrated a parallel relationship between their philosophies of teaching and their ability to motivate students to learn. Their educational philosophy was demonstrated in their performance in the classroom. Award-winning instructors' aptitude for teaching involves the integration of their philosophy with the actual practice of their teaching. We found no variance between these two aspects or strengths of reported behaviors. They demonstrate and communicate well-defined course organization, diagnose and plan for students' needs within their course development, and are initially directive and positive in their approaches with students. They are accommodating and supportive of their students, providing them with extra help and time and urging them to succeed on their own. They pay particular attention to the college environment, "inspect what they expect" from their students (and have high expectations of their students), and demonstrate care and concern for the dignity of the individual student. In Figure 5.4 the award-winning instructors' strengths, or response rate, for the six teaching-learning path-goal concepts are illustrated. The terms defined as factors 1 through 6 respond to the six major themes of the teaching-learning path-goal framework: (1) recognizes and engages students' desire to learn; (2) increases opportunities for educational performance and success; (3) offers positive orientation, guidance, and direction; (4) uses effective performance as an expectation to empower students; (5) works to limit or eliminate learning obstacles; and (6) motivates students to increased satisfaction for and development of learning skills.

Figure 5.4: **AWI Population and Teaching-Learning Path-Goal Means**

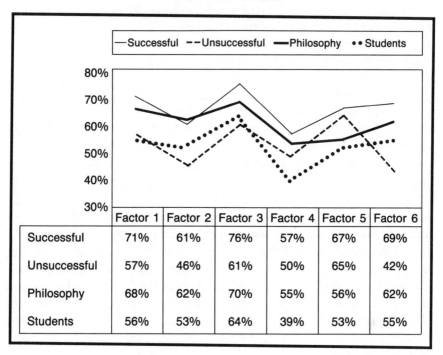

	Factor 1	Factor 2	Factor 3	Factor 4	Factor 5	Factor 6
Successful	71%	61%	76%	57%	67%	69%
Unsuccessful	57%	46%	61%	50%	65%	42%
Philosophy	68%	62%	70%	55%	56%	62%
Students	56%	53%	64%	39%	53%	55%

CONCLUSION

In general, award-winning faculty excel in allowing students input into their courses and their teaching; in their dedication to their role in encouraging students to take responsibility for their own learning; in their ability to match needs to plans, course content, and curriculum; in their insistence on regular and consistent feedback to students; in their ability to motivate students; and in their ability to personalize outcomes and to encourage independence.

By positing a teaching-learning framework that is linked to path-goal theory, instruction becomes focused on the skills and competencies of successful and exemplary instructors as they perform in the classroom. The mystery and guesswork of the classroom experience are eliminated when faculty see the teaching-learning path-goal framework as a basis for course and class planning.

The competencies of award-winning instructors may be employed by any teacher. Both experientially and behaviorally, award-winning instructors have identified their skills and leadership abilities in the classroom. Their special leadership emphases are on motivation, influence, and student orientation. They are instrumental in recognizing student desire and willingness to learn, in increasing student opportunities for successful educational performance, in motivating students to heighten their academic skills, in offering positive guidance and teaching direction, in working to eliminate or limit learning obstacles, and in using high expectations as the key to empowering students to take responsibility for their own active learning.

Thus, one of the major roles of the instructor becomes the act of linking the attributes and competencies of motivation, leadership, and path-goal theory. Now it is important to tie these concepts to experiential learning theory and its implications for teaching styles or archetypes. From the work of Lewin, Piaget, and Jung, Kolb (1984) introduced his learning styles inventory, which demonstrates the effects of experiences and experiential learning on the adult learner's dominant learning style. By integrating this idea with the life cycle theory of Hersey and Blanchard (1982), the Teaching as Leading Inventory was developed to reveal the dominant teaching styles of the award-winning instructors of our study. In the subsequent five chapters, these teaching styles will be discussed.

Chapter 6

Introducing the Teaching as Leading Inventory*

> *There can be no excellence in teaching*
> *if teachers*
> *do not bring to bear*
> *what they know and what they cherish.*
>
> Kerr, 1981

* Joe Barwick, a member of the 1989 Community College Leadership Program, University of Texas, and Department Head of English at Central Piedmont Community College, North Carolina, provided background research for the Teaching as Leading Inventory.

6

*A*lthough experiential learning has been advocated in modern times by educational philosophers from John Dewey to Malcolm Knowles, it is not a recent phenomenon. In fact, the earliest advocates are among the most famous. Socrates believed that to educate was "to draw from within." Education meant to draw out something hidden, latent, or reserved. It implied the bringing out of potential. According to Plato, the image of education was "the turning of the eye of the soul outwards toward the light" (Peters, 1965). Education was the vehicle for developing the potential for wisdom and leadership; thus, the good teacher led the student to his or her own understanding. In the *Symposium*, for example, we are presented with an exemplary teacher, Socrates, who struggles to move his students to choose to aspire and live according to principles, to create order in their experiences, and to understand the meaning of concepts and forms.

Rousseau recalled Socrates's concept of how teaching and knowledge are to be understood. Knowledge could not be imparted mechanically from without, but required the student's active participation. This model of teaching views knowledge as insight, which must be stimulated by a teacher and what a teacher does in his or her encounters with a student. Knowledge is viewed as a process of recollection, stimulated by a desire to recover some hidden insight, and requiring an active effort on the part of the student to remember. Rousseau's contribution to our understanding of the student came in the form of the character Emile, who became a prototype of the learner who was allowed to grow according to his own nature, finding his own insight and readiness.

John Locke, another Enlightenment philosopher, asserted that ideas were derived from sensations and from actual experiences and that they were not innate. Locke postulated that the mind was a *tabula rasa*, a blank tablet on which experiences could write. He believed that the mind could be "a little mended" by the good teacher who could focus on developing a sound mind in a sound body and, later, on knowledge of the world. This view presents the student who is malleable and receptive, whose mind is self-enclosed but open to, and changed by, outside experiences. Locke's empirical view is the source of experiential and interactive approaches to teaching and learning.

And in our own time, Dewey pointed to the need for learners to find interconnections and continuity of experience. The responsibility of the educator, then, was to be aware of the shaping of experience by environmental conditions and to select concrete experiences that were most conducive to growth. Teachers, according to Dewey, should know how to use both physical and social surroundings to contribute and build worthwhile experiences.

William James's educational philosophy contributed the concept of pragmatism. Teachers were warned that they could not "justifiably put things before learners to learn"; they had to try to offer ideas and objects attached to students' interests, with the expectation that interest or a sense of connection would arouse learners to exert the effort required to learn. James encouraged the teacher to attend to the student's "free will" and the student's capacity to choose. For James, the ultimate test of ideas and meaning came from freely initiated action and in a life freely lived.

Each of these philosophers contributes to our knowledge of the meaning of education, and each emphasizes the need to provoke students to overcome self-interests, to achieve some agreement about their goals, and to transcend the narrowness of their lives. To quote Kant, it is necessary to educate in order to empower individuals to use their rational capacities and thus to transcend physical stimulation and causation. The art of the educator lies in allowing the mind to freely choose good aims and goals. This is accomplished at different stages of growth and readiness; hence, Kant saw education as a continuous process, always reaching toward the achievement of freedom (Greene, 1986).

Finally, Martin (1982) reminds us of Dewey's warning of the dangers of separating reason from emotion, thought from action, and education from life. She calls for a liberal view of education that focuses on the development of the person, not simply the development of the mind. Her warning draws attention to the tension between the cognitivists and those with an experiential, or action-oriented, view. This tension is exacerbated by the belief that no philosophy of teaching can be developed that does not take the institution and social contexts into account.

Greene (1986) explains "not only are there problems of schools existing in a nation still ridden by inequities and deprivation, there are problems resulting from the erosion of the public, the growth of privatism, and the felt lack of community" (p. 492). For those who take this position, it is not enough to concentrate on rules and norms; attention must be paid to history, consciousness, and change. Educators must concern themselves with empowering students to make sense of, to conceptualize, to develop perspectives upon, and perhaps to transform their actually lived worlds (Martin, 1982). Teaching exists in the light of its consequences for experience, for conduct, and for actual practice in the world. Good teachers must know something about what they are teaching (or trying to let others learn), must care about what is worthwhile about their teaching, and must be concerned about their students learning what they are trying to teach (Greene, 1986, p.479).

What we know about education after more than two millennia, then, is so simple that it is axiomatic: at the heart of learning is the learner. Or more pointedly, the most powerful learning takes place when the learning environment—controlled primarily by the teacher—recognizes and accommodates the learner's gestalt of experiences, needs, abilities, goals, and pre-existing value for what is to be learned. However, lest the reader be affected by the simplicity of our axiom, we should point out that American business is just now recognizing the same interdependent relationship between success and worker satisfaction. In other words, at the heart of work is the worker. Leaders in the workplace, therefore, now realize that to fulfill the goals of the organization, they must take into account the goals of the workers and somehow bring the two sets of goals into compatibility. Workers do better work when they have some expectation that their efforts will lead to personal satisfaction (Vroom, 1976). Likewise, leaders need to help workers clarify their own needs in terms of the desired organizational outcomes and help ensure their success in attaining them (House and Mitchell, 1974). And through the whole process, leaders constantly appraise the worker's motivational and ability levels in order to provide the kind of leadership appropriate for the worker to be successful (Hersey and Blanchard, 1982).

Putting the learner at the center of the learning, or the worker at the center of the work, then, is not nearly so simple as it seems. However, to approach it scientifically, we need to recognize that there are two general areas of study: (1) how students learn through experience to increase personal satisfaction; (2) how teachers "lead" students through experiential learning to accomplish the educational goals at a higher level of personal satisfaction.

EXPERIENTIAL LEARNING

The Lewinian Model. Adults come to a learning situation with a vast storehouse of prior effective and cognitive experiences from which to draw (Cross, 1981; Houle, 1984; Knowles, 1973; Tough, 1977). But these experiences are not merely recorded in a mental catalog; they have shaped the learner into the person he or she is (Chickering, 1977; Erikson,1959; Jung, 1977; Piaget, 1971; Rogers, 1961). Consequently, not to acknowledge the worth of experience in the learning situation to which the learner has committed is to deny an integral part of the learner's "self." However, to recognize the worth of that experience in forming the learner is also to recognize the worth of experience as a change vehicle in the overall learning process. The teacher who would lead learners to higher achievement of educational goals, therefore, must present those goals in such a way that the learner feels his or her prior experience will have a positive impact on performance. But in addition, the leading teacher must provide new experiences the learner needs to ensure that learner effort results in performance.

In order to benefit from experiential learning, a person must have the opportunity to have concrete experiences, be able to reflect upon those experiences, be capable of formulating abstract "theories" that account for those reflections, and be able to apply and evaluate the theories in similar experiences (Kolb, 1984; Lewin, 1951). Lewin saw this process as a cycle. (See Figure 6.1.)

Figure 6.1: **Lewin's Experiential Learning Model**

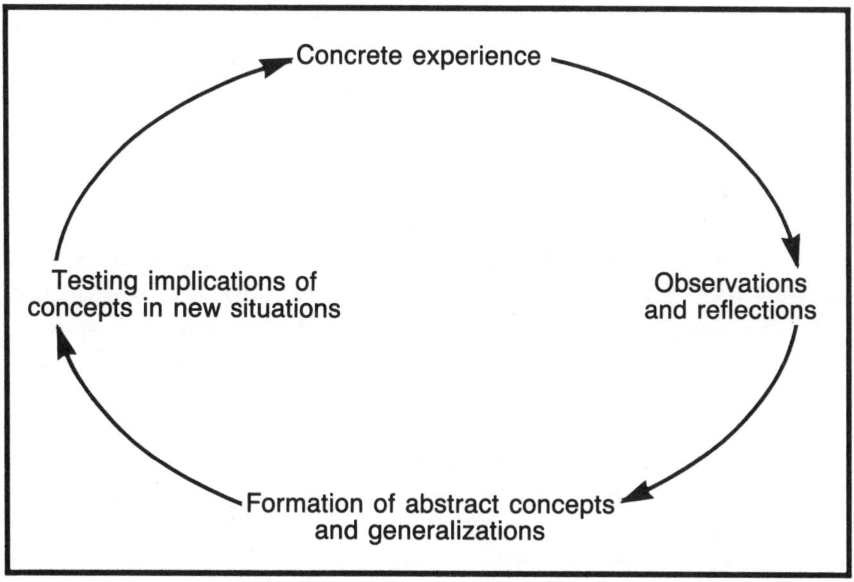

Reproduced by permission, Kolb, 1984

Others, most notably Dewey and Piaget, developed similar models, but their models focused more on how an individual develops over an extended period of time. The importance of the Lewinian model is that it focuses on more immediate aims of learning—that is, to go from concrete experience, through a process of abstracting the experience, to the end result of being able to use the new knowledge. Lewin's Experiential Learning Model is also helpful because it illustrates that experiential learning is only effective when the teacher leads the learner through the complete process.

Kolb took Lewin's model a step further and researched the relationship between the poles of the cycle. Jung's conceptual classification of personality types existing along bipolar dimensions was used as the foundation for Kolb's thinking. What he found was that the poles—i.e., concrete experience vs. abstract conceptualization and reflective observation vs. active experimentation—were in conflict with each other; in other words, there was a dialectic relationship. Consequently, the more a person is oriented toward concrete experiences, the less likely he or she is to form abstract conceptualizations of experience, and vice versa. Likewise, the more a person is predisposed to reflective observation, the less likely the person is to engage in the external activities associated by experimentation. Although experiential learning is a four-stage process, learners appear to have a dominance for the cognitive skills at one stage more than another. Out of this research, Kolb developed his well-known Learning Styles Inventory, which, for purposes of this book, requires closer analysis here.

Kolb's Learning Styles Inventory. According to Kolb's learning model, concrete experience/abstract conceptualization and reflective observation/active experimentation represent two separate dimensions of the learning process. Kolb defines learning as follows:

> Learning is the process whereby knowledge is created through the transformation of experience. This definition emphasizes several critical aspects of the learning process, as viewed from the experiential perspective. First is the emphasis on the process of adaptation and learning as opposed to content or outcomes. Second is that knowledge is a transformation process being continuously created and recreated, not an independent entity to be acquired or transmitted. Third, learning transforms experience in both its objective and subjective forms (1984, p. 38).

The two axes, then, represent the dimensions; and concrete experience, abstract conceptualization, reflective observation, and active experimentation are adaptive orientations. The concrete experience/abstract conceptualization axis is a prehension dimension, in that it represents two opposed processes of grasping the meaning of experiences, either by reliance on actual experience (apprehension) or by reliance on symbolic interpretation of that experience (comprehension). The reflective observation/active experimentation axis is a *transformation* dimension, in that it represents two opposed processes of transforming that grasp on meaning, either through internal reflection (intention) or by manipulating, through experimentation or the like, the external world (extension). (See Figure 6.2.)

Figure 6.2: **Experiential Learning and Knowledge Forms**

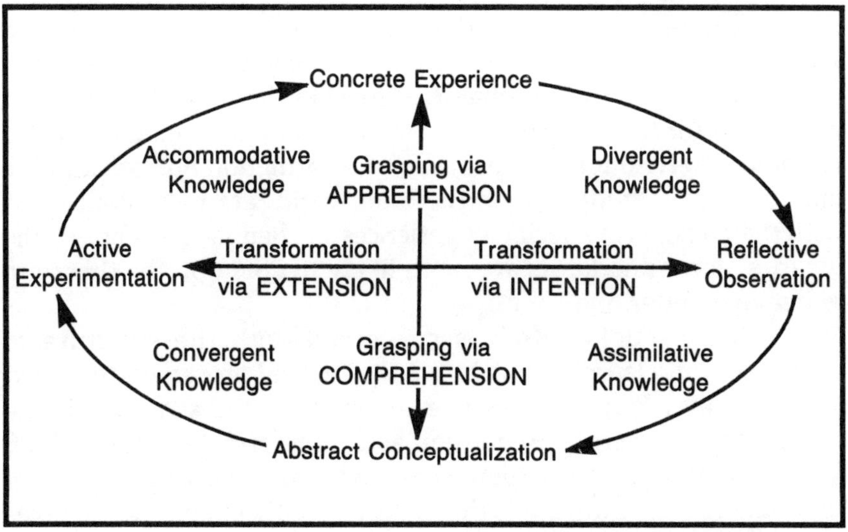

Reproduced with permission, Kolb, 1984.

Remembering that Kolb defines learning as the process whereby knowledge is created from the transformation of experience, we see in the double-axis theory that there are two ways of grasping experience and two ways of transforming it. Because of the interaction of prehension and transformation, there are four elementary forms of knowledge, identified in the quadrants in Figure 6.2. The combination of concrete experience grasped by apprehension and reflective observation transforming experience by intention yields divergent knowledge. The opposite type of knowledge is convergent knowledge. Reflective observation through intention and abstract conceptualization through comprehension yield assimilative knowledge. And its opposite is accommodative knowledge.

Through experience an individual learns to use the adaptive

dimension of either apprehension or comprehension dominantly, and either intention or extension dominantly. Consequently, people have a preferred learning style corresponding to one of the four types of knowledge. Some people are divergent learners and prefer learning situations in which they work outward from experience, seeking possibilities more than solutions. On the other side are the convergent learners. They prefer to use abstract reasoning and direct experimentation to arrive at correct answers or solutions. Those learners who prefer reflective observation and abstract conceptualization are assimilators. They like theoretical models and would like for the facts to fit into them. If they do not, assimilators are more likely to ignore the aberrant information and stick to the theory. Accommodators, on the other hand, are more concerned with the facts, with specific experiences. When facts do not fit the theories, accommodators are more likely to abandon the theory in search of a better one.

At this point, Kolb is concerned with the structure of knowledge and learning more than the cyclical processes described by Lewin and Piaget. However, inherent in the structure is the interaction between apprehension and transformation, the pull of, for example, concrete experiences and reflective observation of experience. Also inherent is the dialectic conflict between the poles of both dimensions. Thus, structure is interaction and conflict, and seeing it as static or fixed would be a mistake. Also, it is important to remember that a person will have relatively higher emphasis on one or two of the learning modes, but will not fall purely into any one of the four.

Kolb's Learning Style Inventory (LSI) is a self-description questionnaire in which the respondent is asked to rank choices according to the word that best describes the way he or she learns. Each of the responses corresponds to one of the learning modes; consequently, the LSI score is derived simply by summing the rank numbers. These scores then can be plotted to show a two-dimensional learning style profile; for example, after a respondent takes the LSI, she is able to plot her particular learning style to discover her dominant pattern of experiential learning as converger, diverger, assimilator, or accommodator.

TEACHING AS LEADING

Knowing a student's preferred learning style is little more than a scientific curiosity, unless the information can be used to help the student reach his or her educational goals. Yet, how can teachers plan for classes when learning styles differ widely among diverse cultural groups, such as the student population of community colleges? And of what avail is this knowledge when community college students so often lack the motivation to act responsibly to bring about high achievement? Again the analogy to the workplace emerges. Studies of successful businesses show that workers are more motivated and have higher satisfaction when they feel personally committed to the goals of the organization (Bass, 1985; Peters and Waterman, 1982). A study of teachers in the City Colleges of Chicago who had demonstrated success by high levels of student achievement and low attrition also revealed the importance of clearly defined outcomes and standards of performance when paired with student participation (Guskey and Easton, 1983). Further studies have verified that excellent teachers are able to clearly articulate the goals of the course and get a high level of commitment from students to reach them (Easton, 1984; Roueche and Baker, 1987). Excellent teachers, therefore, act like excellent business leaders: they help the individuals in the class align their personal goals with the goals of the course.

According to the path-goal theory of leadership (see Chapter 2), leaders are effective, once goals are clarified, to the extent that they have a positive impact on subordinates' motivation, ability to perform effectively, and, thus, ability to derive satisfaction from the work. Unfortunately, there are still many in the community colleges who do not, or will not, recognize the essential role of the teacher in motivating students to achieve. Even Socrates realized that teachers must struggle to "move" their students to aspire to the higher levels of education. And certainly the most effective business leaders do not assume all employees are motivated to achieve high levels of performance simply because they showed up for work on a particular day. Yet, some teachers believe students are either motivated or not (intrinsic), and nothing the teacher can do (extrinsic) will change this state. It is important to remember that motives are internal, but goals are external (Hersey and Blanchard, 1982). The effective teacher, like the effective leader, is the one who can help others to match their motives with their own and the course's goals. Motivation is not always an active process. In fact, motivation is to teaching what attention is to driving a car. There are times when much is needed, and others when relatively little will suffice. The excellent teacher, though, is constantly aware of the signals and is ready with a repertoire of skills to apply to the appropriate situation.

Effective teachers also have a positive impact on the students' ability to achieve the goals. Obviously, this includes much more than providing them with content. First of all, teachers clarify for the students the "path" to the goal. Then teachers help students develop the skills for success; but equally important, they help remove the barriers to success. For example, a student who does not attend class regularly will have difficulty completing the goals of the course, whether that course is American history or integrated electrical circuits. The effective teacher must help the student overcome this negative behavior as well as master the content or skills.

In order to be a leader, according to the teaching-learning path-goal framework, the teacher is in a constant learning mode. Long before the course ever begins, the teacher reflects on desired goals, plans strategies for learning and evaluation, and produces materials for implementing the plans. Once the course begins, the teacher is constantly assessing the group, determining readiness, motivation, interests and other things that could necessitate a change in course activities. And most of all, the effective teacher is aware of each student in terms of ability, progress, needs, and level of satisfaction. In other words, the effective teacher is actively involved every day in experiential learning—learning about the students, about the group, about the efficiency of methods and plans, and about the overall purposes of the course. However, experiential learning in the context of teaching as leading has a fundamental difference from experiential learning in the context of learners acquiring new knowledge or skills. The purpose of this type of experiential learning for the teacher is to increase student success. In other words, the experiential learning is used to directly alter the experience itself (i.e., make the students, group, or course different), thus requiring new learning, further alteration, and so forth. Because of this difference, Kolb's model of experiential learning does not adequately describe the learning process the teacher uses to increase student performance. Instead, we need a model of teacher learning styles that describes the ways teachers view students and the ways they conceptualize course content to achieve results.

In order to build a conceptual framework for teaching as leading, it is necessary to look at what teachers do on a day-by-day basis to adapt to student needs in order to achieve the maximum success. There are two assumptions underlying this approach. First, we assume excellent teachers do, in fact, adapt to student needs regularly. Adaptation may be in the form of making additional hand-outs when students stumble over content, or it may mean calling students in for conferences when their performance is less than it should be. In other words, excellent teachers are constantly examining the interaction between students, content, and methodology, and making changes as needed to get the highest level of performance. The second assumption is that excellent teachers do not lower standards. The purpose of the teaching-learning path-goal framework is to increase students' satisfaction by enabling them to achieve high performance through their own efforts. Lowering standards and expectations would be counterproductive to that effort.

Like experiential learning, teaching as leading involves a four-step process. In the first stage, instructors must involve themselves with learners openly and without bias in new experiences (others orientation). This open involvement with students leads to becoming aware, sensing the need for action, observing the environment, being alert to clues, and discerning results (reflective orientation). The instructor must then think of necessary actions, create solutions in the mind, analyze the situation, develop a plan of action, and think through experimenting and revising anticipated action (task orientation). Finally, the instructor commits to a course of action, commits to goals, decides how to proceed, executes the plan, and evaluates the results (action orientation).

In its broadest context, teaching as leading involves (1) influencing learners individually and in groups to set goals and (2) leading the learners toward goal accomplishment. Therefore, it is congruent with the teaching-learning path-goal framework; to obtain a high level of student performance and, thus, a high level of satisfaction, all stages in the teaching-as-leading cycle must be completed.

Figure 6.3: Teaching-as-Leading Cycle

1.
Others Orientation
1. Feel
2. Care
3. Be Concerned
4. Become Involved
5. Value Others

4.
Action Orientation
1. Commit
2. Set Goals
3. Decide
4. Execute
5. Evaluate

2.
Reflective Orientation
1. Become Alert
2. Sense Action
3. Observe Situations
4. Watch for Clues
5. Discern Results

3.
Task Orientation
1. Think
2. Create
3. Analyze Situation
4. Plan Action
5. Experiment and Change

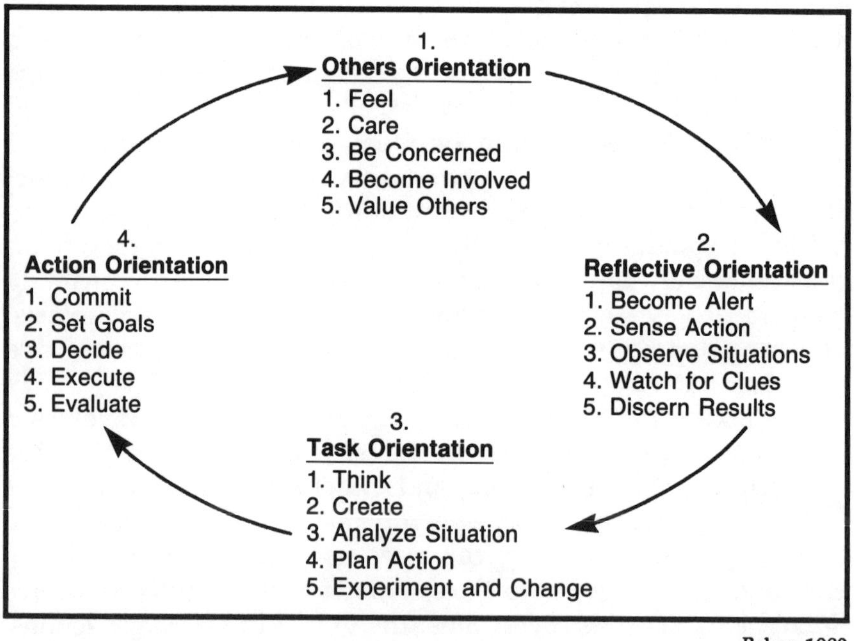

Baker, 1989

One difficulty for teachers as leaders in the learning process results from their natural tendency toward one type of behavior more than another. In our study with the 869 excellent teachers, we found strong evidence of polarity along both axes of the model. High scores for "others orientation" were negatively correlated with "task orientation," and high scores for "reflective orientation" were negatively correlated with "action orientation." Also, there was not a strong correlation from one axis to the other. Figure 6.4 shows the correlation matrix which demonstrates the strong polarity along both axes of the teaching-as-leading cycle.

Figure 6.4: **The Correlation Matrix Demonstrating Polarity**

	Action	Reflection	Task	Others
Action	1	-0.39	-0.29	-0.23
Reflection		1	-0.06	-0.28
Task			1	-0.69
Others				1

The results, therefore, demonstrate that teachers have a pronounced tendency in the way they interrelate learners and content (vertical axis) and in the way they conceptualize and implement learning experiences (horizontal axis). The interaction of these two pronounced tendencies creates the teacher's teaching-as-leading style. These four styles are shown in Figure 6.5.

Figure 6.5: **Teaching-Learning Grid**

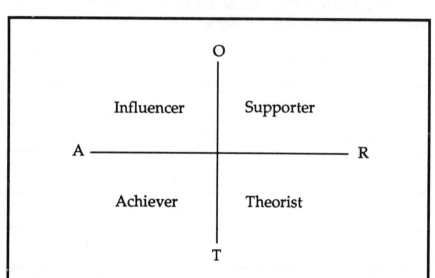

In its broadest context, teaching as leading involves influencing learners individually and in groups to set goals and leading the learners toward goal accomplishment. By combining the teaching-learning path-goal framework with the experiential learning model of Lewin and Kolb, teaching as leading can be envisioned as follows: (1) an immediate experience involving others is the basis for observation and reflection; (2) these perceptions are assimilated into a theory of visualization of realities from which planning and action can occur; (3) these plans and visualizations then serve as guides to the active influencing of others.

As leaders in the learning process, then, teachers must involve themselves with learners openly and without bias in new experiences. These behaviors lead to becoming aware, sensing the need for action, observing the environment, being alert to clues, and discerning results. The teacher must then think of necessary actions, create solutions in the mind, analyze the situation, develop a plan of action, and think through experimenting with and revising anticipated action. Finally, the teacher commits to a course of action and goals, decides how to proceed, executes the plan, and evaluates the results.

As with experiential learning theory, teachers have greater strengths in one stage of the cycle than others. In order to identify this strength, it is necessary to imagine situations in which all four types of behavior would be appropriate and force a choice. The Teaching as Leading Inventory (TALI) is a forced-choice, self-scoring questionnaire designed to alert teachers to their own preferred teaching-as-leading style. Because learning and leading both require all four stages of the cycle, it should not be inferred that one style is superior to another. Excellent teachers are adaptable to student needs and demands of the learning environment, and they must have a broad repertoire of leadership skills from which to draw.

In the compact version of the TALI (Figure 6.6), the reader may learn his or her own teaching style. Six major areas of the TALI are included: teaching, learning, performance, effectiveness, student perceptions, and self-perception. These six areas are derived from the competencies of effective teachers and from the research on teaching and learning. The lead statement appears above questions 1 and 2, 3 and 4, and so on. Replies should be weighted by the respondent so that the number 4 indicates the item that is most like the respondent and the number 1 indicates the item that is least like the respondent. After all scores are indicated, all "A" responses are added as the total T score, all "B" responses are added as the O score; all "C" responses are added as the A score; and all "D" responses are added as the R score. Finally the T score is subtracted from the O score and plotted on the T-O axis in Figure 6.7. The A score is subtracted from the R score and plotted on the A-R axis also in Figure 6.7. The respondent should retain the sign of the subtraction. For example, a T score of 15 subtracted from an O score of 20 would yield a -5. Finally, the respondent draws a straight line parallel to the T-O axis through the marked point on the A-R axis and draws a line parallel to the A-R axis through the marked point on the T-O axis. The intersection of these two lines indicates the dominant teaching-as-leading style of the respondent. In the event that the intersection of the two lines falls toward the center of the grid, and the respondent has difficulty interpreting teaching style, the Figure 6.7a, Enlarged View of TALI, should be used to plot horizontal and vertical lines. Since a whole number does not appear at the intersection of the grid, all respondents will fall into one of the four quadrants of the grid.

Figure 6.6: Compact Version of the Teaching as Leading Inventory

On this page you will find twelve statements related to your teaching style. Examine each statement & the four possible adjacent responses (A,B,C,D) associated with that statement. Weigh the responses according to how well you feel they describe you & enter your ratings in the spaces provided. When you have completed all 12 items, tally your score for each of the four factors by adding all scores in each of the four columns. Place your total for each column in the space provided.

	4-Most like me	3-More like me	2-Less like me	1-Least like me
Teaching—When teaching, I:				
1.	A. rely on logical thinking.	B. express my feelings.	C. am critically involved.	D. observe & watch students.
2.	A. tend to reason out problems.	B. have strong reactions to students.	C. like to try out new ideas.	D. am quiet and reserved.
Learning—I learn best when I:				
3.	A. am thinking.	B. am feeling.	C. am doing.	D. am perceiving.
4.	A. experiment with new concepts.	B. trust my feelings.	C. trust what I do.	D. trust what I see.
Performance—I perform best:				
5.	A: as an intellectual teacher.	B. as a caring teacher.	C. as an action-oriented teacher.	D. as an observing teacher.
6.	A. when I reason out new ideas.	B. when I am receptive & open-minded.	C. when I set goals & pursue them.	D. when I am careful but aware.
Effectiveness—In my behavior toward students, I:				
7.	A. involve them in applying logic.	B. reach out to help.	C. influence them to think.	D. emphasize the meaning of concepts.
8.	A. develop their intellectual skills.	B. develop their emotions.	C. develop them behaviorally.	D. develop their ability to reflect.
Students' Perceptions—My students describe me as:				
9.	A. scientific.	B. humanistic.	C. decisive.	D. perceptive.
10.	A. an analytical teacher.	B. an involved teacher.	C. an influencing teacher.	D. a sensitive teacher.
Self Perception—I see myself as:				
11.	A. thoughtful.	B. involved.	C. committed.	D. aware.
12.	A. a person interested in concepts.	B. a person who values others.	C. an outcome oriented person.	D. a discerning person.
	(Total: **T Score**)	(Total: **O Score**)	(Total: **A Score**)	(Total: **R Score**)

Copyright by George Baker; may not be reproduced or used without written permission, January, 1990.

Figure 6.7: Compact TALI Grid

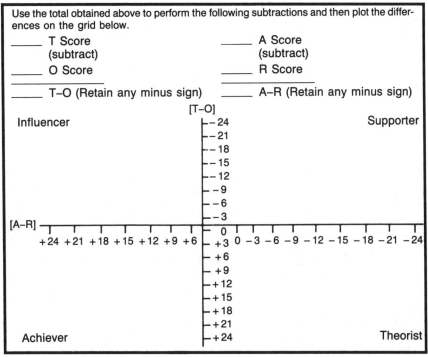

Use the total obtained above to perform the following subtractions and then plot the differences on the grid below.

_____ T Score
(subtract)
_____ O Score

_____ A Score
(subtract)
_____ R Score

_____ T–O (Retain any minus sign)   _____ A–R (Retain any minus sign)

Figure 6.7a: Enlarged View of TALI Grid

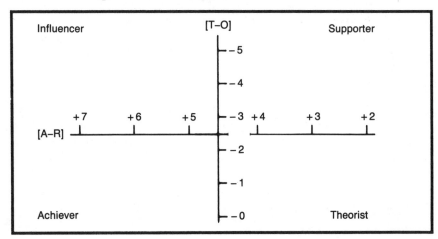

TEACHING AS LEADING INVENTORY AND THE AWARD-WINNING INSTRUCTORS

Many of the award-winning instructors attended the Eleventh Annual International Conference on Teaching Excellence, held in Austin, Texas, in May 1989. Here they were celebrated and awarded medallions for their teaching excellence and their participation in this study. During the conference the award-winning instructors completed the extended form of the Teaching as Leading Inventory (Baker, 1989). Responses were coded and analyzed to form the TALI database. From this rich database we were able to demonstrate teaching styles and to relate the teaching-learning path-goal framework to those teaching styles. Moreover, we were able to carry over our triangulation methodology by incorporating instructors' self reports, students' evaluations, and CEOs' recommendations of their award-winning instructors.

The teaching styles that form the basis for the TALI are meant to point to the teacher's dominant style and to demonstrate his or her opposite and complementary styles as well. Teaching styles are also meant to represent challenges to the instructor to change, to adapt, and to accommodate students' needs. We see the TALI as a predictor of the life cycle that occurs in the classroom. Students are the responsibility of the classroom teacher, and teachers do care about their students. Without examining students' readiness, teachers cannot arouse and engage students' desire to learn; and teachers tend to see learning obstacles as dead ends to student achievement. These are failures the teacher as leader can avoid. We assume that adaptation is the key to teacher-as-leader behavior and that in order to meet contingencies, the master teacher must change his or her style to accommodate the learner.

In the data we present here and in the next four chapters, teaching styles refer to the competencies and actual experiential data related to us by award-winning instructors. Although initially "type-cast," the community college teacher is really a situational teacher who can alter his or her style based on demands of environment, demands of students, or demands of the situation. (This concept of the situational teacher will be discussed in detail in Chapter 11.)

FINDINGS: TEACHING AS LEADING INVENTORY

We found that the instructors who participated in the TALI were mainly (75 percent) Achievers and Influencers; that is, they tended to aggregate toward the action side of the TALI grid. Excellent teachers are action-oriented, whether emphasizing a student orientation or a task orientation. Moreover, almost all of the teaching styles aggregated around the center axis of the grid, which leads us to believe that award-winning instructors find it easy to change and adapt their teaching styles based on situational need. Figure 6.8 displays the distribution and clustering of our TALI participants by style; the difference between the participants' "task" and "others" scores and their "active" and "reflective" scores were plotted to determine their TALI teaching styles.

Figure 6.8: **Teaching-as-Leading Styles**

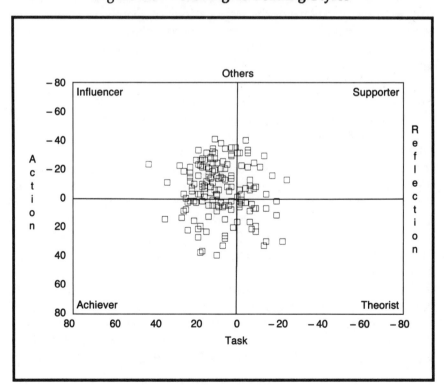

Award-winning instructors were distributed among the four teaching-as-leading styles (see Figure 6.9); in the following paragraphs we highlight the characteristics of each of the styles, and in the following four chapters each of the styles is discussed and participants are showcased.

Influencer: Most (50.3 percent) of the award-winning teachers in this study were Influencers. They commit to clear objectives and are actively involved with students in completing them. Because they are actively involved, they openly seek and exploit opportunities to increase learning. As leaders, they constantly influence learners' beliefs that their efforts will result in performance and that high performance will result in personal satisfaction.

Supporter: Another 12.4 percent of the excellent teachers were Supporters. They listen to students objectively and with an open mind, and they are sensitive to students' feelings. They are constantly gathering information about students, and as leaders they are always aware of the implications of situations they create for teaching and learning. Supporters are also aware of student values and are able to use then to maximize student performance and satisfaction.

Theorist: Some of the excellent teachers (11.8 percent) were Theorists. These teachers constantly analyze quantitative information about individual and group performance and design learning experiences to increase performance. They actively seek more effective ways to organize information and conceptualize theoretical models of the teaching and learning situation. They also conduct ongoing evaluations and assessments of their theories and ideas. Theorists are concerned with designing the best learning situations and environment to ensure that student effort results in performance.

Achiever: Achievers (25.5 percent) are constantly seeking to improve results. They try to create new ways of thinking and doing, and they are continually experimenting with new ideas and methods. As leaders, Achievers set goals for students, evaluate outcomes, and choose solutions that work. Then they try to improve on them by further experimentation, testing, and decision-making. Achievers derive their rewards by getting results. Their role is to find the best way to get the highest performance from the most students.

Figure 6.9: TALI Style Distribution

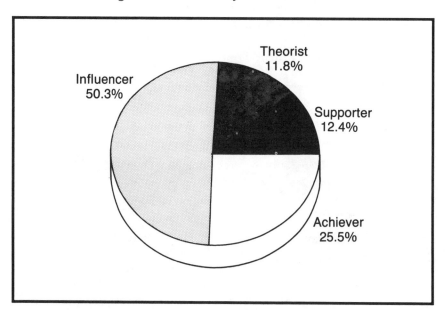

REPORTING THE TALI DEMOGRAPHICS

The TALI population had characteristics that repeated the characteristics of the award-winning instructors' demographic characteristics; we did not learn anything significantly different about them from these data. Even in areas where we expected to find some divergence—for example, the relationship of discipline or subject taught to teaching style—we did not find any unique patterns or statistically significant variations. Variables such as age, gender, ethnicity, fathers' and mothers' education, degrees, and teaching fields did not vary simply because we used teaching styles as a factor. Only in the ethnicity variable did we find any unique patterns, and of course, we must remember that our ethnic distribution with the whole population of participants was only 12 percent. In Figure 6.10, ethnic distribution among TALI styles shows Hispanics only in the Achiever's teaching style, which also demonstrates the highest percentages of minority groups of any teaching style. Because of our actual number of minority group members in the study, we hesitate to comment about this factor; but we note that as Achievers, teachers are active and concentrate on accomplishment of teaching goals.

Figure 6.10: **Ethnic Distribution by TALI Style**

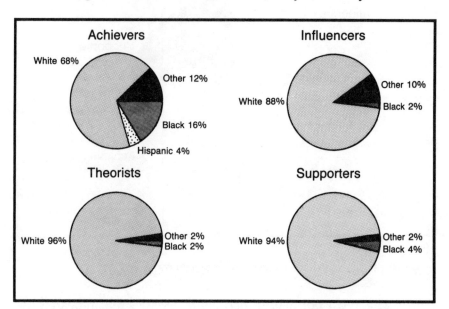

In Figures 6.11 and 6.12 degrees and teaching disciplines by TALI style are reported. All instructors have bachelor's degrees, and the number reporting master's degrees ranges from 75 percent to 98 percent. Influencers and Theorists had the greatest number of doctorates; Achievers and Theorists had a significant number of initial associate degrees.

Figure 6.11: **Degrees Held: TALI Population**

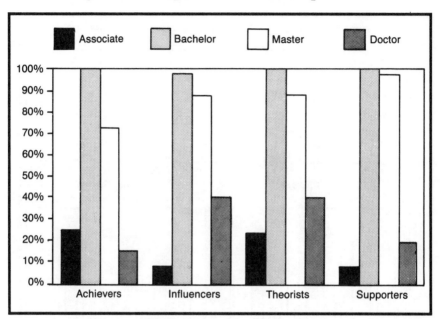

Finally, in a fascinating graphic representation of the relationship between teaching style and teaching discipline, we learn, contrary to Kolb's Learning Style Inventory (1984), where learner's majors can be directly correlated to their learning style, that no such relationship between teaching styles and teaching discipline could be determined. Rather, what we learned was an affirmation of the emphases on teaching as leading and the principle of teaching as a central feature of the community college. In our study, teaching discipline did not affect teaching style (Figure 6.12). What was central to all the instructors we studied was a genuine regard for the ethic of good teaching.

Figure 6.12: **Teaching Fields and TALI Style**

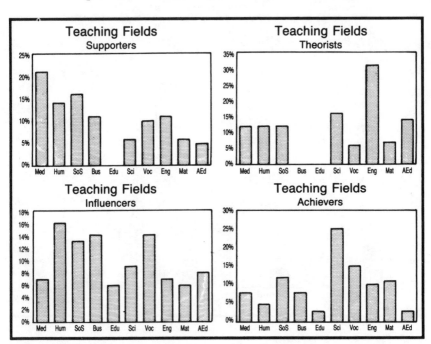

THE TEACHING-LEARNING PATH-GOAL FRAMEWORK:
TALI POPULATION

The TALI population was studied to determine their self-reported explanations of successful and unsuccessful experiences of motivating students and their philosophies. In order to confirm the triangulation process, we also compared the instructors' data to student and CEOs' data. In the following figures, the path-goal strategic functions—abbreviated to read: Arouses Needs, Increases Pay-offs, Clarifies Paths, Clarifies Expectations, Reduces Barriers, and Increases Satisfaction—are reported and related to the written scenarios reported by the TALI population. Two comparisons (see Figures 6.13 and 6.14) are made. In Figure 6.13, the TALI population data that examined the teaching-learning path-goal framework are displayed. Again we make note of the strong concurrence between what teachers talk about and practice (their reports about how they motivate students to learn) and their vision of what teaching "ought to be" (their philosophies of teaching). The TALI population also meets unsuccessful situations head-on; they demonstrate clearly that when the situation demands change, they confront and immediately begin to accommodate the new situation. They are committed to reducing learning obstacles that frustrate and limit students' growth.

Figure 6.13: **Path-Goal Means: TALI Population**

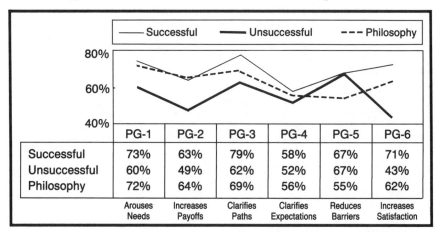

	PG-1	PG-2	PG-3	PG-4	PG-5	PG-6
Successful	73%	63%	79%	58%	67%	71%
Unsuccessful	60%	49%	62%	52%	67%	43%
Philosophy	72%	64%	69%	56%	55%	62%
	Arouses Needs	Increases Payoffs	Clarifies Paths	Clarifies Expectations	Reduces Barriers	Increases Satisfaction

Both students and CEOs also are included in our study of the TALI population and the teaching-learning path-goal framework. Figure 6.14 points out not only instructors' emphases (number of times they reported the behaviors listed in the teaching-learning path-goal framework) about those competencies that strengthen their teaching, but also students' and CEOs' remarks from their evaluations and letters of recommendation. What we have observed from our comparison, i.e., through triangulation, is that teachers' self reports, students' evaluations, and CEOs' recommendations all show concurrence. The successful, unsuccessful, and philosophy percentages demonstrate the faculty response to the teaching-learning path-goal concepts, then student and CEO responses to teaching-learning path-goal framework are given. Although the range of percentages demonstrate as much as a 21-point difference, this range did not indicate statistically unique findings. Rather we used data to compare relationships between faculty discussion of successful motivating experiences and philosophy of teaching, and then compared student and CEO evaluations of faculty. Unsuccessful motivating experiences was not an indicator used for comparisons. What is directly observable is the pattern of concurrence among faculty, students, and CEOs.

Figure 6.14: **Comparing Instructors, Students, and CEOs: TALI Population**

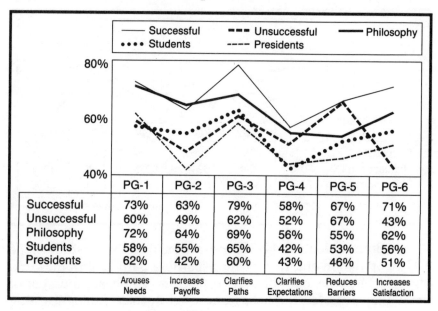

	PG-1	PG-2	PG-3	PG-4	PG-5	PG-6
Successful	73%	63%	79%	58%	67%	71%
Unsuccessful	60%	49%	62%	52%	67%	43%
Philosophy	72%	64%	69%	56%	55%	62%
Students	58%	55%	65%	42%	53%	56%
Presidents	62%	42%	60%	43%	46%	51%
	Arouses Needs	Increases Payoffs	Clarifies Paths	Clarifies Expectations	Reduces Barriers	Increases Satisfaction

SUMMARY

The Teaching as Leading Inventory, developed from the theoretical constructs of Piaget, Lewin, Jung, and Kolb, which point out the significance of experiential learning, was used to complete the teaching-learning identity of award-winning instructors. The TALI population was drawn from the larger award-winning instructors' population to complete our study of excellent teaching. Where the concepts of the teaching-learning path-goal framework gave us teaching themes and explicit attributes or behaviors of exemplary teachers, the TALI broadened our picture of the teacher as leader as one who meets contingency situations by modifying and adapting teaching styles. Four dominant teaching styles were discovered from the interpretation of the Teaching as Leading Inventory; these styles were: Supporter, Theorist, Achiever, and Influencer. These four teaching styles are discussed thoroughly in the next four chapters, and insight into the teaching competencies of the award-winning instructors who participated in the inventory is shared.

Chapter 7

Profiles of Teaching Excellence: Supporters

Philosophy
Characteristics
Strengths
Path-Goal Data and Supporters
Teaching-Learning and Path-Goal
Teaching Fields
Implications

7

The overall role of the teacher is to view the students as teachers and the teachers as students, and to build a trust relationship between the student and the teacher.

Libby Holt
Florida Community College at Jacksonville

My philosophy of the role of the teacher is one of facilitating and mentoring. Teachers are in the classroom for the sake of student learning. We serve as guides for students to follow through the hall of education.

Irma Jones
Texas Southmost College

Great teachers love their subject and their students; moreover, they love the teaching and learning process that unites the two. They use humor effectively and appropriately, adjust their style creatively when that is called for, and renew themselves continually in terms of their subject and their teaching skills.

Mike McHargue
Foothill College

147

*A*bout one-eighth of the instructors who participated in our study displayed the dominant characteristics of the Supporter teaching style (see Figure 7.1). Throughout this chapter, and by reporting the actual voices of faculty, students, and administrators from all over North America, we will concentrate on the Supporter teaching style.

Figure 7.1: **Supporters**

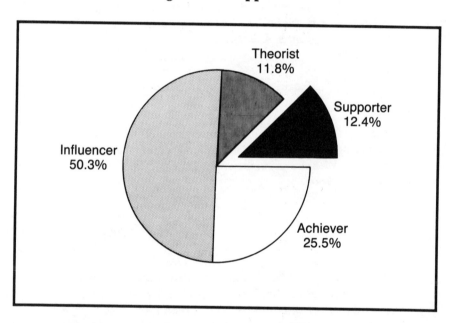

Kay Carl, a communications skills teacher (Blackhawk Technical College, Janesville, Wisconsin), offers this analysis of her own teaching style:

The teacher is a facilitator, a caretaker, an enabler, a creator. The teacher must have patience, endurance, confidence, and a genuine love of others as well as her/his subject matter.

A student in autobody class at Red Deer College (Red Deer, Alberta) seems to agree with Kay Carl as he talks about his teacher, Brad Hemstreet:

> Brad Hemstreet always made the time to go one-on-one with his students. This was a tremendous help to me as I was new to the college and knew no one in Red Deer. I was very nervous in the beginning and very hesitant to begin some repairs I was unsure of. His easy-going attitude and one-on-one help were the biggest differences to my succeeding. Brad really cares about his students.

Edward Luterbach, president of Red Deer College, also spoke of Brad Hemstreet: "Brad understands the need of the teacher to be a representative to the community; his service, assistance, and support in the areas of teaching and faculty development are legend."

PHILOSOPHY

Both of these passages are describing the Supporter teacher. Teachers who are predominantly Supporter in their Teaching as Leading Inventory (TALI) style view learning from the perspective of the learner. They do not, therefore, see themselves as teaching a subject or a class, but as teaching a variety of individuals. What Brad Hemstreet's student called "one-on-one" teaching is a major role of the Supporter teacher and is not viewed as extra or apart from the classroom teaching. For example, a student in Libby Holt's mathematics class (Florida Community College, Jacksonville, Florida) recounted an incident in which she went to Holt's office for help with a math problem. "She was having lunch," says the student. "She immediately pushed her lunch to the side, giving me all her attention." To the Supporter teacher, helping a student who interrupts lunch is as important as preparing a lesson or presenting information to a class.

Because of their focus on individual learners in the teacher-learning situation, Supporters recognize that they are, themselves, ongoing learners. Lincoln Lao, an art teacher (Schoolcraft College, Livonia, Michigan), says, "I always consider myself as a learner, showing students how I heighten my curiosity and proceed to objective investigation. I share learning experiences rather than teaching data." Helen Lowe, a nursing instructor (Amarillo College, Amarillo, Texas), reflects a similar attitude: "Teachers must remain open to learning from students' personal research, educational opportunities, and life experiences." Supporters, therefore, view teaching and learning holistically. They are learners as well as teachers, learning from those they are teaching.

Figure 7.2: Others-Reflective Orientation

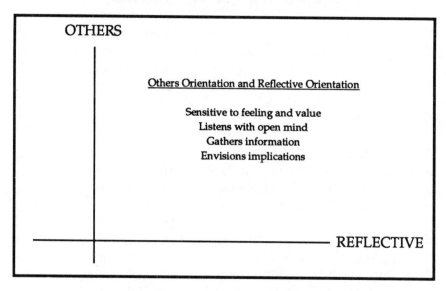

OTHERS

Others Orientation and Reflective Orientation

Sensitive to feeling and value
Listens with open mind
Gathers information
Envisions implications

REFLECTIVE

The primary forces affecting Supporter behavior are others orientation and reflective orientation. Supporters are emotionally drawn to help individual students, but they are constantly gathering and sensing information to help them guide student behavior. Many of the Supporters, for example, use preassessment instruments to determine learner readiness at the very beginning of the term and augment this information with personal information gathered from the students in individual conferences or through some other device. Supporters also continue to gather information about their students as the need arises. For example, Barbara West, a nursing instructor (Broward Community College, Fort Lauderdale, Florida), could not understand why a particular student had failed an exam and wanted to drop the course. She had the student review the exam, question by question, in her office and found that the student had reading problems and also needed glasses. Because of this instructor, both problems were eventually solved, and the student graduated with honors.

Supporters also obtain information by sensing. They are sensitive to student feelings and are quick to detect anxiety, low self-confidence, and other feelings that affect student performance. For example, one of Helen Hammond's nursing students (College of Southern Idaho, Twin Falls, Idaho) admits to being "frightened and insecure" when she started the course. But she further says, "(the instructor) sensed my insecurities and talked to me frankly and kindly. I was encouraged to keep trying, and my grades have been better." Many of the students, in fact, were very open in relating similar experiences where their own feelings would have prevented learning had it not been for a sensitive, supportive teacher. Supporters are also sensitive to values as well as feelings. College exposes students to many experiences for which they are unprepared emotionally. When one of Barbara West's nursing students was given the clinic assignment of providing care to a pregnant 14-year-old, she had trouble maintaining the objectivity required of a nurse. The student credits her instructor with sensing her difficulty and with providing appropriate counsel, thus enabling the student to grow as well as learn.

As we reviewed the student comments on these teachers, we were impressed by the frequency of terms like "caring," "open-minded," "concerned," and "objective." Supporters' students responded to the fact that Supporters do not solve problems; they help people. To balance this others orientation with the reflective orientation, however, Supporters are very aware of the implications of their actions. For example, Ed Tarvyd, a biology teacher (Santa Monica College, Santa Monica, California), talks about the need to make the subject matter interesting and to actively involve the learner in the learning. But he goes on to say why this is important: "The teacher then has the student to work with toward greater ends than just that particular bit of subject matter. One can now work on making that student a whole student, a career-motivated individual, and hopefully a productive and aware person for life." Supporters, then, are sensitive to the needs of students in very personal moments, but they also see the broader implications of the learning experiences and of the kind of support they give to others. In fact, one of Tarvyd's students said, "This understanding professor released the bundled-up anxiety I had been holding and enabled me to feel comfortable and relaxed with a renewed enthusiasm for my chosen career."

CHARACTERISTICS

Figure 7.3: **Supporters and the Teaching-Learning Grid**

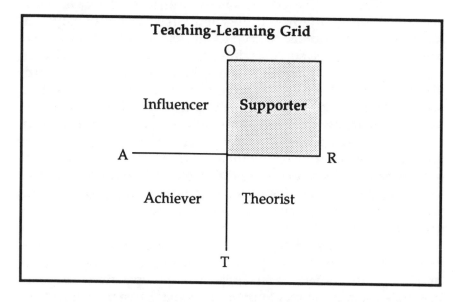

Of the four teacher archetypes, Supporters are the most divergent in their thinking. The combination of others orientation and reflective orientation causes Supporters to be constantly on the brink of change. Although Supporters prepare lessons and work from syllabi, as do other types, they generally think in terms of the success of individual students. Therefore, they are very quick to abandon assignments or lessons that do not foster student success. Through the student comments about Supporters, we constructed an image of a type of teacher who is enthusiastic in that role, whether in a large class or in individual conference. This person enjoys student interaction and is an active listener. Also, Supporters are very spontaneous, relying heavily on their own creativity to maintain maximum student involvement in learning. Because of their focus on individuals more than on subject matter or classes, these teachers tend to form lasting bonds with students.

As divergent thinkers, Supporters tend to view situations from different perspectives, and they are more likely to look for a variety of solutions to problems rather than one answer. Margaret Osborne, a nursing instructor (Mount Royal College, Calgary, Alberta), told about trying to help one of her students develop the skills necessary to conduct a staff meeting, one of the required competencies of the practicum. In personal conferences with the student, Osborne took the role of listener and assistant, providing the student with materials when asked. By being able to shift out of the directive teacher role, this teacher enabled the student to assume the leadership role ultimately required in conducting the staff meeting. The students of Melvin Pasternak, a business communications teacher (Mount Royal College, Calgary, Alberta), were impressed by his belief that there is not always one right answer to learn. Consequently, they were motivated to explore alternatives to find the best answer for each student individually.

As divergent thinkers, Supporters must be flexible. When asked to list words that apply to excellent teachers, the Supporters put terms like "open," "flexible," and "adaptable" almost as often as they put "caring" and "concerned." Their flexibility was not only in their teaching, but also in their schedules. Students felt free to stop by to talk to Supporters about personal as well as school-related problems and were gratified to find someone who, rather than help them find answers, could help find solutions. Supporters are also willing to act on their own emotions. They have a genuine love for people and feel deep compassion for their students. Students will confide in Supporters because they know these teachers care about them and their lives. Joseph Conte (president, Southwestern College, California) praised Charlotte McGowan as a Fulbright Fellow who brought her studies in Latin America and China to her classroom: "Not only has she been a practicing anthropologist and archeologist her entire teaching career at Southwestern College, but she has been an ethnographer of her own students—she understands the culture of her students because she cares about their lives and their learning."

STRENGTHS

Supporters are people-centered and become personally involved in their students' learning. John Britt, an American Studies teacher (Lee College, Baytown, Texas), expressed this best when he told of working with a student who could master the material but who had difficulty writing. When the student's final class project won third place in a statewide competition in historical research and writing, Britt's exuberance was clear. "If I work another 20 years," he said, "I doubt that I will ever again feel such a sense of genuine accomplishment." Supporters thrive on the success of their students. In fact, they are likely to go out of their way to enable student success. We were impressed by the number of students of Supporters who had some type of personal crisis that would have prevented success if not for the caring attitude of the teacher. One of Joanne Miller's business students (Hartnell Community College, Salinas, California) is typical. She says, "Once I was in a serious accident. I got behind in my work, and I was not going to go back to school. She helped me get caught up with my work and encouraged me to stay in school."

Supporters also exploit opportunities to teach. Because they are focused on individuals (others orientation), and because they are constantly assessing the environment (reflective orientation), they are always ready to abandon a plan in favor of a new insight or opportunity. Kay Carl (Blackhawk Technical College, Janesville, Wisconsin) expresses this attitude best.

> I strongly believe that a teacher must be flexible. Teachable moments abound in the classroom. It is important to grab onto these and go with them. It is important to be confident enough to deviate from the lesson plans for spontaneous learning.

It was not a surprise to find that Supporters are good listeners. However, we were impressed by how pervasive this skill was throughout the teaching-learning experience. Students in shop classes learned to solve problems because the teacher listened.

Students who did poorly on an exam or an assignment improved because the teacher first listened to them. Students with a personal crisis or low self-esteem continued in the course and were successful because the teacher took the time to listen and really hear from the students' perspectives. The important fact here is not just that Supporters are good listeners, but that students know they are good listeners and will go to them first when there is a problem that interferes with learning. In fact, some of the students commented about events that took place when they were not even a member of the Supporter teacher's current class. Supporters, it seems, are open and available to all students, not just their own.

As classroom teachers, Supporters often lecture, and they recognize the value of a clear, well-organized presentation. However, for them, lecture is only one way to teach, and they are quick to abandon it if it is unsuccessful. Brian McDonald, a biology teacher (Red Deer College, Calgary, Alberta), told about a course he had over-organized for the students, thinking he was making it easier for them. When it was clear that motivation and enthusiasm were low, he devised a feedback form to elicit comment from the students and found the students resented his "treating (them) like children." This Supporter teacher offered the class an apology and immediately changed the approach. The result was a totally different classroom atmosphere with renewed student motivation to learn. This kind of constant interaction with the class is typical of Supporters. Consequently, they are more likely to use techniques such as group work and individual projects than lecture, although most Supporters expressed a desire for balance. These teachers, however, do not feel they have to be "in charge" of the classroom learning and are quite willing to give students some of the responsibility for what takes place.

PATH-GOAL DATA AND SUPPORTERS

In the four figures that follow, each of the indicators of the teaching-learning path-goal framework for successful and unsuccessful experiences and Supporters' philosophies of teaching are displayed. The Supporters' position in the figure is a heavy black line; other teaching styles are portrayed by other types of lines.

Although there is close convergence along all the behaviors, there are especially similar patterns in the reported strengths in both the successful reports and the philosophies of teaching. For the unsuccessful behaviors the greatest convergence is focused in the "reduces barriers" context (faculty are working to eliminate or at least reduce learning obstacles); the greatest divergence among the styles is displayed in two functions: "increases pay-offs" and "increases satisfaction." The different teaching styles demonstrate their greatest variance in the areas of "having the ability to increase students' opportunities for educational success" and their ability and responsibility to motivate students toward greater involvement in their learning and the development of their learning skills.

Figure 7.4: **Supporters and Path-Goal: Successful Motivation**

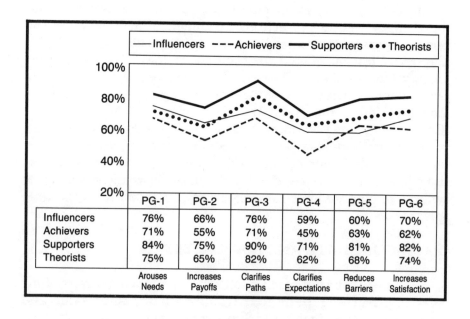

	PG-1	PG-2	PG-3	PG-4	PG-5	PG-6
Influencers	76%	66%	76%	59%	60%	70%
Achievers	71%	55%	71%	45%	63%	62%
Supporters	84%	75%	90%	71%	81%	82%
Theorists	75%	65%	82%	62%	68%	74%
	Arouses Needs	Increases Payoffs	Clarifies Paths	Clarifies Expectations	Reduces Barriers	Increases Satisfaction

Figure 7.5: **Supporters and Path-Goal: Unsuccessful Motivation**

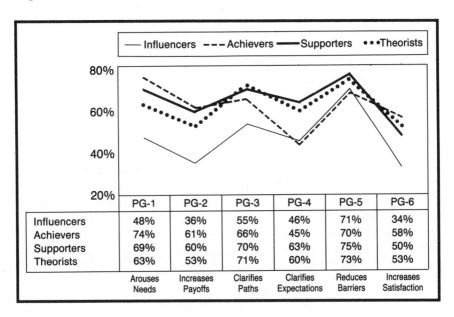

	PG-1	PG-2	PG-3	PG-4	PG-5	PG-6
Influencers	48%	36%	55%	46%	71%	34%
Achievers	74%	61%	66%	45%	70%	58%
Supporters	69%	60%	70%	63%	75%	50%
Theorists	63%	53%	71%	60%	73%	53%
	Arouses Needs	Increases Payoffs	Clarifies Paths	Clarifies Expectations	Reduces Barriers	Increases Satisfaction

Figure 7.6: **Supporters and Path-Goal: Philosophy of Teaching**

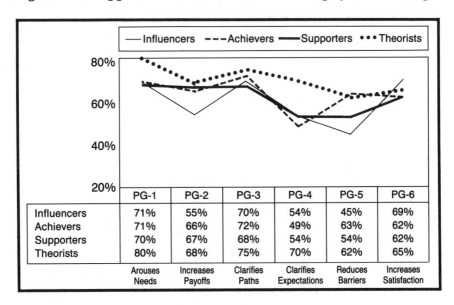

	PG-1	PG-2	PG-3	PG-4	PG-5	PG-6
Influencers	71%	55%	70%	54%	45%	69%
Achievers	71%	66%	72%	49%	63%	62%
Supporters	70%	67%	68%	54%	54%	62%
Theorists	80%	68%	75%	70%	62%	65%
	Arouses Needs	Increases Payoffs	Clarifies Paths	Clarifies Expectations	Reduces Barriers	Increases Satisfaction

In Figure 7.7 both students' and CEOs' input are compared with Supporters' self-reported data. Typically, students and presidents see Supporters with fewer strengths than the instructors report. The spread of the difference between the self-report and others' reports ranges from 11 to 29 percent, with the greatest convergence along the dimensions "clarifies paths," "clarifies expectations," and "reduces barriers." Faculty are perceived as positive and directive, as good role models for expected behavior, and as working hard to reduce learning barriers. Presidents and CEOs see the Supporters' ability to offer structured guidance as their greatest skill; but they are less convinced of Supporters' abilities to motivate students to greater involvement. Students think that Supporters are best at eliminating barriers to learning success and, unlike the CEOs, praise Supporters for their ability to increase satisfaction for learning. Students are especially attuned to the Supporters' consistent and helpful use of feedback, well-defined courses, and directive guidance.

Figure 7.7: Supporters: Self-Report and Student and CEO Reports

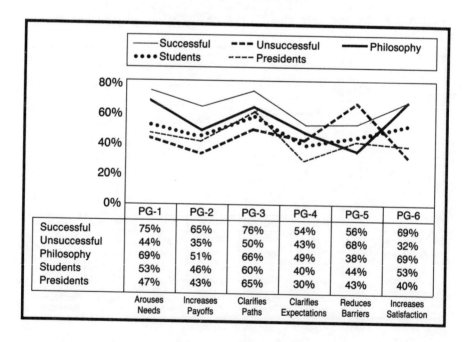

	PG-1	PG-2	PG-3	PG-4	PG-5	PG-6
Successful	75%	65%	76%	54%	56%	69%
Unsuccessful	44%	35%	50%	43%	68%	32%
Philosophy	69%	51%	66%	49%	38%	69%
Students	53%	46%	60%	40%	44%	53%
Presidents	47%	43%	65%	30%	43%	40%
	Arouses Needs	Increases Payoffs	Clarifies Paths	Clarifies Expectations	Reduces Barriers	Increases Satisfaction

TEACHING-LEARNING AND PATH-GOAL

Each of the six themes of the teaching-learning path-goal framework are examined here in relation to the strength that the Supporter reported for each of these teaching characteristics (in the chapters that follow, the order and strength of the teaching-learning path-goal framework also are reported for the Theorist, the Achiever, and the Influencer).

Recognize and Engage Students' Desire to Learn: Supporters arouse student needs by enabling the students to see the value of what they are learning. Ed Tarvyd (Santa Monica College, Santa Monica, California) expresses this well:

> Good teaching does not stop simply with the delivery of subject matter, testing, determination of final grades, etc. It instead transcends to complete involvement of the teacher and student, helping the student make the proper career choices, convincing the student that college definitely is the place to be.

Dan Minock (Washtenaw Community College, Ann Arbor, Michigan) states it more simply when he lists his number one maxim of good teaching: "Help students to need what you are teaching them." Although all of the award-winning instructors indicated that arousing student needs was an important path-goal effort, Supporters are more likely to approach this on the basis of immediate needs than future needs. For example, many of the students who responded to our questionnaire indicated that they would have withdrawn from college had it not been for the timely intervention of the Supporter teacher. Rather than talk about the long-range benefits of college, Supporters helped these students satisfy more immediate needs to complete the course or term. Supporters also want their students to see very practical, immediate applications of what they are learning. Therefore, whether they are teaching philosophy or autobody repair, Supporters attempt to arouse student needs by showing how the knowledge and skills they are teaching have real value in students' lives.

Motivates Student to Increased Satisfaction and Development of Learning Skills: Perhaps because of their focus on individual students, Supporters especially value increasing student satisfaction. Kenneth Boyer, a report writing instructor (St. Louis Community College-Florissant Valley, St. Louis, Missouri), strives to have the students teach themselves, not only because they will retain more content, but because they will become more self-reliant. Supporters are the exact opposites of the "caretaker" teacher in that their goal is to increase student satisfaction by fostering independence, not dependence. Brian McDonald (Red Deer College, Calgary, Alberta) reflects this attitude as he explains the reason why teachers need to be caring individuals: "Students respond to the instructor's concern by feeling more worthwhile and, therefore, are more motivated to learn." A student in Margaret Osborne's nursing class (Mount Royal College, Alberta, Canada) says her teacher "doesn't do the work for you, but rather quietly encourages you, making you believe in your own ability." Throughout the student comments we found examples of great appreciation for Supporters who helped students feel better about themselves and their own abilities. One of Sheran Wallis's dental assistant students has a very typical community college profile—over 30, single parent, limited resources. She remembers when she first came in contact with this Supporter teacher:

> She encouraged me to keep going because she believed in me and made me realize that I was carrying a heavy load and that I should feel proud of myself for my effort and determination. And because of that I decided to enter the dental assisting program. I'm glad to have her as my support. Even when it looks hard I'm looking forward to success, thanks to Sheran.

Increased student satisfaction is part of the bond that forms between Supporters and students. Although the students feel much better about themselves, they fully acknowledge the importance of the personal attention given to them by the Supporter teacher. Sometimes this attention is part of the classroom rather than individual settings. For example, one of Terry Bales's media communications students (Rancho Santiago College, Santa Ana, California) admitted to being very shy and hesitant in class. When she did answer a question, however, she says the teacher "acknowledged, respected, and reinforced my perception of things." Perhaps even without the Supporter teacher being aware of it, this student says she was motivated to do well in the course just because she was acknowledged. Supporters, then, increase student satisfaction in very personal ways.

Offers Positive Orientation, Guidance, and Direction Through Coaching: Supporters also are able to clarify paths to success. This is evident in the way Sheran Wallis (Lake Michigan College, Benton Harbor, Michigan) describes her teaching:

> *I present an order, a structure, a large amount of information, a pathway through a subject matter, a sight-seeing tour with stops at significant attractions. I structure time and evaluate progress based upon experience and standards.*

Because Supporters also value flexibility and creativity, however, neither they nor their students are necessarily bound by structure. Supporters usually have well-organized approaches to course content, but they are spontaneous and adaptable when a presentation is not successful. Consequently, they often have individual or small-group projects as major assignments in the course. Students, therefore, are not regimented into the same learning experiences and precisely the same content.

Supporters also make good advisors. Their focus on individuals, coupled with their value for clear paths to success, enable them to provide guidance and direction for students who sometimes cannot see beyond their immediate schedules. One of Joanne Miller's students (Hartnell Community College, Salinas, California) is typical:

> *Ms. Miller set up a meeting with me to discuss my future here at Hartnell. I was really leery about the type of business classes I should take. Ms. Miller took a few extra minutes out of her busy schedule and went through all the business classes. After meeting with her, I definitely knew what I wanted to take the second semester and even the following semester. Now that I'm*

in my second semester, I just love my business classes, and I have a positive perspective for accomplishing my future goals.

Increases Opportunities for Quality Educational Performance and Success: Supporters increase the personal pay-off for students by enabling them to succeed. One of Libby Holt's (Florida Community College, Jacksonville, Florida) math students, for example, was disappointed with her low test score on the first test. After talking with Holt, the student not only understood what she had done wrong on the test, but says she became a better math student. Evidence is the score of 100 she made on the next two tests. We found similar stories in accounting classes, communications classes, virtually every field. When students went to Supporters to ask for help, they saw immediate results. But Supporters also try to increase the personal pay-off of attending class. Melvin Pasternak (Mount Royal College, Calgary, Alberta) expresses this by saying students expect and deserve Return on Investment (ROI) for time spent in class. Therefore, he tries to present the information in as entertaining a way as possible so the students will enjoy class as well as learn from it. The use of humor was a common trait among the Supporters, and they all indicated a commitment to make each class as memorable as possible. Many of the students reflected this attitude by saying how much they looked forward to each class.

Works to Eliminate or Limit Learning Obstacles: Perhaps because they are sensitive to student needs, Supporters are especially adept at reducing barriers to student learning. Often these barriers are a result of poor reading and writing skills that prevent success on assignments. Supporters typically spot these problems and attempt to match the student with available resources. Some teachers, like Joanne Miller (Hartnell Community College, Salinas, California), take their time to help students learn how to study better and how to read assignments more effectively. David Greenhoe (Glen Oaks Community College, Centreville, Michigan) requires a research project in his modern Asia course. One of his students did not have good library or research skills and told about the extra effort this Supporter teacher took to give him the direction he needed to complete the assignment.

Sometimes the barriers to student success are outside the actual material or skills being learned. Several of the Supporters indicated their desire to break down the usual teacher-student barriers that prevent students from becoming personally involved in the learning. Melvin Pasternak (Mount Royal College, Calgary, Alberta) makes it a point to play ping pong and basketball with students in order to establish rapport. Once rapport is established students are more open to advice and counsel from the Supporter teacher. Community college students often have personal barriers to success. There were several stories about crises, such as surgery or deaths in the family, where the Supporter teacher provided both emotional support and appropriate guidance to enable the student to complete the course. Barbara West (Broward Community College, Fort Lauderdale, Florida) is typical of another kind of help. When a student came to her with financial problems, this Supporter teacher was able to put the student in touch with a hospital scholarship committee and help her obtain some financial support to continue her education.

Uses Effective Performance as an Expectation by Which to Empower Students: Because Supporters value the success of individual students more than classes, they place less value on clarifying expectations than on other path-goal efforts. Throughout the comments made by these teachers, we saw evidence that Supporters want each student to rise to his or her potential. Consequently, expectations of Supporters evolve and are developed based on the readiness, needs, and abilities of each student. This is not to say that all students do not meet some standard requirements and have common learning experiences. Supporters, however, are likely to clarify expectations differently for different students. There was no evidence, on the other hand, that Supporters lower standards. In fact, comments were quite clear that Supporters have high standards and expect the student to achieve those standards. The difference between one student and the next is more likely to be measured in terms of the amount of time and resources the Supporter teacher gives to each—a measure based on student need.

TEACHING FIELDS

As with all four teacher archetypes, we did not find evidence that Supporters occur in some disciplines and not in others. On the contrary, we found Supporters in most fields and at various levels. However, the largest number were in medical fields, such as nursing and dental assisting. There were also Supporters in theoretical as well as applied business courses, in social as well as physical sciences, and in English and humanities courses.

Figure 7.8: **Teaching Fields: Supporters**

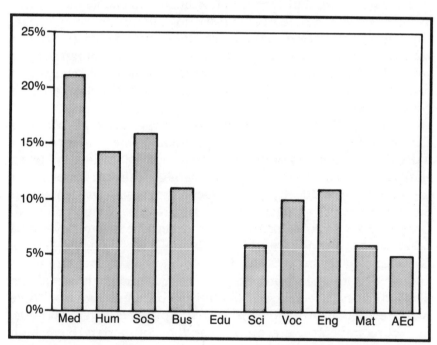

IMPLICATIONS

In a pure Teaching-as-Leading cycle, Supporters belong at the beginning, the point at which community college students enter the teaching-learning process. Supporters are particularly effective with students who have low self-confidence, low self-esteem, or who lack some of the basic skills for success in college. By forming a relationship with these students, Supporters give them the very important message that they are valued and that it matters whether they succeed. Also, because the Supporters thrive on seeing individuals succeed, they are more likely to take time necessary to locate additional resources that might be required to overcome barriers to student success.

Students responded to Supporters throughout their college experience. Often, a student just beginning a math sequence or faced with a research project for the first time will have characteristics similar to students hesitant about entering college. They have prior negative experiences, and they doubt their own abilities. In fact, many of the students who responded to our survey had been in college several semesters or quarters. Therefore, the need for Supporters exists throughout the student's college experience.

It is interesting to note that some of the Supporters teach classes that can be considered double or triple sections. Therefore, we can conclude that Supporter behavior is applied to some students more than others. In a larger class, not all students will need the kind of support and individual attention the Supporter teacher is prepared to give. Nor could the Supporter teacher, with this size student load, give this attention to every student. Consequently, we need to see Supporter behavior as available to help certain types of students, regardless of where they are in the teaching-learning cycle.

Chapter 8

Profiles of Teaching Excellence: Theorists

———

Philosophy
Characteristics
Strengths
Path-Goal Data and Theorists
Teaching-Learning and Path-Goal
Teaching Fields
Implications

8

I describe myself as hard-nosed and often demanding...in the end I emphasize that students must learn to learn on their own—the foundation stone of the truly educated.

James Ardini
Diablo Valley College

Learning and readiness are almost entirely the responsibility of the teacher; we cannot await some mystical moment of learning readiness. It is the teacher in the role of enabler that excites the student with the subject matter and encourages eventual scholarly curiosity and independence.

Stephen Stroud
Modesto Junior College

I cannot accept the idea that it's only what goes on in the classroom that counts. Credibility does not stop at the classroom door, and a teacher's influence does not stop outside the college environment. Integrity is a sweeping concept that intertwines itself with all aspects of life: it demands that I be the best model of mature adulthood I am capable of being.

Shirley Sweet
Blackhawk Technical College

*A*pproximately 12 percent of the award-winning instructors who took the TALI were Theorists (Figure 8.1). Like the Supporters, the Theorists are more reflective than active, but they are also characterized by a dominant preference to place the learning milieu into a theoretical framework or structure; they are apt to include their students in such a framework as well.

Figure 8.1: **Theorists**

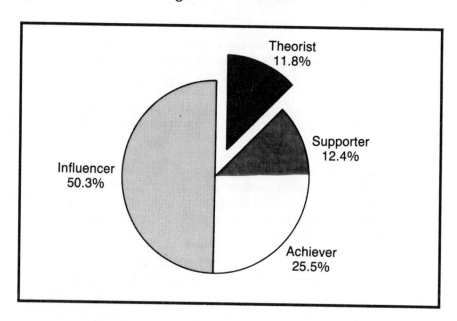

PHILOSOPHY

Theorists approach teaching and learning through a conceptual framework. Somewhere between the learner-centered philosophy of Supporter teachers and the discipline-centered philosophy of Achiever teachers, Theorists see their role as forming content into an organized, integrated whole that will enable students not only to grasp and appreciate the knowledge, but also to understand and master the process of learning. Everything that Theorists do, therefore, has a theoretical abstract base. The following is a paraphrase of Nova Jean Weber's (Cerritos College, Norwalk, California) description of the technique she uses to teach the metaphorical process:

> *In explicating poetry, students revert to a line-by-line paraphrase of the material to be learned, which is worth a zero for the analytical skills I try to teach. I searched for a new way to teach them to analyze and offered a 'dissected frog' as a model for the analysis of a metaphor. Various frog organs (heart, lungs, kidneys) are understood for their discreteness. The importance of dissection to science students is to understand how the individual parts work and how each part must be examined in conjunction with the whole of the frog. Dissection is careful and methodical. I then ask the students to imagine studying a frog by chopping, as a chef might, from head to foot. The students quickly recognize that they could not 'see' the organs, only fragments. I then point out that we do not 'butcher' poetry in attempting to analyze and understand it either.*

As this example shows, Theorists approach the instructional process, as well as the instructional content itself, conceptually. This teaching style produces students who know more (in this case, the metaphorical process) and know more about learning (in this case, analogical learning). Put more simply, Theorists believe that learning begets learners, rather than the other way around. Katherine Staples (Austin Community College, Austin, Texas) demonstrates this point of view in her discussion of the teacher's role:

> *I have seen students in all courses involving language find new mirrors of themselves through their writing, reading, and critical skills. Such students blossom personally and intellectually. Their new confidence gives them daring to try new ideas, new roles, new projects, and new occupations. The role of the teacher, then, becomes one of guide...(and) any strategy which encourages learners to trust themselves and gives them the knowledge, skills, and critical thinking ability to do so logically is a valid instructional strategy.*

Because of their love for their subjects and their love for learning, Theorists tend to believe that students approach the learning situation with the same interest and enthusiasm. Moreover, we found Theorists more often in subjects such as English and the sciences—subjects not always approached enthusiastically by community college students. Mike Cooper (Westark Community College, Fort Smith, Arkansas) typified the problem that Theorists sometimes have when he explained why some of his plans do not work as well as he would like: "Occasionally, I have been unsuccessful when I have planned activities where I have assumed an interest in intellectual learning and growth and found that the (students') primary interest is in doing the paper to get it out of the way with the minimal amount of effort and thought." In our study, however, we found that the excellent Theorists, like Mike Cooper, are able to change student attitudes about learning. Throughout the student comments we found statements such as, "I have never liked English before, but now it is my favorite subject," and "All through high school I avoided physics, but now I hope to take more courses in it." Theorists, then, combine the supportive roles of Supporters and the subject-mastery values of Achievers and turn students into learners.

Figure 8.2: **Reflective-Task Orientation**

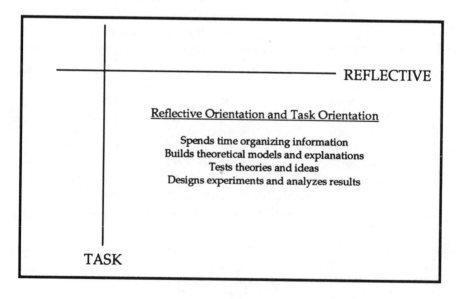

The forces acting on Theorists are a reflective orientation and a task orientation. Therefore, this teacher thinks deliberately and methodically about what he or she is trying to teach and how to teach it. The result is a well-thought-out theoretical model. Mike Cooper (Westark Community College, Fort Smith, Arkansas), for example, explains teaching by presenting a model:

> *A teacher is a coach, setting up the play, helping students walk through it, guiding them as they do so, encouraging them in their effort, diagnosing their weaknesses and working on strategies to correct them, and being firm with those who are not putting forth effort.*

Alice Rasmussen (Lake Michigan College, Benton Harbor, Michigan) described the role of the teacher by constructing a general model composed of several model subsets: the models of police officer, idea reflector, idea stimulator, and role model. Although most of these labels, especially that of coach, occurred in the philosophies of the other types of teachers, they occurred as adjectives. For the Theorists, however, these labels are fairly circumscribed concepts into which they place and organize the attributes of successful teachers.

As Theorists' minds work, so does their teaching. They build models for their students. James Ardini (Diablo Valley College, Pleasant Hill, California) explained to us how he engages his students in the study of physics on the first day of class. He starts with the question, "Why does a satellite orbit the earth?" In the questions and answers that ensue, he constructs for them a conceptual model in which satellites—including the moon—fall to the earth, just as Newton's apples. However, because the earth is forever spinning away, these objects forever miss and, consequently, are forever "falling" around the earth rather than toward it. (We would like to point out that of the hundreds of teachers who responded to our study of excellence, only this Theorist teacher went so far as to draw us a diagram.) Jim VanderMey (Mid Michigan Community College, Harrison, Michigan) builds models slightly differently. He has his English students come in for conferences before they write their essays. As he questions them about their ideas and their plans for completing the assignment, he writes down their responses. At the end, he shows the students what they have said and helps them organize their own thoughts into an appropriate framework.

Theorists, however, do not assume that their theoretical models produce student learning. Their reflection orientation compels them to continually think about what they are doing and how it is working. Rodney Oakes (Los Angeles Harbor College, Los Angeles, California) is an example:

> *Just because I understand a concept or have a certain kind of mastery and am able to present concepts in a well-organized and logical lecture, it does not follow that my students are learning! My job is to continuously find new ways for students to learn. And I must always keep checking to find out if learning is taking place.*

Jim McInturff (East Arkansas Community College, Forrest Park, Arkansas) illustrates one of the ways that Theorists test their theories and ideas:

> *I try to teach and treat students the way that I would like to be taught and treated if I were the student. Whenever I make an assignment, I try to do the assignment along with the students. In speech, I give a speech. In composition, I try to write the assignment to see how the students feel.*

In contrast to the Influencer, who is likely to try anything, often spontaneously, the Theorist designs rather elaborate experiments to test theories and ideas. When describing situations in which they felt they had been successful, these teachers often went into great detail—giving the objectives of the learning task, the rationale behind the experimental methodology, a description of the process, and a list of outcomes. Theorists, then, approach teaching and learning reflectively, working the subject matter and the learning task into a theoretical model, designing a methodology based on the model, and testing the approach to determine whether the goals have been reached. Often, these teachers will use quantifiable data to determine success. However, in contrast to the Achievers, who use data to determine whether students are succeeding in high numbers, Theorists use the data to determine whether the conceptual model is appropriate. The difference is, admittedly, subtle.

CHARACTERISTICS

Figure 8.3: **Theorists and the Teaching-Learning Grid**

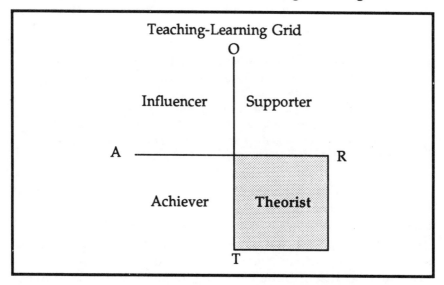

In the Teaching as Leading Inventory, Theorists are opposite Influencers. Whereas Influencers are active doers, quick to try new approaches and often relying on trial and error, Theorists are thinkers, reflecting on what they know and want the students to learn, working out strategies and plans beforehand. Also, Influencers have *accommodator* learning styles, meaning they try to fit new experiences into existing theoretical models. But when they cannot, they quickly abandon the models. Theorists, by contrast, have *assimilator* learning styles; and when new experiences do not fit into existing theoretical models, they tend, at least at first, to discount the experiences. They are not likely to abandon an existing theory in light of new information and experiences until they have conceptualized a new model that accounts for the information and experiences.

It would be inappropriate to say Theorists are not concerned with student success or do not value high achievement. As with all participants in our study of excellent teachers, we found Theorists to have a very high commitment to student learning. However, as a teacher type, Theorists focus on concepts more than student behavior. They are not focused on student needs to the same degree as the Supporter teachers, nor on student performance as much as the Influencer teachers. A student of Bruce Bjorkquist (Conestoga College, Stratford, Ontario) gives an example:

> During one of his classes, Bruce mentioned the difference between knowledge and belief. This sparked my interest. After class, I asked him more about this topic. He said he had taken a course on that very topic, and we proceeded to have a wonderful discussion on knowledge and belief. Following the discussion, I went to the library and researched this subject in even greater detail and learned a lot about it.

Regardless of whether this student developed this interest, to this Theorist the concept is an important one, and the theoretical base on which the learning situation was structured is still sound. The student did, however, develop this interest; and the fact is that students of Theorists frequently become truly awakened to the joy of learning because of the intellectual stimulation of abstract thinking, as well as the contagious enthusiasm of the teacher. Karen Detweiler (Wytheville Community College, Wytheville, Virginia) puts it best:

> A teacher must be interested and enthusiastic about her subject— enough so that when she talks about it, the enthusiasm shows. I feel it is important to convey the feeling, 'I enjoy this, and I enjoy learning new things about this subject so much. How could anyone not enjoy it and not be as interested as I am in this class?'

Because of this conceptual focus on discipline, Theorists have what Shirley Sweet (Blackhawk Technical College, Janesville, Wisconsin) calls "integrity."

> I use the word 'integrity' to mean several things. First, the

teacher guards the integrity of the discipline which is taught.
This means that one must provide balanced views on controversial
subjects and also avoid being trapped into 'pop' wisdom that has
not been honed by rigorous research (but may have enormous
public appeal via mass media). It also means that one must
continually be a learner as the discipline matures and grows.

Tom Hooe (Community College of Baltimore, Baltimore, Maryland) further demonstrates the centrality of the discipline in Theorist teaching when he says, "The community college professor must blend a concern for the sanctity of the content with instructional strategy and style that ensures that student learning does, indeed, take place." The powerful impact of Theorists on students, however, can best be told by students, such as a student in Jim McInturff's literature class:

I had never had much interest in poetry during my life. But with
Mr. McInturff's excellent methods of teaching, he has opened up
a whole new world for me. Because of him, I can now enjoy the
world of poetry, and new insights are mine to incorporate into my
thinking. His love of literature is obvious, and one cannot sit in
his class without becoming enthusiastic about what we are
learning. His creativity spurs his students on to really think.

STRENGTHS

Because Theorists work from conceptual models, they integrate knowledge rather than isolate it. Whereas the Achievers see and value the practical applications of their knowledge, Theorists see and value connections. Darlene Logan (New Mexico Military Institute, Roswell, New Mexico) expresses this:

My attempt to present material in a way that is not isolated and
fragmented, at a time in history when our very lifestyles encourage
specialization and fragmentation, is more difficult. This is
something I have been wrestling with for a number of years. It
requires the teacher to be open and extremely knowledgeable; to
be the eternal teacher and student; to see, make, and encourage
connections; to teach more than a subject to students, but rather

to share with human beings the joy of learning, growing, and strengthening themselves and their concept of themselves and the world and people around them.

Tom Hooe adds that an effective teacher "must have a command of content, not only in his discipline, but also in related bodies of knowledge." This love of learning in the broadest context enables students not merely to apply the knowledge they gain at school, but to integrate it in such a way that they see the process of learning as a powerful tool for personal growth and understanding.

Another strength of Theorists is their use of inductive reasoning. By observing individual behaviors, they are able to construct an experimental model of students' learning needs and design an experimental teaching-learning situation. Yvonne Estes (Austin Community College, Austin, Texas), for example, told us about a situation involving a student who seemed unresponsive to her attempts to instill in him a value for the biology skills she was trying to teach. By observing his writing ability, his attentiveness, his stated reasons for being in school, and the kinds of assignments he seemed to find interesting, she was able to put the skills she wanted him to learn into a context he found relevant and worth the effort required for success. Bruce Bjorkquist (Conestoga College, Stratford, Ontario) described a similar process involving the whole class. Frustrated by the apparent passivity of students during discussions in his ethics class, he took the time to observe the behavior of the class and work the observations into a designed classroom experiment that required the students to deal with an ethical question through both contrived role-playing and real decisions.

Because of their deliberate forethought, Theorists also tend to be highly organized. Throughout the comments from students, we found an appreciation for the clear, systematic presentation of lessons. Mary Beth Monroe (Southwest Texas Junior College, Uvalde, Texas) is an example of this type of teacher:

I must continually search for ways to make the curriculum more simple, yet complete, in presentation and to make the delivery of the curriculum understandable and enjoyable. Therefore, I must stay on top of all discoveries in physics and new pedagogical techniques.

Theorists, then, are able to translate their genuine love and enthusiasm for their disciplines into a rational, precise, and orderly presentation that maximizes student understanding. The students' ability to think about the subject is not clouded by a necessity to reshape the teachers' information.

PATH-GOAL DATA AND THEORISTS

Theorists most closely resemble Achievers in their report of motivating students to learn. This comes as no surprise since both attack teaching from a task-oriented perspective. Like Achievers, they display their greatest strength in their ability to clarify paths to success by offering guidance and direction to their students through structured planning and modelling. Theorists, of all the four teaching styles, report greatest strengths around their espoused philosophy of teaching, and they are especially cognizant of the need to capitalize on a teaching pattern that recognizes the student's desire to learn— although they demonstrate some reluctance to relinquish the learning goal to the student (Figure 8.4). An unexpected finding from Theorists was the vehemence with which they reported both their successful and their unsuccessful experiences; unlike the other teaching styles, the Theorists felt strongly even about their defeats (Figure 8.5). Theorists did not demonstrate variance between their successful experiences and their espoused philosophies of teaching (Figure 8.6).

Figure 8.4: **Theorists and Path-Goal: Successful Behavior**

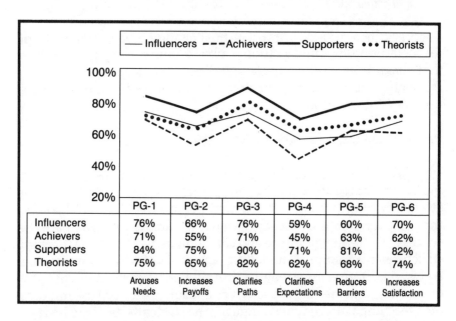

Figure 8.5: **Theorists and Path-Goal: Unsuccessful Behavior**

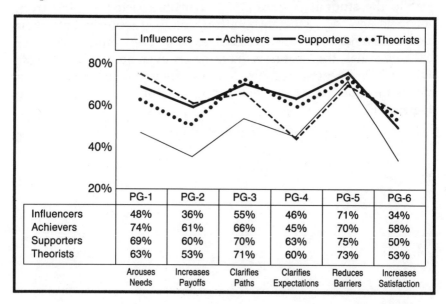

Figure 8.6: **Theorists and Path-Goal: Philosophy**

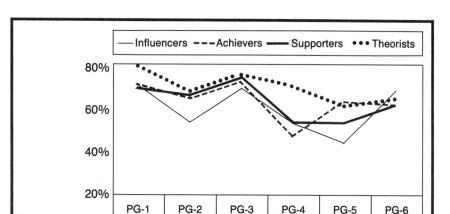

	PG-1	PG-2	PG-3	PG-4	PG-5	PG-6
Influencers	71%	55%	70%	54%	45%	69%
Achievers	71%	66%	72%	49%	63%	62%
Supporters	70%	67%	68%	54%	54%	62%
Theorists	80%	68%	75%	70%	62%	65%
	Arouses Needs	Increases Payoffs	Clarifies Paths	Clarifies Expectations	Reduces Barriers	Increases Satisfaction

Figure 8.7 displays student and CEO perceptions of the strengths of Theorists as teachers. Students who have Theorists as teachers see their greatest weakness in the Theorists' reluctance to give students independence over their own learning; but they are extremely complimentary about their instructors' abilities to positively guide them to greater learning realms by reconfirmation of the goals and objectives of the course they are teaching. Presidents single out the Theorists as the most able instructors at arousing their students to learn through diagnoses, clear definitions of course objectives, and an analytical understanding of their needs. Jess Parrish (President, Midland College, Midland, Texas) said that Julia Flaherty "has every intention of making a difference in students' lives. She carefully plans but remains flexible about the delivery of content and is always cognizant of students' needs." Wayne Wiley was seen as a very thorough teacher by his president, Johnnie Merritt (Central Virginia Community College, Lynchburg, Virginia): "Dr. Wiley is a master at setting and accomplishing instructional goals and evaluating students; he keeps students 'turned-on' by rewarding

their successes and showing them that he genuinely cares about their learning."

Figure 8.7: **Theorists: Self-Report and Student and CEO Reports**

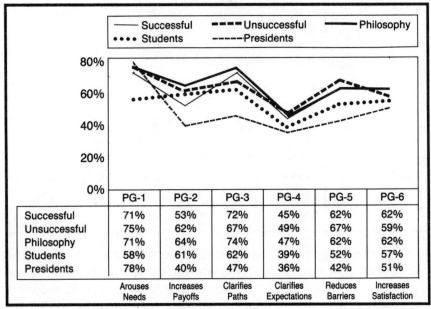

	PG-1	PG-2	PG-3	PG-4	PG-5	PG-6
Successful	71%	53%	72%	45%	62%	62%
Unsuccessful	75%	62%	67%	49%	67%	59%
Philosophy	71%	64%	74%	47%	62%	62%
Students	58%	61%	62%	39%	52%	57%
Presidents	78%	40%	47%	36%	42%	51%
	Arouses Needs	Increases Payoffs	Clarifies Paths	Clarifies Expectations	Reduces Barriers	Increases Satisfaction

TEACHING-LEARNING AND PATH-GOAL

Recognizes and Engages Students' Desire to Learn: Theorists share with the Supporter the primary concern for arousing student needs as a path-goal effort. However, Theorists arouse needs by kindling in students a desire to know more about the subject. Barbara Gill (Community College of Denver, Denver, Colorado) says she tries to motivate students with the goal of a good job or job advancement. But most of all she tries "to instill a love of learning just for the sake of the knowledge and becoming a better person." One of Wayne Wiley's (Central Virginia Community College, Lynchburg, Virginia) American history students illustrates the success Theorists frequently have in motivating students to learn for the sake of learning:

> *While doing a book review of a subject I did not like, nor had the time or incentive to follow through, Dr. Wiley's driving force and example helped me find the time and, much to my surprise, the interest not only to complete the assignment, but to follow through on my own and further research the subject. Thus, I am now well-versed and very much interested in any other materials that relate.*

Offers Positive Orientation, Guidance, and Direction: Again working from a conceptual framework, Theorists help students see the way to successful completion of the learning task. Mary Beth Monroe (Southwest Texas Junior College, Uvalde, Texas), for example, induced the author of her physics textbook to prepare a videotape for her class in which the author explained the philosophy of the course and discussed the nature of the questions the class would be exploring in the course. Robert Wylie (Central Virginia Community College, Lynchburg, Virginia) requires his students to write a poem but admits, "It would be folly to make such an assignment as 'write a poem.'" Instead, he takes the class through a series of steps that naturally culminates in a finished poem. Theorists are organized and systematic, and they give the students a clear sense of direction toward learning goals.

Works to Eliminate or Reduce Learning Obstacles: Theorists place a high value on reducing barriers to students' performance, but this usually involves barriers specifically between the student and the content. Supporters, by contrast, are likely to attempt to reduce barriers outside the teaching and learning context, such as financial problems. An unusual example, but one that illustrates Theorists' focus on subject matter and conceptual orientation, comes from one of Julia Flaherty's (Midland College, Midland, Texas) students. The student went into this teacher's office after reading a biography of Andrew Jackson. She was clearly upset that one of her heroes from grade school history lessons seemed undeserving of the honor.

> *She listened to me attentively. Finally, she said, 'Those of us who like to learn a lot are in danger of forgetting the grandeur of the past or of minimizing it. We are in danger of becoming cynical and of losing our faith in the future. Don't let it happen. America has a great history!' I was satisfied. No matter what happens, I must learn. I must learn to consider the past at its real value, in some cases to even reconsider it.*

Whatever comes between the student and his or her potential joy in learning, the Theorists' subject dependency forms a preventive barrier that the student may use as a reference point.

Motivates Students to Increased Satisfaction and Development of Learning Skills: In path-goal theory, satisfaction occurs when the rewards for student performance match the student's expectations. To the Theorist, learning is inherently rewarding and mastery is satisfying by nature. This belief is implied in the statement by James Ardini (Diablo Valley College, Pleasant Hill, California):

> *At the bottom, I emphasize that [students] must learn to learn on their own—the foundation stone of the truly educated. They gradually learn that true motivation to learn comes not from a cheap and flashy teaching technique, but from the self-mastery of a discipline and themselves.*

Throughout the comments from the students of Theorists, we found support for this belief. Students did find genuine delight in learning and real satisfaction with their accomplishments as learners.

Increases Opportunities for Quality Educational Performance and Success: Students do not, however, enter the Theorist's classroom with a burning desire to learn, any more than they enter any other teacher's. This desire has to be sparked, then tended, through the teacher's example and dedicated effort. Karen Detweiler talks about personal pay-offs in terms of the nonreaders she has had in her reading improvement courses. As the students begin to see progress, they come to believe achievement is possible. Gradually, they realize there is hope for change in their lives. With this recognition they are willing to spend hours each day and, therefore, are able to reach a sixth- and seventh-grade reading level in a little over a year.

Uses Effective Performance as an Expectation to Empower Students: Theorists are clear in their expectations of students. They expect them to learn and to learn to love learning. However, recognizing that community college students usually need something a little more tangible to work toward, they communicate to students the goals and standards of the learning tasks. A student of Nova Jean Weber (Cerritos College, Norwalk, California) shows a typical way Theorists accomplish this:

> *I remember how hard it was for me to write. I sat in my chair writing and thinking of things to say on paper. She would suggest topics that motivated me; and between much writing and her checking and marking up my paper in red ink, I could see the whole picture of what was expected of me.*

Theorists, then, work from conceptual models. Therefore, students must usually go through a process of discovery to fully grasp the teacher's expectations. This is not because the teacher does not have those expectations clearly in mind. Quite the contrary! The discovery process is a result of the abstract nature of the Theorists' expectations and the difficulty in communicating abstractions clearly and concretely. Theorists, for example, would not be satisfied to expect a five-paragraph essay described in terms of specific objectives. And yet, by expecting the student to write an essay that shows analytical thinking, Theorists greatly increase the difficulty in communicating to the student exactly what he or she should do.

TEACHING FIELDS

Theorists reported a wide variety of teaching fields, and we could not predict or define teaching behavior based on their teaching fields—Theorists do not fit neatly into particular fields or disciplines. Although our chart shows some preponderance in the fields of engineering and the sciences, no statistically significant findings about the Theorists and teaching fields were found.

Figure 8.8: **Teaching Fields: Theorists**

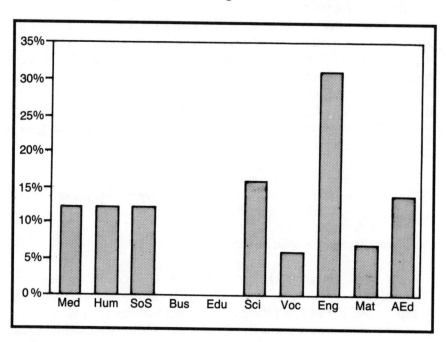

IMPLICATIONS

In the teaching-as-leading cycle, Theorists are best for those students who have advanced beyond the nurturing care of the Supporter, but who are not yet ready for the driving, competitive demands of the Achiever. Through Theorists' love of a subject and enthusiasm for learning, the students discover that learning is something that goes beyond rote behaviors for accomplishing specific requirements. Instead, they see that learning is something they are quite capable of doing for themselves and that they can find great satisfaction in it for its own sake. Once they discover this about learning and develop confidence in their own abilities as learners, they are ready to test themselves against the standards of Achievers. With success in that arena they can ultimately challenge the "personal best" approach of the Influencer teachers.

As with all four archetypes, however, Theorists must be

adaptable to their students in order to get the most and best student learning. Within each class there are students with diverse needs and a wide range of motivational and cognitive readiness. Theorists provide an important, often pivotal, learning experience for community college students, but the impact, as always, is dependent on the match between the teacher's style and the student's place in his or her own learning cycle.

Chapter 9

Profiles of Teaching Excellence: Achievers

———

Philosophy
Characteristics
Strengths
Path-Goal Data and Achievers
Teaching-Learning and Path-Goal
Teaching Fields
Implications

9

In the end, the role of the teacher is to make students understand that (a) if they put in the effort, most likely, they will succeed splendidly, and (b) developing intellectual curiosity in one area will stimulate their appetite for knowledge in other areas.

Jorge B. Gonzalez
Miami-Dade Community College

Occasionally, a teacher must mentally spar with students instead of simply being the fountain of knowledge. Sometimes, this means the teacher is the loser, but even then students feel they are also a part of what the teacher teaches.

Henry Castillo
Temple Junior College

*O*ne-fourth of the teachers in our study were Achievers (Figure 9.1). Although Achievers are characterized by their task orientation, they are energetic, active teachers who want to see student participation in their classroom environment; Achievers are focused on mastery of content but are likely to embue content mastery with great enthusiasm, confidence, and spirit.

Figure 9.1: **Achievers**

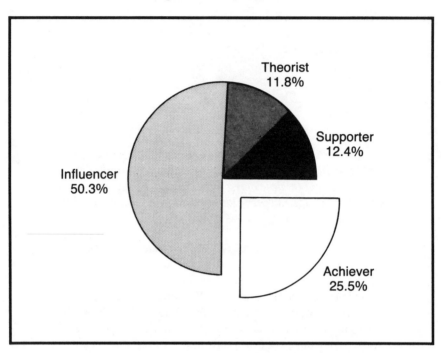

*I possess facts or skills that the students need, and I structure
situations so that the students can acquire these facts or skills. ...I
feel most comfortable, however, when I abandon traditional
authority and become a fellow struggler in pursuit of whatever
certainty or truth the discipline promises. I try to model a kind
of academic literacy that is more than just the ability to read and
write. It is a vocabulary, a set of structures for testing reality, a
way of knowing* (David Humphreys, Cuyahoga Community
College, Cleveland, Ohio).

*My number-one joy is to creatively and enthusiastically share
my knowledge, experience, talent, and energy with [students].
My basic philosophy is that students learn best when they are
productively and happily involved in the learning process and
when the knowledge is relevant* (Teresa Thomas, Southwestern
College, Chula Vista, California).

PHILOSOPHY

These quotes exemplify the teacher that we classify as "Achiever." In the Teaching as Leading Inventory, the Achiever is opposite the Supporter. Although they strongly value the learner in the teaching and learning situation, Achievers view their role as teachers of content; therefore, their purpose is to enable students to master content. The primary requirements for effective teaching in the Achiever style are genuine love for the subject and the systematic thinking skills necessary to pass it on to the learners. Achievers, like excellent community college teachers in general, are also learners. However, when they think of themselves as learners, they do not think in terms of intra-personal needs, as Supporters do. Instead, they think in the more specific terms of learning styles. Bob Norden (Community College of Denver, Denver, Colorado), an honors accounting instructor, demonstrates this point of view in his statement of the role of the teacher:

> *The role of the teacher...is that of a practiced learner. I try to maintain a student perspective by teaching classes as I would want someone to teach them if I were the student. A primary role of the teacher is to maintain enthusiasm in the classroom. By creating a positive atmosphere that allows for intellectual growth, the exchange of ideas, and the development of the tools to solve problems, the teacher can improve the learning process.*

As the name Achiever implies, then, Achievers are focused on mastery. When they take the students' perspective—as they often do—it is to better understand how to organize and present content. Students are motivated by success, according to the Achiever, and student performance will result from student effort. Therefore, when students come to an Achiever with problems in learning the subject matter or skills, the Achiever will present different learning strategies until the student finds one that enables learning. Robert Xidis (Johnson County Community College, Overland Park, Kansas) explains this philosophy:

> *In addition to conveying and interpreting course content, I*

believe that a teacher ought to share various ways of learning. I don't think teachers should just expect students to learn the material they teach; I think teachers ought to demonstrate different techniques for mastering material and explain various learning strategies. In other words, I think the role of the teacher includes demonstrating how to learn, as well as telling students what to learn.

The goal of the learner is to master content; the purpose of the Achiever is to design teaching-learning strategies that enable the learner to reach that goal. With this focus, Achievers approach the teaching-learning process as scientists. Like the Theorist, the Achiever hypothesizes theories to guide teaching decisions rather than relying on sensitivity to feeling, a Supporter strength. Mark Lewine (Cuyahoga Community College, Cleveland, Ohio), for example, is typical of the Achiever when he describes an assignment in his "Social Problems" class:

I require a term project designed to both integrate concepts and provide an opportunity for personal community application. As my research indicates that students have an extreme aversion to writing term papers, I spend most of the first week...in an orientation process culminating in student selection and positive commitment to the assignment and the course.

Unlike the Supporters, who see themselves as helping people solve problems, the Achievers see themselves as helping learners learn what they have to teach. School, then, is a very special place, but a place with a focus and singular purpose. As Jerry Long (Wharton County Junior College, Wharton, Texas) says, school is "a center where those who possess knowledge, experiences, and sensitivities meet with those who wish to gain knowledge, develop experience, and hone sensitivity."

Figure 9.2: **Task Orientation/Active Influencing**

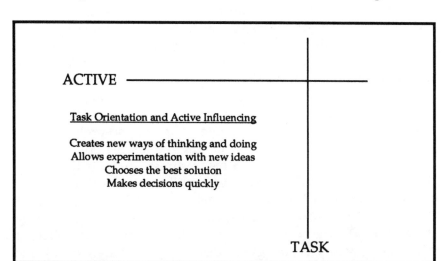

The primary forces affecting Achiever behavior are task orientation and active orientation. Consequently, they are very focused on what it is they are trying to teach and on how well the students are learning it. If students are having difficulty, the Achiever is likely to try different strategies but not change the essential task the students are expected to master. Achievers, in other words, believe very strongly that they are teaching something of great value and that students will be rewarded by learning it. The excellent Achiever, then, receives personal and professional satisfaction from actively influencing students to succeed—at high levels and in high numbers. The student comments clearly demonstrated the willingness of these teachers to spend as much time with individual students as necessary to enable individuals to succeed. However, the teachers' comments overwhelmingly supported our belief that excellent Achievers measure their own success by the numbers of students, rather than individual students, who perform in their courses at a high level of achievement.

Like the Supporter, the Achiever is innovative and seeks new ways of thinking and doing. However, more like the Theorist than the Supporter, the Achiever experiments from a theoretical base rather than a sensing or feeling base. For example, David McCarthy (University of Minnesota Technical College, Waseca, Minnesota), a welding instructor, discovered a way to use his dual role as teacher and advisor to enhance teaching and learning. He developed a 25-item questionnaire for his freshmen advisees, but distributed it in the early part of "Introduction to Agricultural Mechanization," a course he teaches to the freshmen advisees. He then summarized the data and used them in interviews with the students about their study habits, problems with the course, general goals, and problems with transition to college life. By combining the teacher-advisor roles, this teacher formed bonds with his freshmen students that lasted throughout their college experience. The theoretical base for experimenting and innovating is also evident in Mark Lewine's (Cuyahoga Community College, Cleveland, Ohio) explanation of the purposes for the peer group tutoring process he introduced in his large introductory sociology classes: "to mix independent and dependent learning modes, increase student motivation, encourage success orientation, develop study skills, and increase student performance and learning as measured by test scores." Achievers do not experiment just for the sake of change, but rather to find a better way to enable students to learn and always with a clear idea of what they expect to accomplish.

These experiments may be elaborate or relatively uncomplicated. Mary Jane Wheeler (Cuyahoga Community College, Cleveland, Ohio), an anatomy and physiology instructor, developed the "Multi-Method Approach to Anatomy and Physiology," which includes videotapes, visuals, computer-generated reviews, and games to enhance the lecture method and accommodate a variety of learning styles. Starr Weihe (St. Petersburg Junior College, St. Petersburg, Florida), a zoology instructor, turned a lecture course with 90 students into a discussion course. Both of these approaches increased students' active participation in the course and resulted in increased student performance. The Achiever, then, is quick to experiment and to seek new ways of thinking and doing. However, because these teachers are driven to achieve high levels of student success, their experimenting is to find a better way, not simply to find another way. One of Dave Humphreys's (Cuyahoga Community College, Cleveland, Ohio) students made his first 'A' in an English class because his teacher found a better way:

> *I used to have a hard time expressing my ideas on paper until Dr. Humphreys introduced me to the MacIntosh and the system of separating the creative process from the editing process. With the Mac I don't have to worry about spelling and can concentrate on the ideas. Because of this new technique, I earned the first 'A' I have ever had in English.*

One of Burlin Matthews's (Iowa Lakes Community College, Estherville, Iowa) students shows the convergent nature of Achiever thinking in describing how the teacher works with students on the college farm. The student says, "He works with you and asks your opinion, and we then decide together what the best way is." Achievers do not take decisions away from students; but because they are looking for solutions in their experimenting, they can be decisive. When Harold Albertson's (Richland College, Dallas, Texas) students became frustrated in a robotics class, they naturally wanted the teacher to solve the problem. Recognizing that problem-solving skills were an important dimension of the learning experience, this teacher told the students to consider themselves on the job and in charge—in other words, with no one but their team to rely on for answers. By acting decisively, the teacher influenced high performance from the students on the task, as well as in the area of problem-solving.

CHARACTERISTICS

Figure 9.3: **Achievers and the Teaching-Learning Grid**

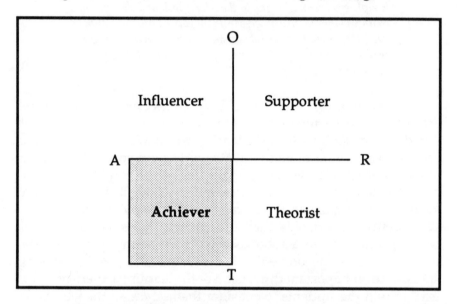

Achievers, as opposites of Supporters, are the most convergent thinkers of the four teacher archetypes. Their personal satisfaction is related to student performance, so they are quick to seek a better way of teaching. Achievers, however, always work from a plan. That is, they are not always in a state of experimentation. As convergent thinkers and solution seekers, they are very goal-oriented. The following statements indicate the strength of this orientation:

> *The entire semester has been geared toward taking a common goal and making the greatest achievement possible* (student of Stephen Stroud, Modesto Junior College, Modesto, California).

> *My philosophy of the role of the teacher has two basic parts, high expectations and student involvement. As the teacher, I must set goals for class achievement* (Carolyn Harris, Midlands Technical College, Columbia, South Carolina).

I believe that a teacher must set standards of excellence in the classroom and demonstrate ways for the students to reach these standards. These goals or standards must be attainable for the student (Paul Ausmus, Howard County Junior College, Big Springs, Texas).

Similar to the Theorist, the Achiever has great confidence and faith in the plan and the goals, and, when students are unsuccessful, will attempt first to change what the student is doing rather than change the teaching-learning situation. Robert Xidis (Johnson County Community College, Overland Park, Kansas), for example, responded to his students' low performance on an essay by putting all the essays, along with his comments on each one, on reserve in the library and asking each student to go through the whole set before attempting the next assignment. By giving the students additional materials to use in understanding the course expectations, this teacher was able to increase student performance without altering the course itself. Many of the Achievers set up study groups and review sessions, arranged tutoring, and did other things, to enable the students to accomplish the goals of the course. When large numbers of students do not perform well, however, the Achiever will abandon the plan in favor of one with a greater likelihood of success.

Achievers, though creative, do not rely on creative insight to guide their changes. Instead they employ systematic thinking. Robert Peetz (Midland College, Midland, Texas) shows this kind of thinking in his attempts to solve a three-part problem. He wanted his criminal justice students to have a better understanding of the law; he wanted them to develop some tangible skills that would be useful after college, and he wanted to help increase utilization of campus resources. The result was a required, two-hour seminar on how to prepare briefs using the campus law library and the implementation of assignments in several courses requiring those skills and resources. This kind of systematic thinking is also seen in the Achiever's teaching behaviors. A student in Mary Perks's (Northern Oklahoma College, Tonkawa, Oklahoma) algebra class expresses her appreciation for the teacher's systematic approach to helping her master the bane of many algebra students—the word problems:

> *Mrs. Perks went step-by-step through each situation, developed graphs, tables, or formulas for each problem, and made the class aware that most problems are similar in their step-solving procedure. My confidence in my abilities has definitely been increased through her efforts.*

Pat Turner (Howard Community College, Columbia, Maryland) advises teachers: "Organize the curriculum so that the student knows what is useful and important, in what order the material is best learned." The convergent nature of Achiever thinking, then, derives from a firm commitment to goals and a belief that there is a best way to get there.

Perhaps because they focus on goals and relate goals to student mastery of content, Achievers tend to think of themselves as subject-matter specialists. That is, they do not think of themselves as teachers in the broad sense that they are prepared to teach anything at anytime. Their teaching is a product of the way they feel about a specific discipline or content area. George Frakes (Santa Barbara City College, Santa Barbara, California) states this point of view unequivocally: "To have effective learning, one must first establish the instructor's love of learning and excitement about his/her field." Mary Knapp (Alvin Community College, Alvin, Texas), a court reporting instructor, demonstrates this excitement by going to various classes in the department, just to talk about interesting experiences she has had on court reporting assignments. The result is that other students become interested and committed to learning this body of knowledge and skills. Throughout the statements of the excellent teachers, and reflected throughout the comments by students, we saw enthusiasm and excitement about the subject. Achievers love to teach because they love what they know.

STRENGTHS

If looked at from only a single perspective, the subject-matter orientation of the Achievers could appear out of step with the student-centered mission of the community college. However, for the excellent Achievers, the value of the knowledge and skills they teach is a special strength because they insist that students see the practical applications for them. Pat Turner (Howard Community College, Columbia, Maryland), for example, begins the "Introduction to her Laboratory Science" course with guest speakers who are lab technicians in the community. They explain to the students how this course prepared them for the jobs they hold—jobs the students expect to hold, as well. One of Elwood Schapansky's (Santa Barbara City College, Santa Barbara, California) physics students explains why he is so motivated to learn physics: "[The teacher uses] practical examples and demonstrations of how the things we learn apply to the everyday things that surround us." James Gray (Miami-Dade Community College, Miami, Florida) sums up this value in his explanation of the role of the teacher: "I want students to know from a historical perspective why things are the way they are. I encourage them to relate historical facts to present-day events."

Another strength of the Achievers is their use of hypothetical-deductive reasoning to improve teaching and learning. Through this approach, Achievers are often able to solve multi-faceted problems systematically and construct solutions that last. In other words, they are less concerned with "quick fix" approaches to problems concerning one or few students, and more concerned with problems in the broader scope of course mastery for all students. Carolyn Harris (Midlands Technical College, Columbia, South Carolina), for example, was concerned because clinical chemistry students did not seem personally involved in the laboratory experience. She noticed the lack of an inquiring attitude on the part of the students and their "recipe" approach to lab assignments. As a result, she designed a student lab prep assignment in which a student not only presents and explains a lab experiment to the rest of the class, but is also responsible for inventorying supplies and equipment for the assigned lab, obtaining specimens and quality control materials, preparing reagins, and maintaining everything under proper storage conditions. A similar example comes from Jack Spohn (Centennial College, Scarborough, Ontario), a mathematics teacher. When he was notified that some of the first-year nursing students were having trouble with the calculations in pharmacology, instead of arranging tutoring (a Supporter technique), he designed a two-hour, noncredit course, in which he could teach math from library nursing books. The course has worked so well that he has been asked to design similar courses for other programs in the college. Because Achievers are such analytical problem-solvers, their solutions often result in new and lasting ways of doing things.

Perhaps as a by-product of their deductive, analytical approach to problem solving, Achievers are also very rational and objective in their dealings with students. George Terrell (Gadsden State Community College, East Gadsden, Alabama) reveals this belief in his explanation of the role of the teacher:

> I think students should feel that all of them are equal in the eyes of the teacher and that no favoritism is being shown to anyone. If every student is treated exactly the same and they know that whatever they earn is what they will get for a course grade, then they can set their own goals and work toward what they feel is realistic for them.

Ron Pulse (Laramie County Community College, Cheyenne, Wyoming) further reflects this attitude when he says a teacher should be realistic and honest about a student's future. The fact that Achievers act with objectivity, as well as talk about it, is seen in one of Mr. Pulse's student's recollection of an event in which this Achiever put the student on the right track to success. When the student went to the teacher to discuss why he was not doing well in the class, he remembers the teacher saying, "I'm speaking as a citizen of the city, and I think you are drinking and partying too much!" According to the student, there were no further problems with his performance in the course.

Achievers, then, love what they teach and value it for its practical meaning. The truly excellent ones, believe students can learn it, will be enriched by it, and will receive personal satisfaction from mastering it. Their role as teachers is to design systems that enable mastery at a high level, systems designed with the belief that all students can succeed.

PATH-GOAL DATA AND ACHIEVERS

Achievers feel most successful at clarifying paths to student success; they encourage student effort with constructive feedback, and they identify and affirm student responsibilities—they are great coaches (Figure 9.4). Philosophically, they most espouse their need to engage their students in active learning before they point the way through guidance (Figure 9.6). They are highly displeased and even frustrated when they cannot use their energies to motivate students or encourage them to become self-motivators (Figure 9.5).

Figure 9.4: **Achievers and Path-Goal: Successful Behavior**

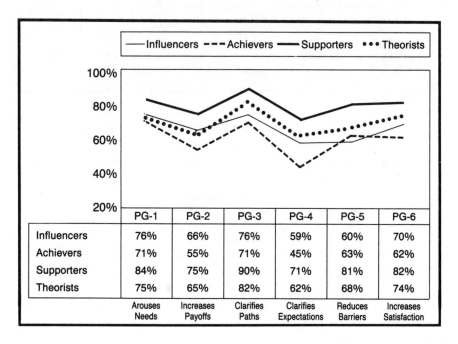

	PG-1	PG-2	PG-3	PG-4	PG-5	PG-6
Influencers	76%	66%	76%	59%	60%	70%
Achievers	71%	55%	71%	45%	63%	62%
Supporters	84%	75%	90%	71%	81%	82%
Theorists	75%	65%	82%	62%	68%	74%
	Arouses Needs	Increases Payoffs	Clarifies Paths	Clarifies Expectations	Reduces Barriers	Increases Satisfaction

Figure 9.5: **Achievers and Path-Goal: Unsuccessful Behavior**

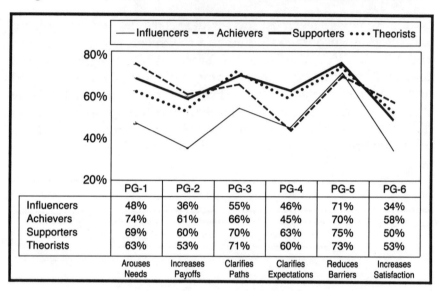

	PG-1	PG-2	PG-3	PG-4	PG-5	PG-6
Influencers	48%	36%	55%	46%	71%	34%
Achievers	74%	61%	66%	45%	70%	58%
Supporters	69%	60%	70%	63%	75%	50%
Theorists	63%	53%	71%	60%	73%	53%
	Arouses Needs	Increases Payoffs	Clarifies Paths	Clarifies Expectations	Reduces Barriers	Increases Satisfaction

Figure 9.6: **Achievers and Path-Goal: Philosophy**

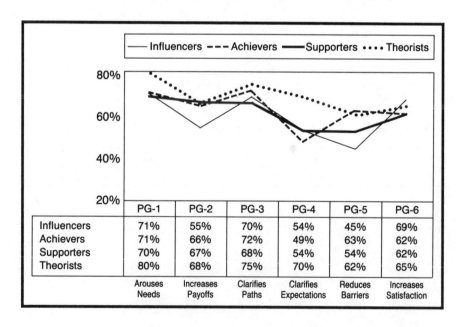

	PG-1	PG-2	PG-3	PG-4	PG-5	PG-6
Influencers	71%	55%	70%	54%	45%	69%
Achievers	71%	66%	72%	49%	63%	62%
Supporters	70%	67%	68%	54%	54%	62%
Theorists	80%	68%	75%	70%	62%	65%
	Arouses Needs	Increases Payoffs	Clarifies Paths	Clarifies Expectations	Reduces Barriers	Increases Satisfaction

Presidents compliment the ability of Achievers to accomplish what they set out to do: they report satisfaction with Achievers' abilities to encourage students to learn and rate them as top-notch teachers. Achievers demonstrate the greatest range of difference between their discussions of motivating experiences and their philosophy of education probably because they place extraordinary value on their ability to motivate and arouse students to succeed in college. Students demonstrate a rather consistent attitude about their Achiever instructors, although they report they do not always live up to the expectations that Achievers have of them. Rather than demonstrate a discouraging view of this weakness, students admire Achievers precisely because they have such high expectations of their students. Stephen Mittelstet, president, notes with praise the accomplishments of Harold Albertson (Richland College, Dallas, Texas):

> If I were to select one educator who, in my estimation, exemplifies the philosophy and spirit of the community college, that person would be Harold Albertson. Dr. Albertson participated in the Building Communities report and personifies the teacher the commission is seeking: he is a mentor and a scholar. He is a creator and a person who always pursues excellence. He makes his courses a dynamic laboratory of learning and accomplishment for students.

Figure 9.7: **Achievers: Self-Report and Student and CEO Report**

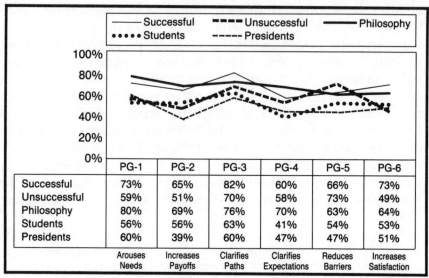

	PG-1	PG-2	PG-3	PG-4	PG-5	PG-6
Successful	73%	65%	82%	60%	66%	73%
Unsuccessful	59%	51%	70%	58%	73%	49%
Philosophy	80%	69%	76%	70%	63%	64%
Students	56%	56%	63%	41%	54%	53%
Presidents	60%	39%	60%	47%	47%	51%
	Arouses Needs	Increases Payoffs	Clarifies Paths	Clarifies Expectations	Reduces Barriers	Increases Satisfaction

TEACHING-LEARNING AND PATH-GOAL

Offers Positive Orientation, Guidance, and Direction: Because of their commitment to high student performance and achievement, Achievers believe strongly in the use of objectives and alternative ways for students to reach them. Donald Wheeler (Cuyahoga Community College, Cleveland, Ohio) exhibits this attitude in his statement of philosophy:

> I believe that a teacher must provide to the student a list of performance objectives that the student must master in order to successfully complete the course. I believe in providing the student with 100 percent of the information by as many learning avenues as possible.

Whereas Achievers and Supporters both recognize the need for alternative paths, the two styles are different. The Supporter is likely to create an alternative pathway when confronted with an individual student's special needs. The Achiever, on the other hand, is more likely to build multiple pathways into the course and expect all students to choose from among them. Robert Peetz summarizes this difference in his statement of the role of the teacher:

> *Because not everyone responds to the same stimuli, teachers must be able to evaluate what works for the majority, or what best accomplishes the goals of that particular course. As courses have different objectives, standards of learning, and material, approaches to learning must be flexible.*

Individual students do, in fact, recognize the impact of the Achiever's means of clarifying paths. One of Anna Mae Tichy's (Mt. Hood Community College, Gresham, Ohio) students is typical when she says her instructor motivated her by using an accurate assessment of her skills and giving her direction as to where she needed to improve. In other words, Achievers clarify paths by helping students adapt to pre-existing and appropriate plans for learning.

Recognizes and Engages Student's Desire to Learn: Although Achievers value practical applications of what they teach, their love for their disciplines compels them to want to arouse student needs for learning in a broader context. Willie Quindt (Western Nebraska Community College, Scottsbluff, Nebraska) expresses this in his personal philosophy:

> *As a teacher I strive to instill in the student the never-ending need for the spirit of inquiry, the acquisition of knowledge and understanding, and thoughtful formulation of worthy goals.*

To put it more simply, Achievers attempt to arouse in students the needs they have in themselves. For the excellent teachers, this works. One of James Gentry's (College of Southern Idaho, Twin Falls, Idaho) students admits that he was not happy when he had to take a history course. However, the student says this teacher "teaches with an enthusiasm and knowledge that few teachers have." Because of this, the student says this teacher makes students want to learn, and history has now become a personal hobby of his. One of Beverly Fite's (Amarillo College, Amarillo, Texas) students says her teacher taught her: "You need to learn as much as possible, and there is always room for more learning." The Achiever's love for his or her subject, therefore, pays off in increased student motivation to learn.

Motivates Student to Increased Satisfaction for and Development of Learning Skills: The Achiever believes that satisfaction is directly tied to performance; and in their courses, performance is directly tied to mastery. The Supporter increases satisfaction in personal ways, by requiring a minimum standard for all students and encouraging all students to do their best beyond that standard. The Achiever increases satisfaction by focusing on a high standard and pushing all students to try for it. Joseph Cochran (Wytheville Community College, Wytheville, Virginia) is typical when he says, "Course work should be rigorous and the standards high." But also typical of Achievers, he believes the majority of students will rise to the level of his expectations, as long as he can make those expectations clear.

To the Achievers, learning is itself intrinsically satisfying. Therefore, they do not think in terms of helping students find personal satisfaction in who they are or in their current accomplishments; they prefer to direct students into the specific satisfaction of learning. Starr Weihe (St. Petersburg Junior College, St. Petersburg, Florida) states this almost matter-of-factly in her explanation of the role of the teacher:

> With effective instruction, students will identify what needs to be learned, will be motivated to research additional information, and finally will understand that learning is a perpetual process which brings much pleasure and satisfaction.

Because Achievers believe learning is inherently satisfying, they believe the primary tasks of the teacher are to clarify the paths to performance and to arouse the students' needs for learning. Satisfaction naturally follows. Kenneth Bishop (Itawamba Community College, Fulton, Mississippi) is an instructor whose president, W.O. Benjamin, sees as one who brings a high degree of satisfaction to his students: "Ken sets high expectations, but his students are never those who set the standard for complaints; rather, almost in a single voice, they express admiration for his work, and then seem to work harder to meet his expectations. Almost always they report how surprised they were to find themselves wanting to do more."

Works to Eliminate or Reduce Learning Obstacles: The examples of barriers mentioned by the Achievers and their students were almost exclusively related to the specific teaching-learning situation. Whereas Supporters are likely to help students overcome barriers outside the teaching-learning situation but impacting on it—e.g., personal crises or reading problems—Achievers are concerned only with barriers within their span of control. If a student has a reading problem, for example, the Achiever is more likely to direct the student into an existing alternative learning strategy designed for course mastery, such as tapes and visuals, than to help the student get into a developmental reading course. One of Robert Norden's (Community College of Denver, Denver, Colorado) students admits that her performance in class suffered because she was "disillusioned with accounting." She was turned around, however, by her teacher's ability to motivate her to succeed in his Accounting III class. That is, the teacher did not attempt to deal with the personal aspects of disillusionment; instead, he pushed her to improve her performance and feel good about it.

Achievers recognize the necessity of alternative teaching strategies to enable student success. Therefore, they build into their courses many systems to reduce barriers in learning. Also, because they see themselves as providing students with a rewarding body of knowledge or skills, they are less likely to become involved in, or know about, dimensions of their students outside their shared teaching-learning environment. Supporters get to know their students as people. But even the students who form lasting relationships with the Achievers are forever "students."

Uses Effective Performance as an Expectation to Empower Students: Mary Perks (Northern Oklahoma College, Tonkawa, Oklahoma) best expresses the Achiever's attitudes about expectations:

> *A demanding teacher, in terms of the depth of mastery required*
> *by the students, as well as the amount of work required of the*

students, enables far more learning to take place than a teacher who coddles the students by not expecting their best efforts and work. Students do what is expected of them. Good teachers expect and demand their students' best!

One of Teresa Thomas's (Southwestern College, Chula Vista, California) students shows the student side of the Achiever's expectations:

Ms. Thomas treated all her students as if they were all equally intelligent, which motivated us to do well. She expected superb work from her students....We were all expected to do labs and turn in labs that were of professional standards. Ms. Thomas was preparing us for what lies ahead.

Perhaps the trademark of the Achievers is that they do indeed expect students to perform. In fact, so pronounced is this expectation that it is implicit in their pathways to success. Achievers use performance objectives to direct students toward mastery of content and skills at a high level rather than a minimum level. Therefore, their expectations are clarified, they believe, by everything they do in class and by every assignment they give. "Clarifies expectations," then, was not at the top of their path-goal efforts because they cannot clarify the path without including the expectations. Such is the nature of the Achiever.

Increases Opportunities for Quality Educational Performance and Success: At the risk of oversimplifying, we could say that students of Supporters have increased pay-offs by feeling better about themselves and having meaningful relationships with their teachers. Students of Achievers have increased pay-offs by being awakened to the wonder of learning and the enjoyment of a body of knowledge. A student of Robert Xidis (Johnson County Community College, Overland Park, Kansas) says he has grown to understand literature in a way he never understood it before. One of Elizabeth Brett's (John C. Calhoun State Community College, Decatur, Alabama) students says that because this teacher pushed him to read books that he, at first, did not like, he is now reading books on his own that he never would have opened before. For

David Humphreys (Cuyahoga Community College, Cleveland, Ohio), "If the alchemy is right, students leave the course with a genuine excitement for learning." To the Achievers, the students' personal pay-offs are increased as they become more involved in the subject. Enthusiasm for the subject is contagious, and we heard over and over from the students that the teachers' obvious excitement about what they were teaching motivated the students to want to learn more. Many of these students began the courses with apprehension, even dread, but quickly realized how much they could gain by increasing their effort.

TEACHING FIELDS

Achievers are active in every teaching discipline, although they appear to have greater numbers in the sciences, vocational, engineering, math, and social sciences areas. Again, like Supporters and Achievers, they do not demonstrate any proclivity toward teaching fields based on their teaching style.

Figure 9.8: **Teaching Fields: Achievers**

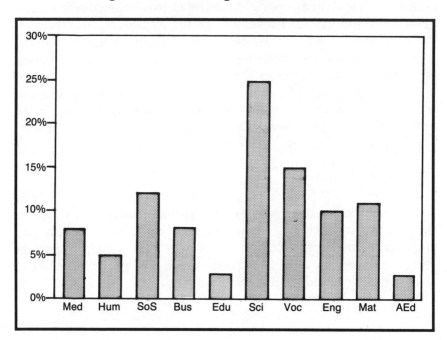

IMPLICATIONS

Although Achievers teach beginning students, advanced students, large classes, small classes, and most disciplines, their particular strengths best fit those students who are able to make a high commitment to learning. The Supporters are best for the entering student who is taking those important first steps in gaining self-confidence to pursue an eduction. The Theorists are best for those students who have taken the first tentative steps and who are testing and developing the systematic thought processes required in a learning environment. Achievers, though, are best for those students who have resolved personal aspects that interfere with learning, have made appropriate decisions concerning their educational goals, and who are, therefore, in a state of readiness to devote the time and energy to learning expected by these demanding teachers.

Achievers are a special asset to community college students because they back up their high demands with systems designed to enable high student performance. Although they will not take responsibility for student performance, they believe effort leads to performance, and they will assume some responsibility for motivating students to put forth that effort. Therefore, these teachers often play key roles in helping students see how much they are capable of achieving. Students of these teachers often go on to perform well in four-year colleges and in their careers. Thus, they continue to achieve once they have learned they can.

Chapter 10

Profiles of Teaching Excellence: Influencers

———

Philosophy
Characteristics
Strengths
Path-Goal Data and Influencers
Teaching-Learning and Path-Goal
Teaching Fields
Implications

10

The teacher is in a role of 'forever' student. The love for and desire to learn is a lifestyle. Nothing is separate—not teachers and students nor teaching and learning.

Sue Foy
Laramie County Community College

The number one rule for the teacher is that the student is the first priority. Rule number two is to remember rule number one.

Steve Zabetakis
Hagerstown Junior College

*T*he majority teaching style is the Influencer style. Over one-half of the instructors who responded to the Teaching as Leading Inventory inquiries were Influencers. Their dominant teaching style is active and student-oriented. Influencers are teachers who have finely honed intuitive skills; they are, as their name connotes, experts in shaping values, attitudes, and beliefs among their students. That they orient those behaviors toward educational goals is a given for Influencers.

Figure 10.1: **Influencers**

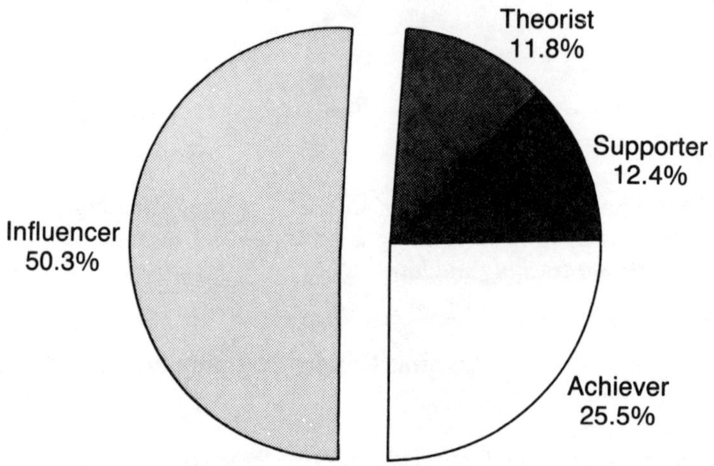

PHILOSOPHY

Teachers who are classified as Influencers on the Teaching as Leading Inventory are concerned with individual students; however, like Achievers, they focus on mastery learning. Therefore, the Influencer attempts to motivate all students to high levels of performance, but takes great satisfaction from the special individuals who overcome the most and reach the farthest. Tom Vance (Central Piedmont Community College, Charlotte, North Carolina) shows the Influencer's philosophy on motivation:

> It is rarely a single incident that motivates students, but a strong, never-say-die attitude on the part of the instructor to help the students overcome seemingly insurmountable obstacles that block their way to success…The good teacher must constantly fill each class with subject matter that challenges the student to grow and to reach a little farther than he first thought he could. And,

each day should present a new challenge—none of this treading water!

Even though Influencers are enthusiastic about the subjects they teach, they love the actual act of teaching, most of all. Of all the Teaching-as-Leading types, Influencers are the most driven by student growth and change. As their title implies, these teachers are actively involved in influencing this growth. Although they believe the student is ultimately responsible for his or her performance, they hold themselves responsible for providing the motivation and means to succeed. One of Mel Carter's (Community College of Denver, Denver, Colorado) students illustrates the difference:

> *Without Mel Carter's commitment to help his students succeed, I do not believe I would have completed the semester. He was sympathetic to my personal circumstances, but was quick to remind me that my own success was determined by discipline and hard work. He is passionate about this belief and unselfish about sharing his experience and ideas with his students. I am convinced that without his relentless and compassionate devotion to his students, which included me, I would not have tasted the fruits of success, which were a result of my own hard work.*

Between the Supporter's commitment to people and the Achiever's commitment to subject matter, then, is the Influencer's commitment to learning.

Figure 10.2: **Active Influencing—Others Orientation**

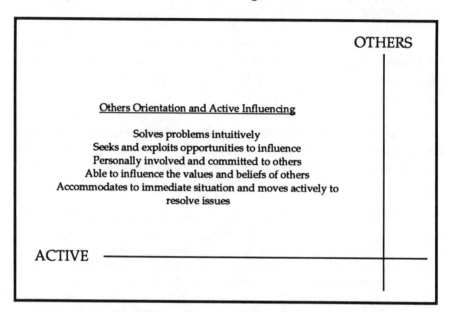

The forces behind Influencer behavior are active influencing and an others orientation. Influencers are the opposites of Theorists, but combine many aspects of both Achievers and Supporters. For example, Influencers are able to develop plans to guide actions, but are impatient with too much reflection. They prefer to act. As a result, these teachers tend to have a great deal of energy, both in class and out. This desire to act is reflected in the belief that learning itself is also active. Therefore, Influencers involve students in the learning process as much as possible.

Influencers are constantly poised to take advantage of opportunities to increase student learning. For example, after class, Nancy Shaw (Midland College, Midland, Texas) helped one of her students master a difficult concept. In the next class meeting, another student asked a question about the same concept. The first student, though notably shy, volunteered to answer the question. The teacher seized the opportunity by inviting the shy student to the board to explain the concept, which she did. According to the teacher, the student generated more positive discussion than she herself could have. Paul Kaser (Kings River College, Reedley, California) was asked to teach conversational and written English to a group of older Hispanic adults. Upon realizing that some of the students could barely write in their own language, he developed oral history groups that brought together students with various levels of native literacy and English skills. The students with low-literacy and English skills told stories about themselves while the other students recorded and translated them. The result was greater commitment from all the students because they were able to teach each other.

Excellent Influencers see opportunities where others see threats. The pay-off to teaching and learning, though, is that opportunities often lead to additional opportunities. This is exemplified in Tom Osborne's (Rancho Santiago College, Santa Ana, California) history class. Students in this class are required to write a letter to a public official or media representative urging a particular action on a public issue. Knowing that one of his students had expressed an interest in educational issues, this teacher encouraged her to fulfill the assignment by writing to William Bennett, then Secretary of Education. As a result of the letter, the student received a call from Bennett in which he expressed gratitude for the letter and explained the actions he planned to take regarding the issue. Osborne then used this opportunity to instill in other students the true value and responsibility of "We the people...." It is important to note, however, that Influencers' readiness to seize opportunities is not exactly the same as Supporters' openness to the "teachable moments." Supporters are willing to take opportunities to teach students what the students may suddenly appear to need. Influencers, by contrast, are open to those opportunities that will increase student performance within the discipline.

However, Influencers see their influence as extending beyond the particular goals of the course. They define success in terms of student growth and change. Bobbie Van Dusen (Guilford Technical Community College, Jamestown, North Carolina) recognizes that as a developmental reading instructor, her "greatest challenge is to motivate students to develop good study habits to make needed changes in attitude, in addition to improving their reading skills." As Steve Zabetakis (Hagerstown Junior College, Hagerstown,

Maryland) says, "Outcomes are the result of successful efforts that were not always originally planned in the instructional program. Not only does the teacher influence the student, but on many occasions the student influences the teacher." Influence, then, is an interactive process between teacher and learner, in which both are enriched. When George Williams (John C. Calhoun State Community College, Decatur, Alabama) introduced one of his students to the wonders of marine biology, she became so enthusiastic that she went on to take a double major in biology and English. Moreover, she has now written a textbook for science teaching. Seeing this student's success further inspired this Influencer to continue pushing other students beyond their limits.

The interactive nature of influence is supported by Influencers' personal involvement in the learning. Cynthia Hayot (Kennedy-King College, Chicago, Illinois), for example, puts her students into groups to discuss certain assignments. She then sits with each group during the discussion to see and hear the discoveries that occur. The result, as she says, is a pleasant learning experience for all. Because of this personal involvement, students relate to the Influencers as leaders in learning, and are, therefore, motivated to higher levels of performance. Ray Von Caldwell (Central Piedmont Community College, Charlotte, North Carolina) takes his botany students on a field trip to his farm. Thus, he teaches and at the same time shares a part of his life. One of Chris Walters's (Eastern New Mexico University, Clovis, New Mexico) students attributes her success in child psychology to the fact that the teacher explains the concepts in terms of the successes and failures she has had in her own family. The student says, "We know that even though she's a teacher, she is a person first, and we have a lot in common."

By being willing to be personally involved in students' learning, Influencers are, in fact, able to influence more than just student effort. They influence beliefs. One of Melvona Boren's (San Juan College, Farmington, New Mexico) Native American students was shy and insecure in class; however, because of the teacher's efforts, she gradually came to see herself as a successful student who was capable of high levels of performance. Now in a successful position, she wrote to her teacher to express her gratitude:

I never realized what school could mean to me. I never knew there was a world like the one you have shown me. My dad didn't believe I should get an education, but my mother insisted that it was important. You have shown me how right my mother was.

Throughout our study of Influencers, we found similar testimony from students. Where Supporters provide counsel and empathy that enable students to feel worthwhile as human beings, Influencers provide motivation that compels students to try and to grow through their own successes. The following comment from one of Kay Frazier's (Clark State Community College, Springfield, Ohio) students is typical:

Mrs. Frazier sat down with me and said: 'You have to believe in yourself because I believe in you.' She gave me the motivation that I needed to succeed in court reporting. Without her confidence in me, I wouldn't have succeeded in this endeavor.

Influencers can influence beliefs because they believe strongly in what they do. Achievers believe in the value of the knowledge and skills they teach; therefore, they believe that students will find learning to be rewarding. Influencers, though, believe the rewards come from meeting the challenge of learning through performance.

CHARACTERISTICS

Figure 10.3: **Influencers and the Teaching-Learning Grid**

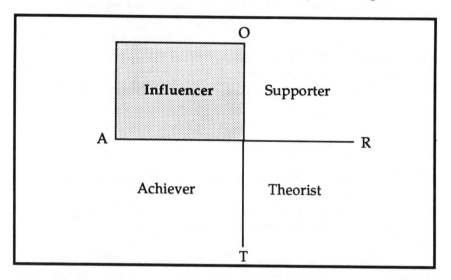

In Muriel Tyssen's (Lee College, Baytown, Texas) statement of her teaching philosophy, she wrote the following postscript:

> *I hate this kind of essay. It lends itself to glittering generalities and marginal sincerities. I like my job. I like it enough to do it well. I am proud of the way I do this job. Maybe this quality is the only one that counts.*

This comment demonstrates an essential characteristic of Influencers—they are doers. Although they will freely discuss their students' successes, they do not like to reflect. Their teaching style is based on positive action. They actively motivate students, actively engage them in the learning process, and actively inspire them to stretch beyond their reach. James Coleman (Community College of Baltimore, Baltimore, Maryland) is an example of a teacher who acts. One of his students recalls a turning point in her learning:

> *After mid-term, I had decided to drop this course because*

I wasn't making the grades that I wanted to make. Mr. Coleman called me at home to talk to me about my grades. He was so optimistic about my ability to do the work that I changed my mind about withdrawing. I started to study a little harder and a lot longer. Eventually, the pieces fell into place.

Influencers do not allow students to be passive about their learning, and they do not permit themselves to be passive about students' commitment to succeed. Larry Foreman (San Diego City College, San Diego, California) puts it this way:

I pursue teaching with a passion. I immerse myself totally into the experience—in and out of the classroom. My basic philosophy is simple: inspire the students to perspire.

Because of this predilection for action, rather than reflection, Influencers are always quick to try new approaches. Their basic learning style is that of accommodator, and, as such, they are always trying to fit new information into existing schemes or theories. However, unlike the Theorists' assimilator style, Influencers tend to quickly abandon pre-existing schemes when they do not accommodate new experiences and go in search of better ones. Pamela Howell (Midland College, Midland, Texas) expresses this tendency metaphorically: "I certainly have some objectives in mind; however, I am willing to alter, change, and steer when I have to in order to come in to port." Robert Wotring (Washtenaw Community College, Ann Arbor, Michigan) is also typical of the Influencer when he says, "I have 10 ways to explain everything. So, when I feel that one approach is failing, I try another." Influencers do not have to rely on their own creativity to think of new approaches. They are enthusiastic conference participants who will experiment with any idea that offers the promise of increasing student learning. Art Lindenberg (Schoolcraft College, Livonia, Michigan) attended a conference session on collaborative learning. He found the session to seemingly match what he was trying to accomplish in his own teaching. Consequently, by the beginning of the next term, he had completely redesigned his course in short fiction. As a result, he was able to achieve greater student success.

Of course, not all experiments work as well as hoped. When asked to describe situations in which they did not feel successful, Influencers often told of failed experiments. But that is the nature of the teaching-as-leading style. In lieu of a reflective orientation, Influencers approach change largely through trial-and-error. They keep the experiments that work, for as long as they work; however, they are quick to abandon any experiment that does not produce better student participation and performance. Sometimes this experimentation seems deliberate, as with Melvin Schwartz (Miami-Dade Community College, Miami, Florida):

> I try to be creative and innovative in the development of methodologies that meet students' learning needs. When students have great difficulty in learning, the responsibility often falls on me because my strategies are not refined enough to satisfy their educational needs. I try anything and everything to assist my students in discovering their skills and talents.

At other times, Influencers' experiments seem completely spontaneous. The following example is a situation described by one of David Brown's (College of DuPage, Glen Ellyn, Illinois) students:

> During a class session we were discussing the atomic theory. Halfway through the period, my instructor jumped up on the top of the table and gave us his loud and enthusiastic interpretation of an exploding atom. From that day on, I never forgot the atomic theory.

Regardless of how Influencers experiment with new ideas, we found strong evidence that they involve others in the campaign to increase student learning. In Carol Maudlin's (Cowley County Community College, Arkansas City, Kansas) sociology courses, she provides her students with multiple objectives and lets each student pick the objective he or she wishes to achieve and the appropriate method with which to achieve it. At the end of Carolyn Neptune's (Johnson County Community College, Overland Park, Kansas) algebra course, she has students write notes of advice and helpful hints for distribution to new students the following term, thus letting the students use their accumulated wisdom to help prepare other students for the learning. Bob Rose (Mount Royal College, Calgary, Alberta) provides a good example of how Influencers involve others in their attempts to increase student learning. This teacher divides his students into feedback teams consisting of six members each, with one member selected as a representative. In bimonthly meetings, the teacher gets feedback from the team representatives on methods of instruction, content, and other aspects of the course. Therefore, Influencers consider every idea and every person a potential resource to improve teaching and learning.

STRENGTHS

Influencers, because of their others orientation, resemble Supporters in their sensitivity to the learning environment. However, the difference is that the sensitivity is less emotion-based, less aware of feelings and personal needs, and more cognition-based, aware of the level of understanding present. Dean Russell (Washtenaw Community College, Ann Arbor, Michigan) explains it this way:

> A teacher should constantly be aware of the classroom attitude; and if things are not as they should be, he should attempt to inject into the situation something that will change it. A teacher must imagine himself as a student in the classroom—listening, watching, and taking part. He must constantly ask himself: 'Am I learning in this classroom?'

The importance of this strength to student performance is seen in a situation recalled by a machine shorthand student in Camille Cargill's (Amarillo College, Amarillo, Texas) class:

> I came to class feeling as though I would never succeed because the machine was not coming along as I thought it would. I thought the problem had to do with me and not the fact that the machine and the theory were hard to learn. My instructor sensed that the class was struggling and thereafter gave us the most encouraging and motivating talks. It helped me tremendously.

The combination of intuition and willingness to try new ideas makes Influencers particularly adaptable to new teaching and learning situations. Daryl Herrman (Glen Oaks Community College, Centreville, Michigan) recalls encountering a student in her basic writing class whose dyslexia made content mastery difficult. This teacher's response was to enroll in a program that trained educators to work with dyslexic students. After completing the program, she became the student's advisor. She watched this student receive her associate degree, then go on to receive a bachelor's degree. Ruth Hatcher (Washtenaw Community College, Ann Arbor, Michigan) remembers trying to teach basic English in a program for high-risk students. Instead of worrying about the low-preparedness and motivation of the students, she felt "challenged to make writing real" for them by approaching literacy with situations relevant to the students' lives. Therefore, situations that are threatening to many teachers are opportunities and challenges for the excellent Influencers, who thrive on pushing students to perform and get results.

Another reason Influencers are particularly adaptable to new situations is that they are risk-takers. Beverly Terry (Central Piedmont Community College, Charlotte, North Carolina) was one of the first teachers at Central Piedmont to volunteer to teach via the experimental interactive television. The fact that a young mother with a handicapped child was able to take Accounting I at home and make an A+ made it worth getting used to microphones, bright lights, and being on camera. Robert Malcolmson (Mohawk College, Hamilton, Ontario) walked out of his criminal law class in the middle of his lecture on gambling offenses and returned with playing cards and poker chips. During the next hour, the teacher set up a lottery, played poker with the students, and secretly induced one or two students to cheat at poker and get caught. At the end of the class, the teacher told the students to go home and read the codes to see if they could tell which ones had been violated—90 percent could. In his criminal justice class, Jerry Larson (Iowa Lakes Community College, Estherville, Iowa) has instituted Kingsfield Day, named after a principal character in the TV series, "Paper Chase." On this day, students must dress professionally and be prepared to be questioned by a professor who is absolutely intolerant of shoddy student performance. Throughout the teacher's role-playing, the students learn how well they are able to perform when the demands are truly high.

By some standards, Influencers are unorthodox. Their commitment to student performance is so great, however, that they are willing—and likely—to try almost anything. One of the things that enables these teachers to take risks is their comfort level with learners. Here again, their others orientation is an advantage. James Sasser's (Central Piedmont Community College, Charlotte, North Carolina) summer tour course in North Carolina history is an example. More than 40 students, ranging in age from 18 to 70, sign up for his course, which includes several day-long bus trips and two weekend trips. Many Influencers, in fact, teach courses in which they are with students longer and more intensely than in usual class courses. These courses are usually very popular because of the student's level of comfort with the Influencer. One of Larry Pilgrim's (Tyler Junior College, Tyler, Texas) students describes his feelings about a class:

> While sitting in Mr. Pilgrim's class, I feel very comfortable. He creates such a suitable atmosphere for learning that students actually look forward to attending class and learning.

Because of their comfort with people and their fundamental belief that students can and will perform, Influencers tend to use group work very effectively. Therefore, we analyzed the comments from these teachers and their students to gain insights into their teaching practices. We found that almost all of them either described or implied some kind of group activity. Russ Flynn (Cypress College, Cypress, California) created group projects in order to develop teamship and camaraderie as a way of improving class attendance—which it did. Nancy Laughbaum (Columbus State Community College, Columbus, Ohio) uses groups in her writing skills class to generate ideas for writing. Influencers cited group work as a means to enhance the atmosphere of the class, and thus increase learning, student responsibility, and creativity. Of all the techniques used by these teachers, group work was the most common by far.

With all this flexibility in teaching, however, it would be easy to assume that Influencers do not have a clear plan concerning what they want to accomplish. However, our analysis of the materials indicates quite the opposite. Shirley Gilbert (El Paso Community College, El Paso, Texas) is a typical example:

> I decided to really challenge the students. I included the usual computer lab projects; however, with each successive project I withheld direction more and more, leaving the student to decide on the final output. On the final project, students would select the subject for the project, develop the computer model, write the appropriate documentation, and demonstrate the finished project to the rest of the class.

At the beginning of the class, the students complained about the final project in all the predictable ways. However, because of the teacher's "planned" reduction of structure, by the end of the quarter the students were not only capable and willing to work on their own, it seemed natural to them. One of Shea Lynn Nabi's (Midland College, Midland, Texas) students comments on her flexibility in class, but at the same time says, "She is extremely organized; therefore, there is no wasted time. The student knows what to expect." Influencers have very clear ideas about what and how much they expect students to learn. They also work from plans designed to result in high student achievement. At the same time, however, they are flexible and adaptable, but only in terms of methods. For example, they strongly believe in the value of humor in the classroom, and the students often commented that this made the class sessions enjoyable. There was never any doubt, however, that these teachers take teaching and learning very seriously.

PATH-GOAL DATA AND INFLUENCERS

Influencers feel strongest about their abilities to clarify paths for successful student behavior and their emphasis on engaging students in an active, enthusiastic pursuit of learning (Figure 10.4). They are the most remorseful, of all the teaching-as-leading styles, about their inabilities to motivate their students—but especially about the actual loss to the student in terms of achievement and future performance, and their obligation for and responsibility to capitalize on student experience as a guide to motivate their behavior (Figure 10.5). They also demonstrate some disparity between their actions and their hopes, especially because they want to be accountable for decreasing and eliminating obstacles that inhibit student success (Figure 10.6).

Figure 10.4: **Influencers and Path-Goal: Successful Behavior**

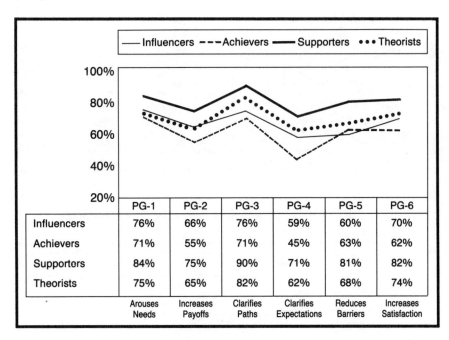

	PG-1	PG-2	PG-3	PG-4	PG-5	PG-6
Influencers	76%	66%	76%	59%	60%	70%
Achievers	71%	55%	71%	45%	63%	62%
Supporters	84%	75%	90%	71%	81%	82%
Theorists	75%	65%	82%	62%	68%	74%
	Arouses Needs	Increases Payoffs	Clarifies Paths	Clarifies Expectations	Reduces Barriers	Increases Satisfaction

Legend: —— Influencers - - - Achievers ▬▬ Supporters • • • Theorists

Figure 10.5: **Influencers and Path-Goal: Unsuccessful Behavior**

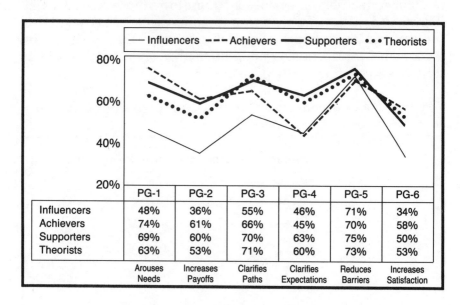

Figure 10.6: **Influencers and Path-Goal: Philosophy**

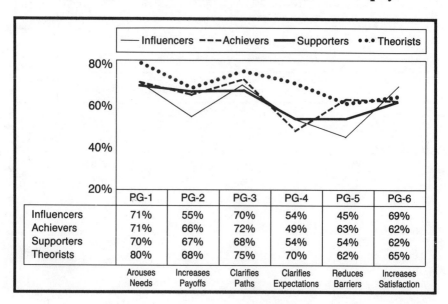

Presidents seem concerned about Influencers' dispositions that make them sensitive to aiding students in their learning process; moreover, presidents seem to expect Influencers to work to decrease learning obstacles and to clarify their expectations to students. Students reflect the concern of the CEOs and need feedback, standards for behavior, and a model they can emulate (Figure 10.7). The president of Vancouver Community College, Paul Gallagher, praised John Parker's achievements: "Independence of learning is John's teaching mission. When students complete his classes, they are convinced they can do more and better than they had thought; he has high expectations for himself and for others, and he works to realize those expectations."

Figure 10.7: **Influencers: Self-Report and Student and CEO Report**

	PG-1	PG-2	PG-3	PG-4	PG-5	PG-6
Successful	73%	65%	80%	61%	72%	72%
Unsuccessful	60%	49%	59%	51%	65%	39%
Philosophy	69%	65%	65%	53%	53%	60%
Students	59%	56%	67%	44%	56%	58%
Presidents	62%	44%	62%	45%	48%	54%
	Arouses Needs	Increases Payoffs	Clarifies Paths	Clarifies Expectations	Reduces Barriers	Increases Satisfaction

Legend: —— Successful ∎∎∎∎ Unsuccessful ▬▬▬ Philosophy •••• Students ----- Presidents

TEACHING-LEARNING AND PATH-GOAL

Works to Eliminate or Reduce Learning Obstacles: To the Influencer, reducing barriers to student performance is the most important teaching-as-leading effort in the path-goal model. This value is best expressed in David Rowlands's (Harry S. Truman College, Chicago, Illinois) philosophy of teaching:

> *Some educators might argue that it is the student's responsibility to want to learn and that as long as the teacher has presented the information in a meaningful way, it is not the fault of the professor if the student is unsuccessful. My personal philosophy is that if the student failed to learn, the teacher failed to teach.*

Therefore, as a leader in the learning situation, Influencers believe they are responsible for student performance. That is not to say they are responsible for student effort—without which performance is impossible. However, whenever low motivation affects effort, Influencers take responsibility for motivation. In fact, the comment students most often made concerning their performance and the teacher was that the teacher motivated them. Influencers reduce other barriers, as well. One of Cecil Nichols's (Miami-Dade Community College, Miami, Florida) students is typical of the type of learner who performs better for Influencers. She admitted to being so shy that she could not ask questions in class. However, she tried harder in the class because the teacher stayed after class to answer questions, called her by name on the second class day, and once wrote her an encouraging letter. Janet Hastings (Washtenaw Community College, Ann Arbor, Michigan) realized that some students in her algebra classes have "math inferiority complexes" because they cannot do math quickly in their heads. So she begins each class day with a few minutes of arithmetic to help these students develop skills and confidence. One student wrote of the success of this approach:

> *I have felt a failure in math all of my life. Ms. Hastings has constantly encouraged me and stated that all I lacked was confidence—not skill. As a result of her efforts and mine, I have a 98 percent average for the year.*

Offers Positive Orientation, Guidance, and Direction: Influencers also believe that clarifying the path to success is a highly important teaching-as-leading function. Sue Foy (Laramie County Community College, Cheyenne, Wyoming), in fact, defines her role in terms of this function: "As a facilitator, I watch for the individual's potential. I show him his potential and systematically take steps to help him realize his potential." One way Influencers exercise their sense of responsibility for student performance is by breaking the learning process into incremental, manageable steps. Although very few instructors mentioned specific or behavioral objectives, many talked about individual lessons or units. Also, Influencers use frequent tests and other means to track student progress, as well as provide many opportunities for students to experience success.

Motivates Students to Increased Satisfaction: Influencers believe that only high achievement can produce satisfaction. Bill Banks (Texas State Technical Institute, Amarillo, Texas) writes of his feelings concerning a student who had to retake his course because she did not work up to her potential. He says, "I learned that I had to be hard in order to be fair. Giving in would not have been fair to this student." The second time in the course, the student turned in work of professional quality. Charlene Felos (Cypress College, Cypress, California) has her advanced students assist in teaching the beginners. Because they are in this role due to their success as learners, these students immediately develop a sense of confidence about what they know and, therefore, accept responsibility for the success of their beginner. However, one of Marjorie Schuchat's (Brookhaven College, Farmers Branch, Texas) students probably best sums up the students' feelings about this teaching-as-leading function:

> *In my attempt to write the best possible research paper, my teacher made herself available every step of the way to read, re-read, and re-read my work. She was always encouraging me and suggesting ways to better myself. Thanks to her dedication and encouragement, I received an 'A,' and more importantly, a feeling of satisfaction.*

Melvona Boren (San Juan College, Farmington, New Mexico) is a teacher James Henderson, president, brags about, explaining that the U. S. Secretary of Education presented her with his Award of Excellence. We learned that Melvona "has found new ways to establish harmonious relationships with students. She accepts her students as individuals and makes sure that each is able to achieve special and unique goals. She 'activates' her students to think for themselves and to become highly productive in and out of the classroom experience."

One of the things we were very pleased to find in researching the Influencer was the number of students who decided to continue taking more course work in the discipline—or even better, decided to follow in the teacher's footsteps and become a teacher. Clearly, Influencers have a powerful impact on students.

Recognizes and Engages Student's Desire to Learn: Influencers also increase student performance by identifying and stimulating student needs. Robert Radueche! (Modesto Junior College, Modesto, California) says, "Everyone has desires and expectations; therefore, I try to find out what they are and work with the student to enhance and develop them." Students are also aware that these teachers are able to increase their need or desire to learn. One of Judith Parks's (Tyler Junior College, Tyler,Texas) students explains it this way:

> *It is obvious the teacher loves what she does, which sparks the interest of her students to learn everything they can. She makes everyday class attendance a pleasure. Even difficult material becomes fun. Her class has greatly increased my interest in the subject area and has deepened my commitment to my chosen field of study.*

John Venesile (Cuyahoga Community College, Parma, Ohio) believes it is his attitude—that the students' failure is his failure—that makes students "want to learn so as not to disappoint [him] or themselves." In fact, this Influencer was particularly impressed with his students' commitment and performance during a particularly difficult assignment. When he asked what made them give such obvious extra effort, they responded that they did not want to disappoint him—they wanted to be a reflection of him.

Increases Opportunities for Quality Educational Performance and Success: Influencers not only arouse students' needs in the learning situation, they also make the effort personally rewarding. They believe that performance will result in higher levels of student satisfaction, so they reward students for increased effort that produces performance. One of Svea Craig Mason's (Mount Royal College, Calgary, Alberta) students was spending long hours in the drafting lab on a particularly difficult assignment, feeling like "he was going nowhere." After he expressed his frustration to his teacher, she made it a point to stop by the lab every hour to check on his progress and encourage him. One of Angèle Dion's (Sir Sandford Fleming College, Peterborough, Ontario) French students finds each class rewarding because this is one teacher who "pays attention to everyone, not just the smart people." From Don Bailey's (Westark Community College, Fort Smith, Arkansas) music class, a senior citizen says she obtained a new interest to entertain, and a shy student says he achieved the confidence to do jazz improvisations.

Influencers realize that the satisfaction students derive from high performance is relative to the amount of effort they put into the task. Therefore, these teachers want to see maximum effort on all the incremental steps leading to the ultimate achievement of learning. Even the group work Influencers so often use for task completion has a way of increasing effort by increasing personal pay-offs. Diane Martin Jordan (Eastfield College, Mesquite, Texas) points out that collaborative learning teams not only encourage critical thinking and build confidence, but give students a sense of belonging to a community of learners. Henry Bagish (Santa Barbara City College, Santa Barbara, California) was so disappointed in his students' performance on the first test, he told them that if they performed better on the next one, he would cancel the first grade and double the second. As he explains, "Most *do* improve; and that, after all, is what I am really after."

Uses Effective Performance as an Expectation to Empower Students: Like Supporters, Influencers do not always express their expectations to all students in the same way. However, the consistent message to all students is "whatever is your best, you must surpass it." These expectations, however, reflect the teachers' demand for quality. In terms of actual course requirements, Influencers are specific and, like the Achievers, have a single standard for all students. As Ron Ridgley (Brunswick College, Brunswick, Georgia) says, "Courses should contain no surprises. Students need to know what is expected of them." In an "Introduction to Composition" class, a course where students often complain that they do not know what the teacher expects, Rita Gress (Guilford Technical Community College, Jamestown, North Carolina) eliminates the guesswork by "publishing" the best examples of last term's students' work in a booklet that is distributed to students the following term. These students, therefore, not only have clear models to use, but can see that their performance could result in their own work being published.

TEACHING FIELDS

Clearly Influencers represent every teaching field and discipline. No one field is markedly represented over another (Figure 10.8).

Figure 10.8: **Teaching Fields**

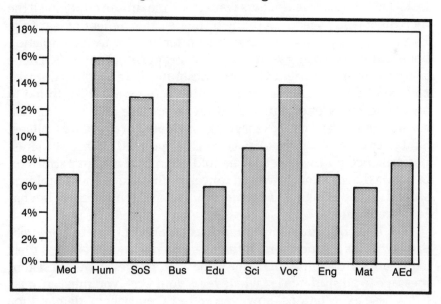

IMPLICATIONS

Influencers are best for those students who, for whatever reason, have low motivation, but who, at the same time, have a personal need to experience success. Whereas the Achievers' students most often said, "The teacher motivated us to succeed," the Influencers' students said, "The teacher motivated me." Therefore, the Influencers' others orientation is particularly suited for students who somehow feel alone in the learning environment and have not yet identified themselves as a member of a learning community. These students may have an external locus of control that makes them particularly susceptible to the demands of these aggressive, unyielding teachers.

As more and more community colleges in the next decade adopt the model of Miami-Dade Community College and others in holding students to high standards of performance, and even separating those who do not perform, the role of Influencers will become more pronounced. These teachers appear to have a personal mission to eradicate mediocrity and underachievement. Therefore, students who are passing, yet are unfulfilled and appear to be drifting from course to course—with little direction or commitment— are the students who are likely to experience the most change with Influencers. Because these students (as, indeed, all students) appear in all points of the community college curriculum, it is difficult to place the Influencer on the teaching-as-leading cycle. However, with much caution to the reader about oversimplification, we offer the following scheme as a way of illustrating the archetypes as stages:

- The Supporter introduces students to the human community of learning. He or she is a caring person who will put students' needs above his or her own. The Supporter gives students the message that help and resources are available for whatever problems they may have.
- The Theorist introduces students to the science of learning. By observing this teacher, students begin to see learning as a systematic, programmatic process governed—to the extent possible—by rational

choices. It is goal-directed, and ends are achieved one step at a time.

- The Achiever shows students the need for a high commitment to learning in order to achieve the personal satisfaction obtained through high performance. These students see that a learning community is demanding, competitive, but highly rewarding. At this point in the cycle, students begin to see the enormous potential of an education.
- The Influencer shows students that locked inside every person is a larger, more capable person trying to get out. Students, therefore, come to realize that performance is ultimately a truly personal thing. They find that it is not circumscribed by extrinsic limitations, but attainable by individual effort. Therefore, these students have the attitudinal skills and self-confidence to confront their futures and succeed.

Chapter 11

Toward Situational Teaching

In the final analysis,
the task of the excellent teacher
is to stimulate apparently ordinary people
to unusual effort.

K. Patricia Cross, 1984

11

The contemporary studies of leadership remind us of the interdependence between the leader and the follower and of the goal of leadership—that obligation that bends leadership toward achieving the needs of the follower and toward the eventuality that the follower will become the leader. Perhaps there is no better place for this kind of leadership than in the classroom.

The classroom, without its obvious political sway and impending societal pressures, lends itself to the fulfillment of the implications of leadership. Here the teacher is the leader, with the knowledge and skills of his or her discipline for guidance. The interdependence between the teacher and students is a given in a classroom. Neither actor can play out his or her role without the other, and both teachers and students agree to the outcome of their interdependence. The teacher uses knowledge, motivation and interpersonal skills to guide the student in the curriculum; students react to those skills by employing their own abilities and aptitudes to enhance their education. The classroom becomes a meeting ground between teacher and student, a place in which the goals of the teacher and the goals of the student merge to become a single goal. Student and faculty aptitude, ability, performance, motivation, and reward are as much a part of the classroom as is the curriculum; and from our view, these elements are co-dependent—good situations demand both. Each of these characteristics contributes to the teaching and learning environment.

Examining the competencies of award-winning instructors has made us even more aware of the singular role of teachers in the

243

classroom as they guide students toward their educational goals. Acknowledging the strategies of teachers as leaders—leaders who recognize and engage their students' desire to learn, increase opportunities for their educational success, offer guidance and direction, eliminate or reduce learning obstacles, and motivate and empower students—has made us aware of the dynamic quality of the teaching-as-leading experience and that teaching does not just happen. Effective teachers plan, strategize for success, analyze the environment and situation, and adapt and accommodate their behaviors because they can accurately read and assess students and situations.   To do these things well, teachers must be leaders. President John E. Hawse, Hawkeye Institute of Technology, Waterloo, Iowa, clearly expresses his perception of faculty member Gareth D. Downey's leadership style:

> Mr. Downey has a long-term commitment to teaching. He makes a difference in students' lives. He has a positive attitude and believes that success breeds success. Viewing students as whole individuals, helping them achieve their goals, making students accountable for their learning, and setting high expectations are more of Mr. Downey's outstanding attributes. The characteristics of developing an excellent learning environment, rewarding students for desired behaviors, developing student confidence, approaching students with a friendly, business-like attitude, and satisfaction about learning are part of his dedication to education.

Leadership is based on a continual re-examination and review of the goals of the leader-follower relationship; and when exigencies or challenges or crises lead to dysfunction of existing situations, teachers should rise to new levels of leadership. It is then that leaders must become situational leaders; that is, they must consciously and willingly change their style to meet the demands and challenges of the teaching situation. For the teacher in a leadership role, the styles of teaching—Supporter, Theorist, Achiever, and Influencer—are patterns that signal the need for action. They provide the bases for teacher behavior and student responsibility that lead to student action. We contend that instructors may shift their leadership style to that which best suits the needs and readiness of the student.

Further, we offer the teaching-as-leading styles as clues for the behavior of faculty as they are thinking about ways to better accommodate their students' needs.

DEFINING TEACHING-AS-LEADING STYLES

In the previous five chapters we developed the teaching-as-leading concept, employing the Teaching as Leading Inventory (TALI) as a means for determining four characteristic teaching styles. These styles were illuminated through the written responses of teachers, students, and college CEOs. The four chapters on the teaching styles—Supporter, Theorist, Achiever and Influencer—supported the idea that each teaching style may be displayed along two orthogonal poles: student and task orientation, and reflective and active orientation. All teaching, especially the teaching of adult learners, should be predicated on assumptions about the learners' developmental levels or their readiness to learn. We believe that teachers will be more successful when they consider students' motivational levels, develop a teaching-as-leading style that is appropriate to the developmental level of the student, change their behavior to fit the situation, and then motivate and influence students toward personally satisfying educational goals. Motivational teaching style and situational teaching are essential aspects of the teaching realm. The idea of situational or contingency teaching suggests that teachers can change, modify, alter, or re-assess their teaching style throughout the entire segment of a single course, and that this accommodation of teaching styles is dependent on student readiness to learn.

We have defined teaching as leading as an influence process where faculty members work cooperatively with students to accomplish the goals of the learning environment—which include the curriculum, the social context, and the motivation or drive to continue and excel in higher education. The thesis behind the teacher as leader focuses primarily on the ability of the teacher to influence students toward higher motivational levels so that they may become more independent learners. But to influence and motivate students to reach for higher educational goals and to derive satisfaction from this process is not an easy task. Influence has a cognitive dimension that may allow the teacher to demonstrate either successful or unsuccessful behaviors in motivating the performance of the student. Also, teachers can be effective or ineffective in influencing the attitudes, commitment, and feelings of the students toward themselves, their teachers, and the curriculum.

As previously discussed, we would define a teacher leadership style as a pattern of behaviors that the teacher employs with students, particularly as perceived by the students themselves. Obviously, we are interested in the reported patterns of behaviors by the instructors, but more so in conjunction with their students' perceptions. The ultimate goal of the leadership dimension would be that students, the faculty member, and the college administration would come to see the faculty member's pattern of behaviors consistently. One of the purposes of this study has been to help faculty members see themselves as leaders in the classroom— leaders who must always be aware of their responsibility to the followers and who must discover ways to enhance or change their teaching-as-leading style.

An examination of the Johari Window (Hall, 1973; Luft, 1961) may serve to clarify the idea of perception and its relationship to the teaching and learning structure. The four windows of this model describe perceptions of individual behaviors. We are reminded of the self-perception and public perception of the individual; and we can apply these perceptions to the student and teacher. Figure 11.1, perceptions by teachers and students concerning teacher behavior, are classified according to the concepts of private behavior, public behavior, precognition behavior, and blind behavior. If our behavior as teachers is private, we tend to work and teach without the affirmation or confirmation of student understanding or comprehension. If our behavior is precognitive, then neither the teacher nor the student is communicating, or sharing, or focused on their commitment to teaching and learning. If our behavior is blind, then although students recognize and react to the instructor, the teacher himself does not have a grasp of what he does, does not do, or should do to make the teaching-learning situation more worthwhile. If our behavior is public , then our actions are more dialectical in nature—some (but not all) of our behavior is known to us and to our students, and we are both reaching to make our behavior more appropriate within the teaching-learning structure. In the Teaching as Leading Inventory (Chapter 6), both the perceptions of students and the perceptions of instructors are an integral part of the information-yielding discovery of a person's dominant style of teaching.

Figure 11.1: **Johari Window**

PRIVATE BEHAVIOR Known to self Unknown to student	PUBLIC BEHAVIOR Part known to self Part known to students
PRECOGNITION BEHAVIOR Unknown to self Unknown to students	BLIND BEHAVIOR Part unknown to self Known to students

Adapted from Luft ,1961 & Hall, 1973

Recommended, of course, is that teachers increase their public window and diminish the less known and less understood dimensions of their behaviors. Thus, a continuum of teaching-as-leading behavior might be indicated. By examining the poles of the Teaching-as-Leading Grid, we reveal that teacher behavior follows a continnum along a student-oriented/task-oriented line, or an action-oriented/passive-oriented line (see Figure 6.5, Chapter 6). Although the orthogonality of the poles is important theoretically, we recognize and encourage traveling the direction of the continuum in order to meet the demands of situations that confront teachers and that necessitate change and adaptability. Thus, a teaching situation that may call for greater teacher attention to students' basic skills would ask a teacher to move along the task-student continuum and focus, initially, more on the students than on the task. Moreover, if we consider the importance of empowering the teacher (see Chapter 12), then we may find the administration working actively to make institutional changes to support the needs of teachers and their students.

THEORETICAL BASES FOR SITUATIONAL TEACHING

Tannenbaum and Schmidt (1958) suggest that there are forces in the teacher, in the students, and in the teaching-learning situation that drive or call for differing teacher behaviors. For example, if the faculty member assumes that students are underdeveloped or not ready for individual freedom in the classroom, he might become directive and make all the decisions for class activity. (Generally, this behavior is most often found early-on in the development of a course; the teacher sets the curriculum, writes a syllabus, and has expectations that this format will be implemented.) At the opposite end of the teaching continuum, if the faculty member sees students having high maturity levels and readiness to accept greater responsibility, she might encourage them to design their own curriculum and/or move beyond the normal cognitive limits of the course.

Directive Teacher Behavior. Directive teacher behavior can be defined as the extent to which a teacher's communication with the students tends to be oriented to the student; the teacher offers guidance and coaching by explicitly directing the students' behaviors. For example, the directive teacher:

- spells out precisely the student's role in the teaching and learning process;
- tells the learner what to do, where to do it, when to do it, how to do it, and how performance will be evaluated;
- closely supervises the learner's performance through constant observation and feedback;
- provides early and continuous planning and organizing of the curriculum and expectations for students;
- constantly communicates learning objectives and priorities;
- provides clear orientation toward the teacher's and the learner's role within the classroom;
- sets, announces, and insists on timetables and deadlines for performance;
- demonstrates strong orientation toward methods

of evaluation;
- provides close and continuous observation and supervision of student's work (Hersey 1984; Hersey and Blanchard, 1982).

Supportive Teaching Behavior. Supportive teaching behavior can be defined as the extent to which the teacher engages in two-way communication with the student. A pattern card of supportive teacher behavior includes:

- listens to students' learning problems and needs, and provides support, encouragement, and specific instruction on task;
- engages in constant interaction with the students that is teacher-oriented and teacher-directed; involves the students in the decision-making process to the extent to which this process relates to student performance;
- listens to the followers' problems, whether they are curriculum-related or not;
- praises the follower for adequate or superior performance;
- seeks the students' suggestions or inputs primarily around how to accomplish learning goals;
- encourages or reassures when the learner is not as successful as expected;
- communicates information about the total expectations of the instructional program;
- discloses personal information about the teacher to the extent that it might motivate the learner;
- facilitates learner problem solving and moving students to higher levels of learning (Hersey, 1984; Hersey and Blanchard, 1982).

BUILDING A FRAMEWORK FOR LEARNING

The themes in the framework for learning are included in Figure 11.2. In the upper right-hand, or first, quadrant, the instructor sees students as immature and is highly supportive and highly directive toward student performance; student needs are great and development is low. In quadrant two, the teacher is more directive, and since support had been previously demonstrated, the teacher would favor direction over support; students seem more motivated as their development is beginning to increase. In quadrant three, the teacher moves to very highly directive or task-achievement on the part of the learner and de-emphasizes support; the learner's development level seems good, but self-esteem or perception of learning level remains weak. In the final quadrant, the teacher moves toward low support and low direction, assuming that in order to move the student toward higher empowerment and individual responsibility for learning, the instructor has to withdraw some individual guidance.

Figure 11.2: Directive and Supportive Behavior and Teaching Styles

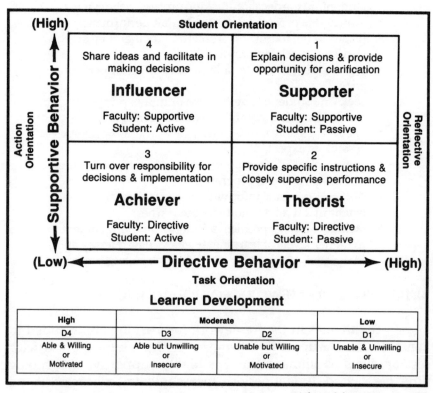

Adapted from Hersey, 1984

In the Supportive teaching-as-leading style, we assume that the teacher desires to establish an early relationship with the student, enhancing the student's motivation and setting high expectations for future work. Researchers strongly suggest that the first two or three sessions of the course focus on both attitudinal and learning needs of the students (Baker, 1982; Roueche and Mink,1980). The Supporter identifies learner problems primarily through assessment; sets goals and explains the curriculum to the student; develops action plans to deal with students' learning problems; is consultative with followers about their attitudes and needs; explains very carefully his or her teaching philosophy and what will be covered; makes early efforts for students simple, but demanding, so students can experience early successes; provides immediate feedback for early success; and praises and supports students' initiatives. The faculty member makes final decisions about procedures and solutions to curriculum problems, but only after communicating with students.

The Theorist would tend to identify problems; set goals and define roles; develop action plans to solve problems; control decision making about what, how, when, and with whom; provide specific direction about how students can learn the theory; initiate structure; be very directive about deadlines and responsibilities; and closely supervise and evaluate the work of followers.

The Achiever would move into the arena of high achievement orientation by defining the learning problems with followers' involvement. An extremely important aspect to consider here is the setting of curriculum objectives collaboratively, allowing followers to develop an action plan, and involving the learners in making decisions about how problems will be solved. The faculty member, while continuing to provide feedback to the learner, would force the feedback to higher level expectations in order to empower the student to learn. The Achiever allows followers to evaluate some of their own work, e.g., identifying a problem with the student's work and requiring the student to find the problem and correct it. For the Achiever, faculty and students are very heavily involved in the curriculum, and the faculty member will move toward the idea of recognizing student learning by celebrating exceptional performance with learners. One important idea here would be to find some exceptional performance for most learners so that the celebration idea could be a broadly applied technique.

The Influencer would be moving toward an action-oriented and a student-oriented perspective; the assumption is that learners are ready to take responsibility for much of their own learning. As an Influencer, the faculty member would tend to involve followers in problem-solving and goal-setting around the curriculum. However, the follower, in many cases with the faculty member's guidance, would define how the task would be accomplished. This aspect of the course would require a teaching environment in which the student is performing and the faculty member is coaching. While the tasking side of the Influencing contingency style is present, the supporting style is not absent. The faculty member would continue to have group-oriented meetings, democratically held with much student involvement, and would be instrumental in making the responsibility for acceptable performance the students' responsibility. This portion of the course might be characterized by more one-on-one relationships with learners in order to identify their particular learning problems and their particular learning needs. As was true in the Achiever example, students should be able to evaluate much of their own work after broad feedback from the faculty member, since in this style it is the desire of the faculty member that the student become very mature in understanding the curriculum and dealing with it.

Figure 11.3 demonstrates the assumptions of the contingent teaching model that follows a simple pattern of learner development and teaching style within a classroom situation. (We emphasize that this is a theorized model, not an empirical one; in other words, we see it as a valuable model, but its development was not an object of this research.) As students enter the course, it is assumed that a supportive teaching style would be motivationally enhancing. As the student progresses to higher levels of competence and higher levels of commitment, the faculty member would enhance the theoretical portion of the course.

Figure 11.3: **Contingent Teaching Model**

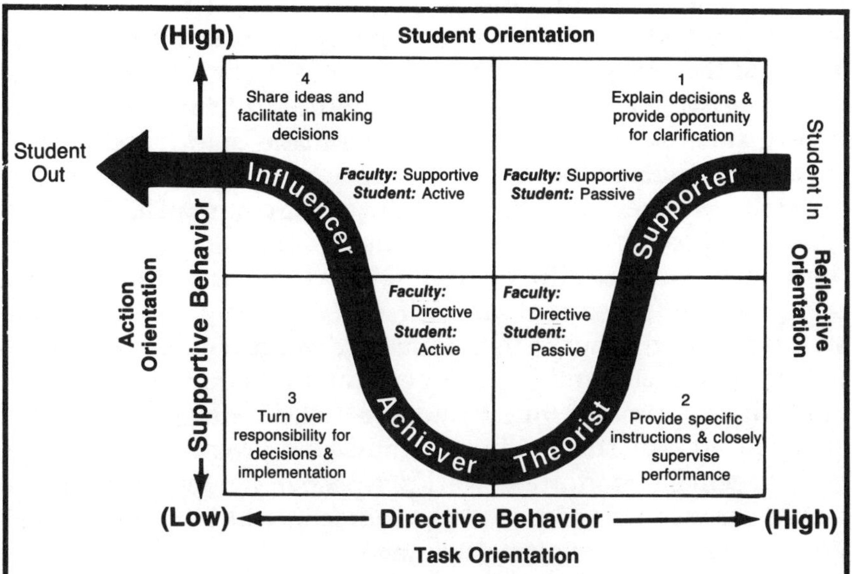

Learner Development

High	Moderate		Low
D4	D3	D2	D1
Able & Willing or Motivated	Able but Unwilling or Insecure	Unable but Willing or Motivated	Unable & Unwilling or Insecure

Adapted from Hersey, 1984

As the student demonstrates increasing competence and higher levels of commitment, the faculty member would move toward a student-active orientation where high levels of achievement, both on the faculty side and the student side, are evident. Finally, as students mature toward the end of the course or program and are developing high levels of competence and high levels of commitment, the faculty would move to the influencing style, where the responsibility for performing is shifted to the student and the faculty member becomes more of a coach and a one-on-one counselor and director.

There are other factors that must be considered over and above the readiness or developmental level of students. We argue that Supporter style of teaching be employed when the assumption is that students are uncommitted to the learning task, have low levels of competence, are not accustomed to working independently, and need the group involvement of the other members of the class. The Theorist approach to teaching may be used when the teacher has limited time, when responses must be made quickly, and when students are inexperienced but are to some degree committed through earlier involvement with the instructor in the course. The Achiever style would be appropriate when students are becoming competent, motivated, and confident and when they are seeking new opportunities to demonstrate their skills. Finally, the Influencer style is appropriate when individuals are competent but when they may vary in their confidence to perform on their own. This style might be appropriate in situations in which students have not experienced full success in the course or program and need encouragement. From a teamwork perspective, influencing behavior would occur in that portion of the course in which individual and group efforts must be most encouraged.

LIFELONG LEARNING AND THE TEACHING-LEARNING CYCLE

While teaching as learning depicts four distinctive styles of teaching, it should be emphasized that individual students vary in skills, abilities, and developmental readiness; they tend to spread out along all dimensions of the developmental structure (see Figures 11.2 and 11.3) in their readiness to learn and their commitment to education. While faculty might think of the situational teaching model as a general approach to teaching students in a group, it should be recognized that the motivational process is personal for each student; and while the faculty has a general approach to the entire group, a personalized approach to each individual is certainly necessary to achieve an effective teaching-learning situation for most learners.

While we have focused primarily on the behavior of the teacher, it is also necessary to consider various levels of development of the learner. In the model presented in Figure 11.3, we defined learner development as including two aspects: varying levels of competency and varying levels of commitment. Competence is the ability of the student to accomplish task-relevant requirements for the teacher, based on the acquisition of knowledge and skills within the curriculum. Competence is also described as skillfulness in transferring lessons learned from the classroom to the job or to responsibilities in life. A commitment is defined as the motivational drive of the student and the confidence or self-concept that a student has about his or her ability to perform.

In Figure 11.3 we described four developmental levels for learners. Although we know that development is more complex than our model would suggest, we choose to limit our discussion to the development of competency and motivation, or self-concept about one's performance. In our model we assume that under low levels of development students would have low competence for the actual curriculum program being presented by the faculty, and based on their previous experiences in college might have anything from a low to a high commitment for learning a particular program. Research supports the idea that students demonstrate higher commitment to courses where they see an immediate pay-off and an immediate ability to apply the skills to other aspects of their lives (Baker, 1982; Knowles, 1989). And as we have described earlier, when low levels of readiness exist, the Supportive teaching type tends to work best initially; under moderate levels of readiness we would move to the Theoretical approach. As students demonstrate variable commitments or motivations to a course , and as they gain some degree of competency, it might be time to move the classroom environment to an Achiever orientation. Finally, as students move to high competence and high commitment, it would be appropriate to move to the more student-centered, student-active orientation of the Influencer style.

Integration of our research is warranted, and here we present a shift in our thinking—we move from a linear format to a cyclical one to express the concept of teaching and learning and its situational construct. In this depiction of the Teaching-Learning Cycle (see Figure 11.4), we employ the conceptual structure of situational teaching, the teaching-as-leading styles, and the ideas of student development and readiness. The Teaching-Learning Cycle is derived both from theory (Burns, 1978; Halpin, 1956; Hersey, 1984; Hersey and Blanchard, 1982; House and Mitchell, 1974; Yukl, 1989;) and the conclusions drawn from the data in this study.

Figure 11.4: **The Teaching-Learning Cycle**

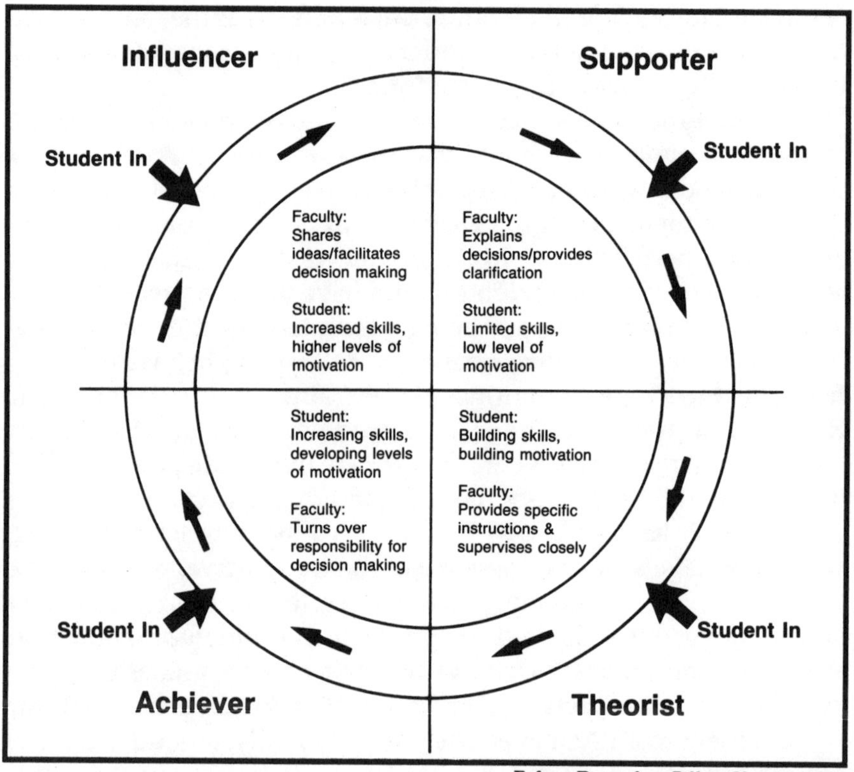

Baker, Roueche, Gillett-Karam, 1990

In the Teaching-Learning Cycle, an awareness of the central role of the student provides the basis for the construct. Students enter community college and their separate classes with varying abilities and skills. We have learned that exemplary teachers in community colleges are concerned about the level of development of their students and that this concern affects their teaching style; for example, we know from our research that although an instructor may have a dominant teaching style, in those cases where his or her teaching meets generally with unsuccessful responses, the instructor can and does modify the approach almost immediately to accommodate students' needs and levels of readiness. For example, we have learned that generally the first response of a teacher is to recognize and engage the student's desire to learn subject matter or content; but when challenges arise, the instructor's strategic function immediately changes to become one of limiting or eliminating frustrating obstacles to learning and then of developing new strategies for successful and motivating behavior.

When considering the Teaching-Learning Cycle, it is assumed that as the student enters the higher education environment, he takes the first step in a subsequent giant leap toward lifelong education. Learning is and should be a lifelong experience for all learners; we are all students, constantly entering the learning cycle. For this reason, we do not show the "student out" consequence natural to a linear structure, or as a consequence of completion of a course. We posit the idea of philosophers and community college experts (Astin, 1978; Cross, 1981; Gleazer, 1980; Knowles, 1989; Roueche and Baker, 1987) that education is a lifelong process. We underscore this idea at a practical level that would support the challenges of a changing workplace, a changing society, and a changing world—all of which demand more and more education, expertise, and know-how from lifelong learners.

Further, we expect that the community college teacher values the community college ethic, that he or she is motivated by a philosophy of providing an egalitarian opportunity for students in higher education and is thus committed to providing for the needs of a culturally and educationally diverse population. These dedicated and excellent teachers demonstrate perhaps their greatest strengths in their ability to modify, alter, and accommodate their teaching style to match the readiness of their students.

SUMMARY

In the Teaching-Learning Cycle, we are closely aligned with the general aspects of motivation theory and leadership theory as they apply to the concept of teacher as leader in the classroom. Our assumption is that most of us apply teaching techniques and styles that have proved successful over time—e.g., the teaching and the curriculum development styles of those who taught us in our disciplines.

Further, we apply teaching styles that we perceive students need. In each case we, as teachers, have three options in motivating and causing students to become competent: to attempt to match our teaching style to the developmental level of our followers; is to undersupervise, or undermotivate; or to oversupervise our students by maintaining a more autocratic or inappropriate style throughout the entire course. It is obvious that the intent of this discussion is to assist teachers to move toward the idea and goal of matching a classroom leadership style to the developmental level needs of learning. In determining the developmental level of our students, we should ask ourselves the following questions:

- Are the student's task knowledge and technical skills high, moderate, or low?
- Is the student's ability to transfer skills from the class-room—such as planning, organizing, decision making, and problem solving—to the job, high, moderate, or low?
- Do students express desire or enthusiasm to accomplish the task assigned, or is this desire or enthusiasm low?
- Do the students demonstrate competence, that is, a feeling of self-assuredness, to accomplish the learning task; and is it high, moderate, or low?
- Is the performance of students as they move through the course better, worse, or unchanging?

Our argument is that analysis of these learning requirements should lead us to become more analytical about choosing particular leadership styles to fit particular situations, rather than assuming that a constant style will be effective for learners as they move through our courses. We should assume that many new learners have experienced disillusionment in their previous learning situations. We can assume an increased responsibility for the outcome of our students. We can also assume that as the semester or quarter progresses, learners will become reluctant to have totally directive teachers and will want to take over some responsibility for their own learning. Finally, we should assume that as students mature, their ability to become peak performers will be enhanced through their own motivation, as well as through the teaching style and the interpersonal relationships we as teachers model with them.

Disillusionment on the part of the learner can occur any time during the course. However, typically it evolves from the discovery that learning tasks are more difficult than students were prepared for; or around the idea that the learning task was not relevant to their particular needs; or around the idea that the more they learn, the more they realize they need to learn more. Finally, since human nature is operating in the classroom, students may explain poor performance by saying that the teacher has not provided the kind of direction and support that they needed when they needed it.

Teacher-as-leader behavior can vary around teaching styles in three ways. First, the amount of direction that the teacher provides to the student varies in all four teaching styles. Second, the amount of support that the faculty member provides to students varies through the life cycle of the course or program. And finally, the amount of learner involvement in making decisions about how he or she will learn varies throughout the course. We have argued that with low levels of readiness and development, the teacher will need to be more Supportive initially; and as the course progresses the faculty member will quickly need to become more Theoretical, while at the same time demanding higher levels of performance on the part of the learner. As the student matures, the assumption is that use of the Achiever and Influencer styles may be determined by increases in the amount of learner success. In all four styles the teacher is responsible for designing the course of instruction to include instructional goals and outcome measures; observing and monitoring performance giving fair, timely, and appropriate appraisals; and providing both group and individual feedback that includes praise for proper performance on a timely basis.

No doubt the future of community college teaching will center more and more on the progress institutions, CEOs, faculty, and students make in their drive toward achieving the objectives of community college education. In many institutions, faculty and student programs are already underway that lend themselves to achieving a teaching and learning community. They serve as examples for others to follow.

Chapter 12

The Future of Community College Teaching

Good Teaching: The Hallmark of the Community College
Recruiting Minorities
Setting the Framework for Innovation in Teaching and Learning
Retention and Recruitment
Professional Development
Faculty Renewal
Part-Time Faculty
Governance
Rewards
Future Success
The Teaching-Learning Path-Goal Framework
The Situational Teacher

*Human history becomes more and more
a race between
education and catastrophe.*

H. G. Wells

12

*I*n the book *Access and Excellence* (Roueche and Baker, 1987), Miami-Dade Community College (M-DCC) was showcased as one of the leading colleges in America. Critical to its excellent reputation was the attention paid to the needs of its particular college community and the students it was drawing from the community. The faculty and the students were significantly empowered by the reforms and changes made to the core curriculum, to the developmental curriculum, and to student advisement, assessment, and retention. The college administration, faculty, and students, united under the leadership of their president, worked for several years to consciously and dramatically change the teaching-learning environment to increase student success. By their example, the programs at Miami-Dade Community College heightened the awareness for change in most community colleges. Colleges were challenged to study and adapt the reform practiced by M-DCC to their own institutions.

But Miami-Dade was not the only cutting-edge institution; other community colleges in North America also have established reforms that may serve as exemplary models. A call for revitalization and reform of the community college remains critical for the 1990s and beyond. What is common to all the innovations we mention is the emphasis on teaching and learning, and the ability of the CEO to recognize and empower faculty by supporting them to take responsibility for student success with excellence.

We support and reiterate the recommendations of the *Building Communities* report (1988), which includes the following guidelines

263

for college reform and success:

- Good teaching must be assured as the hallmark of the community college movement, with students encouraged to be active, cooperative learners through the teaching process.
- Community colleges should increase the percentage of faculty members who are Black, Hispanic, and Asian. Efforts should be made to identify and recruit future teachers from among minority students in high schools and colleges and to provide financial assistance to those planning to teach in community colleges.
- Every college should commit itself to the recruitment, retention, and professional development of a top quality faculty.
- Every community college should establish a faculty renewal program in consultation with the faculty, supported by at least 2 percent of the instructional budget.
- An innovative teachers' fund should be developed to provide small grants to faculty members for the improvement and/or new development of teaching strategies and programs.
- Every community college should have policies and programs for the selection, orientation, evaluation, and renewal of part-time faculty. (However, the use of part-time faculty should be limited to assure that the majority of credits awarded by a college are earned in classes taught by full-time faculty.)
- Strong presidential leadership is required to build community. Community college presidents should not only be effective administrators, but they must also inspire and convey values and vision. The president should be the foremost advocate for teaching and learning at the college.
- Faculty leaders should participate actively in governance, and substantive leadership development experiences should be made available for faculty and administrators.

GOOD TEACHING: THE HALLMARK OF THE COMMUNITY COLLEGE

Teaching as Leading is a celebration, in the form of research and information of good teaching in the community colleges of North America. Our study is dedicated to the women and men who make community colleges the educational institution of opportunity for all people.

It is the regularized and significant celebration of such teaching and those who perform the teaching that we especially applaud. At the annual International Conference on Teaching Excellence, sponsored by the National Institute for Staff and Organizational Development (NISOD), participants meet to support excellence in both teaching and learning. In May of every year, teaching excellence is celebrated through more than 100 presentations by master teachers and others in the college setting who epitomize the values, creativity, and expertise expected from exemplary instructors (Roueche, 1989). Throughout the year, NISOD's activities and programs are based on the premise that teaching excellence is a result of concerned and focused leadership, increased awareness and use of adult learning principles, and a profound commitment to knowing students. NISOD embraces a broad definition of teaching excellence, one that requires that the measures of excellence be adapted to reflect the nature of students, the demands of the setting, and the creativity of the faculty and administration. Its publications, *Innovation Abstracts*, *Linkages*, and *Celebrations*, distributed to the consortium members, are intended to promote practical and innovative teaching tips, program successes, and administering practices.

RECRUITING MINORITIES

Despite the nation's rising ethnic population, the number of Black and Hispanic graduate and undergraduate students in colleges and universities has shown a steady decline. Alarms over the potential problem that this statistic demonstrates abound, but to date little has been done to change the situation. However, at Santa Fe Community College, Florida, a program has been developed and operationalized that could become a model for recruiting both Black and Hispanic graduate students and future faculty members on campuses across North America.

The program, which names Santa Fe Community College Fellows, works in cooperation with the University of Florida to recruit and attract Black doctoral students to the university, at the same time helping the community college develop its own Black faculty members. The University of Florida recruits doctoral students on a nationwide basis as a goal to increase minority graduate students. While working for their doctorates, they are encouraged to apply for Santa Fe Community College Board of Trustees Fellowships, each carrying a $9,000 stipend for the academic year and $1,500 for the summer. In exchange for the stipend, tuition, and fees at UF, the students serve as adjunct faculty at the community college in the English, math, chemistry, humanities, and physical sciences departments. They are required to teach four courses over a 12-month period. In addition to their teaching duties, the Fellows assist in advisement, counseling, recruiting, and retaining minority students at the college. Since its inception in 1986, 10 doctoral students have participated in this inter-institutional cooperative effort. One Fellow was extended an offer of full-time employment upon graduation and is now a full-time faculty member at the college.

At Prince George's Community College (PGCC), Maryland, the applicant pool for professional positions must be representative of the percentages of minorities in related occupations within the region. The college institutional research office has developed a set of indices for minority employment, based on census data. If the applicant pool is not representative of minority involvement in related occupations in the work force, the position is advertised again. Moreover, in order to increase the college's contacts with minorities in the community, PGCC regularly meets with a group of minority representatives of civic organizations, fraternities, sororities, churches, and businesses. This group acts as an advisory council to the college, advising it of the availability of minorities for faculty and administrative positions. Finally, PGCC and Bowie State, a predominantly Black four-year college, have a faculty exchange program to increase the number of minorities on campus.

In California, the legislature—acting on behalf of all the California community colleges—passed Bill 1725, which addressed long-range community college reform. This bill requires districts to have a minimum of 75 percent of their courses (hours of credit instruction) taught by full-time faculty. Districts are required to authorize career resource and placement centers; programs for staff development and improvement must be created; and a faculty and staff diversity fund has been allocated to administer an affirmative action initiative and to assist districts in identifying, locating, and recruiting qualified members of underrepresented groups. The legislature has mandated that 30 percent of all new faculty and staff hires be representative of minority groups by 1992-1993.

The issue of who attends college and who teaches college students is one of interest in the teaching-learning environment. Data from the Education Department indicated that minority students were more likely to attend community colleges than were white students. About 43 percent of Black students, 56 percent of American Indians, and 55 percent of Hispanics attending college were enrolled in community colleges. That number for whites was 36 percent. But we should also be aware of the pipeline that is our promise for future minority faculty: Blacks earned fewer degrees in 1985 than 1977; bachelor's degrees earned were down by 2 percent; master's degrees decreased 34 percent. While 20 percent of Blacks were enrolled in historically Black colleges, 40 percent of Blacks who earned bachelor's degrees graduated from Black colleges. Hispanics, Asians, and American Indians earned more degrees in 1985 than in 1977, at all levels. But except for the Asian populations, these groups also lost enrollment at the graduate level. "Long-range plans for increasing the flow of students in the pipeline may be the best strategy for colleges and states serious about increasing the number of minority faculty" (Linthicum, 1989).

Frederick Community College, Maryland, has joined area institutions to form the Frederick Alliance for Creative Education, whose primary concern is providing opportunities for higher education to minorities in the community. High school seniors are selected by the public schools to take courses in the community college, paid for by the college's foundation. Students are monitored and encouraged to continue their studies at one of the area's four-year colleges.

Madison Area Technical College, Wisconsin, hosts a Minority Pre-Collegiate Program for junior-level minority high school students. The program extends through their senior year in high school and encourages borderline students to graduate from high school and attend college. The summer program offers a class-opportunity of 15 hours a week and a work-opportunity of 20 hours a week in jobs in which minorities are usually not employed. Counselors, parents, and faculty work cooperatively in this program.

The Emerson Electric Company provides tuition and aid to minority students to attend St. Louis Community College (SLCC), Missouri, as pre-engineering students. In a joint program developed by SLCC and the University of Missouri, community college graduates are eligible to attend the university's Rolla campus to pursue an engineering degree.

City College of San Francisco, California, has enrolled Hispanic and Black students in a Math Bridge Program that provides special instruction to strengthen their preparation for transfer to a four-year institution. Black and Hispanic professionals serve as role models, lecturing on careers in science, engineering, computer science, and other math-related fields. A grant from Pacific Telesis Foundation funds the coordination and evaluation of the program.

Valencia Community College, Florida, has signed agreements with five historically Black colleges to encourage academically talented minorities to complete four years of college. The scholarship program will cover two years at Valencia and the remaining two years at one of the five colleges. The program specifically recognizes that the majority of Black students begin their higher education at the community college and earn degrees from traditionally Black colleges.

SETTING THE FRAMEWORK FOR INNOVATION IN TEACHING AND LEARNING

Miami-Dade Community College: The Teaching and Learning Project at M-DCC (Jenrette, 1988) has three goals: to improve the quality of teaching and learning at the college, to make teaching a professionally rewarding career, and to make teaching and learning the focal point of college activities and decision-making processes. Timing was a critical factor, considering the predictions of significant numbers of faculty retirements over the next decade and the increasing numbers of nontraditional students seeking higher education. To improve teaching and learning, and to encourage faculty to take a leadership role in the process, the college had to capitalize on the expertise of the current faculty and student body, provide information and support, raise the status of teaching as a profession, and reward the type of performance they valued.

The products and programs that emerged from the Teaching/Learning Project included a values statement, which became the logo of college publications, catalogs, and manuals. New faculty were oriented to the college and its policies through pre-service training and mentoring, and faculty were required to take graduate-level courses in effective teaching and learning and in classroom research—then these courses were modularized and used in faculty workshops. Videotapes exploring classroom feedback and cultural differences in learning styles were produced for faculty use; funding for endowed teaching chairs was announced; standards were established to appropriately equip and maintain classrooms and labs; recruitment of new faculty was tied to written statements of values and excellence; statements of faculty excellence were translated into criteria for promotion and student feedback and evaluation; and linkages between administration, faculty, staff, and students around the issues of teaching and learning and the support necessary to accomplish excellence in that milieu were continued.

Statements of faculty excellence provide a common understanding of what it means to perform in an excellent manner at M-DCC. This common understanding is used to guide development of the assessment process for new hires, evaluation of portfolios for tenure decisions, and progression through the academic ranks. The combination of articulated faculty excellence standards and established faculty advancement policies and procedures will allow each faculty member to evaluate his or her own performance and to decide upon a plan for his or her professional development.

New faculty are involved in an intensive orientation. The first two days feature a college-wide agenda in which the president, campus vice presidents, faculty senates consortium president, and others discuss and orient new faculty around M-DCC history, mission, and values. Presentations include a review of benefits, a student profile, the faculty governance constitution, and the chair's role in supporting faculty. On the next three days of the week-long orientation, participants report to their assigned campuses. Tours are conducted, and campus leadership is introduced. Meetings with mentors are initiated; department schedules, procedures, and expectations are reviewed.

Courses in "Classroom Research" and "Effective Teaching and Learning" are taught by University of Miami faculty from curriculum developed collaboratively with two Teaching and Learning Project subcommittees at M-DCC, the Classroom Feedback and the Learning to Learn committees. The University of Miami has included these two courses in the core requirements for the Ph.D. and Ed.D. of higher education and has made them part of a three-course certificate program in college teaching that will be made available to faculty and graduate students of the University of Miami. The college will assume tuition costs.

Virtually every element of the Teaching and Learning Project raised issues related to faculty development and support. A unified Teaching-Learning Resource Center exists on each campus to meet three areas of needs: the continuation of traditional staff and program development opportunities; a core program, consistent college-wide, designed specifically to implement the outcomes of the Teaching and Learning Project; and support for instructional design, including classroom research and expanded applications of technology.

By June of 1989, 33 chairs, each valued at $75,000, were endowed by corporate and individual donors, bringing M-DCC one-third of the way to the goal of 100 endowed chairs. The Faculty Advancement Procedures Committee has as its task recommending a process and criteria for the awarding of chairs.

RETENTION AND RECRUITMENT

Sault College of Applied Arts and Technology (Ontario): Sault College follows a set of strategies for increasing the validity of hiring college faculty. Selection strategies include: weighing job qualifications of applicants in which points are given for education and experience; inviting candidates to present a 15-minute lesson on a subject that he or she would be teaching; following the presentation by a structured interview; having applicants participate in a written exercise (e.g., addressing a problem situation with a student or colleague); and verifying applicants' references. Critical to these strategies is for search committee members to gather data to develop a realistic perspective to make good hiring decisions, reinforcing the importance of feedback to the hiring process of faculty.

PROFESSIONAL DEVELOPMENT

Humber College (Ontario): The most important resource at Humber College is the faculty, and faculty development is an administrative arm of the college organization. The values and goals expressed by the administration, which center around the ideas of leadership and empowerment of individuals, are: "To empower and free people, to create a sense of putting them in touch with their greatness, to separate them from their limiting structures, to encourage them to dream and discover their untapped potential, and to allow them to take risks" (Giroux, 1989). The vehicle for melding personal goals and institutional goals is the Human Resource Development Program. Linking the right person with the right mentor equals organizational development—not just staff development; since the readiness of potential leaders depends on individual differences, those differences are taken into account. Coaching and mentoring are modified by the degree of direction the potential leader needs: the "leaper" needs little direction, the "seeker" wants to change but does not know how, and the "follower" has a dormant potential that calls for prodding. Partnerships at all levels are encouraged; thus, the model for organizational development is decentralized, and all components of the college have input into the system.

Yukon College (Yukon Territory): Finding a suitable professional development program for college faculty at Yukon College became part of the challenge of helping existing faculty acquire credentials more compatible with the new mandate of the college. This mandate charged the college with delivery of postsecondary vocational, technical, and academic programming to the Yukon's adult population, which meant delivery of services to 16,000+ adults who live in 16 communities spread over the territory's 482,415 square kilometers. The faculty development program sought to meet certain basic criteria, which included flexibility, accessibility, credibility, relevancy, manageability, and economy. The program also had to be offered locally and on a part-time or continuing education basis. The program became a one-year program of senior undergraduate work with appropriate emphasis on the methods of teaching adults (the University of British Columbia's Diploma in Adult Education). This program, dealing with the issues and concerns of teaching adults, underscores faculty commitment to the community and to their own growth.

FACULTY RENEWAL

Santa Fe Community College (New Mexico): Faculty are involved in a program that promotes teaching excellence and increases faculty commitment. Both full-time and part-time faculty come together in a "Faculty Forum" each semester to discuss issues of immediate interest and concern. "Faculty Forum" effectively promotes tough problem-solving, familiarization with other college programs, faculty interaction with their peers, and discussion of new, different, and innovative teaching strategies. Faculty experience a deeper commitment to teaching and a greater sense of "ownership" from this participation. Santa Fe Community College believes that by providing experiences for faculty to learn from one another in professional activities, a vital sense of belonging to the academic community is supported.

PART-TIME FACULTY

Austin Community College (Texas): The design and implementation of the Mentor Program has helped serve the ever-increasing numbers of part-time faculty at Austin Community College, a multi-campus, multi-site institution. Realizing the value and the growing numbers and responsibilities of part-time faculty, the college sought ways to facilitate faculty's orientation and adaptability to the role of community college instructors. The Mentor Program was designed to produce a mentoring relationship between new faculty members and experienced faculty members from the same department or division, in a non-supervising or evaluative relationship. Guidelines for the program include: a planning meeting in which the new faculty member and his or her mentor establish mutual agreement on the objectives of the program; and a work plan for accomplishing them. Most important, program policies demonstrate concern for the new faculty member's professional life and offer recognition to faculty who serve as mentors.

New Mexico Junior College (New Mexico): New Mexico Junior College operates according to a strict policy of not forgetting the needs of part-time faculty after they have been hired. The college established a staff development program specifically designed to serve these instructors. The components of this program take into consideration the identification of potential part-time candidates, hiring procedures, in-service training, and support services. This program works for New Mexico Junior College as it strives to hire good people, offers them a solid support program, and continues this professional training. These services prove positive when, occasionally, a part-time instructor will come in with a smile and say, "I did not know you would do this for me."

GOVERNANCE

Foothill-DeAnza Community College District (California): Foothill-DeAnza is focused on people; it believes that community colleges "ought to be people-building, rather than people-using institutions" (Greenleaf, 1973). In its Committee of Thirty-Two, all governance and decision-making is accomplished in an open, democratic meeting of all college constituencies. The district administration is not separate from the campus administration or the faculty, staff, and employees of the college; all function together in a single governance body whose decisions are final and complete in that group.

St. Petersburg Junior College (Florida): The Access, Community, and Excellence in Teaching Commission (FACET), named by faculty governance and represented by teaching faculty, instituted a work plan to define the educational values and standards of the college and to explore ways to enrich teaching effectiveness. In their statement of academic excellence, the faculty proclaim their drive to educate students by striving for a quality learning experience; to provide access to students of varying learning levels; to help students achieve goals through counseling, tutoring, and mentoring; to commit to improvement through professional development; to diversify academic programs through development and review; and to develop sensitivity to the needs of culturally diverse and nontraditional students. St. Petersburg sees leadership as a concept that is as much a part of its faculty's role as it is the president's. They seek to develop effective, responsible leaders as role models in the community, in the area of organizational development and assessment, in the acquisition and application of technological advances, in the abilities to develop and employ innovative teaching and learning methods, and in initiating programs designed to meet current and emerging social needs.

Riverside Community College (California): Developing an understanding of the interdependence of each campus job was the outcome of strategic planning at Riverside Community College. The process, involving input from many constituencies (internal and external), brought about a highly visible changed attitude in college personnel. More important, widespread input resulted in a congruency of campus values, primarily centered on students. Supporting student centeredness were the values of teaching excellence, improved learning environment, and the reinforcement of tradition.

REWARDS

In our study, college leaders responded differently to our request to identify award-winning instructors. Whereas some CEOs did not respond at all, others responded enthusiastically by nominating several instructors. Peters and Waterman (1982) believe that, in any given organizational setting, about 10 percent of the employees are performing at an excellent level and about 10 percent are performing at an unacceptable level. Peters believes that we spend the majority of our managerial energy worrying and often doing something about the 10 percent who are marginal performers. Instead, we should be providing influence and motivation for our top performers and empowering these performers to influence the quality of the 80 percent who most often are capable of enhanced and often excellent performance.

The tendency in Western society is to perceive rewards as a scarce commodity. Community colleges tend to recognize a teacher-of-the-year; however, in a college employing 150 faculty, the odds of recognition are 150 to 1. If the intent of recognition is to increase performance of the person selected, as well as those not selected, research tells us that both objectives are often doomed to failure. The Porter and Lawler Model (see Chapter 2), realizes that the performance of the selected teacher is or is not enhanced based on the personal analysis of the individual and on the personal satisfaction derived from recognition. Research supports the idea that only a small portion of the non-winners will perceive that the probability of receiving recognition is worth an increased effort in performance. This argument supports a wider recognition model that would have several categories of rewards and increased probability of enhancing motivation and performance of those selected for recognition and those not recognized. It would be important for colleges to recognize the 10 percent or so who deserve recognition and enhance the motivation of the 80 percent, many of whom will respond to professional development that can lead to future recognition.

Cerritos College (California) and *Santa Barbara City College* (California): These colleges not only celebrate teaching excellence and provide awards to outstanding faculty and programs, but they praise excellence by publishing and widely distributing brochures and catalogs that focus on teachers and their successful programs. At Cerritos College, most outstanding faculty and faculty honor roll award recipients are the subjects of biographical and photographic sketches that celebrate their teaching excellence; moreover, in a separate publication, Cerritos College talks about successful retention strategies, focusing on what exemplary instructors do to keep their students. At Santa Barbara City College, an annual faculty lecture series honors a faculty member, chosen by colleagues to deliver an address on a scholarly subject of general interest. Selection is based on outstanding classroom teaching and unselfish, dedicated faculty service to the college. The lecture is published and distributed throughout the college. Santa Barbara also publishes a magazine highlighting the year's best programs and instructors. The magazine gives details of the program and displays photographs of the instructors and scenes from the actual classes and programs that have won recognition.

Midlands Technical College (South Carolina): Midlands Tech rewards and encourages faculty scholarship with many programs—such as the Author's Reception, the Program Reward for Innovative and Creative Excellence (PRICE), and the Incentive Travel Program. A reception honors a faculty or staff member of the college who has published an article in a significant journal or presented a paper to professional peers at a regional or national meeting; it brings together participants to celebrate the scholarship of an employee. In the PRICE program, competition to complete an innovative project carries with it a monetary reward. The travel program offers matching travel funds to a faculty member if he or she is presenting a paper and other funding is depleted. Midlands encourages its faculty and staff to accomplish "firsts," or something unexpected; and they do so by motivating, challenging, and rewarding their learning community.

Central Piedmont Community College (North Carolina): At Central Piedmont, the "quality circle" concept has provided a vehicle for group goal setting and brainstorming for common purposes. Fostering bonding relationships throughout the college, the quality circles focus on issues that primarily improve services to students, such as a staff development plan for computer literacy, a financial aid policy to encourage student retention, and an improved registration process for foreign students. The quality circle process provides a positive, rewarding component of sound educational management at Central Piedmont: it encourages communication and provides positive recognition for the efforts of employees at all levels.

FUTURE SUCCESS

What we've learned from excellent faculty and from the

pioneering efforts of selected community colleges is that people and institutions are doing the right things well. But we also know that the efforts of community colleges in general do not meet this benchmark of quality and development. Success in the teaching and learning environment of the community college must be a mandatory goal for all community colleges; colleges must be willing to spend money, resources, time, and effort to make good on the promises of egalitarian education for all people. If the open-door concept is a promise of community college education, then community colleges must develop their most important resources—their instructors and their learning community.

In the framework of the teaching-learning path-goal concept and in the concept of situational teaching styles, we offer our own path toward excellence for the learning community. Moreover, we suggest that without support and empowerment from the college administration and a college culture that values and supports the learning community, enrichment of goals of the community college may not occur. These goals should include: the promise of opportunities for the underrepresented and undereducated, a continued pathway for vocational and technological careers and jobs; emphases on good teaching as an essential ingredient for undergraduate education; and special attention to improving students' educational skills.

The Teaching-Learning Path-Goal Framework. The characteristics of the exemplary community college instructor include the ability to recognize and engage students' desire to learn, and the ability to offer positive orientation, guidance, and direction to students as they seek to clarify, then achieve, their educational goals. Effective teachers know the value of analytical and experiential diagnoses about their own teaching patterns and meeting the needs of their students. The right things don't just happen; they are accomplished through the emphases that exemplary instructors pay to their philosophy and practices of teaching and learning. They are committed to the ethos of egalitarian education, and it drives their teaching and learning philosophies. Effective faculty know the abilities of their students, are able to apply that information to their curriculum, and periodically review the changes that occur in the classroom among groups and individuals in order to adapt and accommodate situations. They diagnose students' skills, they offer clear and concise syllabi and course goals, they accommodate students' needs, and they offer positive direction and clarity to achieve results in the classroom. As faculty provide regular feedback, students are constantly apprised of their standing and can easily learn what is necessary for continued development and greater achievement. By valuing teaching and learning, the effective instructor recognizes that a failure syndrome is predictable when students meet learning obstacles and barriers; thus, working to reduce and eliminate teaching and learning barriers is a strategic function of the effective college instructor. Although they provide extensive help and important attention to the details of "studenting," excellent instructors have high expectations; they expect, as classroom leaders, to raise students to higher levels of thinking and acting and toward taking responsibility for their own lifelong learning.

The Situational Teacher. Teaching, like all professions, draws many personalities, is characterized by diversity in cultures and disciplines, and is known for its demand for autonomy. Yet, for all their diversity, teachers obviously have commonalities. Our research found that exemplary teachers who responded to the Teaching as Leading Inventory constitute four teaching styles. Each of the teaching styles have dominant, complementary, and opposite behaviors attached. And each teaching style is attached to the readiness and developmental levels of students. Supporters define a teaching style in which high people-orientation and a low level of student development may be used to facilitate students who bring limited skills and preparation into the college classroom. Supporters view learning from the perspective of the learner; they are sensitive to feelings and values, are good listeners, and use the information they gather about student needs to implement imaginative programs. Theorists focus on task, spending time organizing information, building theoretical models, and testing theories and ideas; because they are enthusiastic and show appreciation for teaching, they infuse this interest and enthusiasm in their students. Achievers are enablers, viewing both their own role and their students' roles as ones in which content must be mastered. They create new ways of thinking, allow experimentation with new ideas, and make decisions quickly, usually choosing the best solution. Influencers are great motivators; they are great believers of moving students to maximizing their potential. They are driven by student growth and changes and are actively involved in influencing this growth.

The teaching-learning framework and the teaching-as-leading styles are interrelated and co-dependent. Dominant teaching styles predict the emphases of the teacher, but excellent teachers are able to shift their teaching styles depending on the developmental level of their students and thus employ the dynamic of leadership as the creative force that drives their teaching. For teachers and students to accomplish their goals, they must be empowered.

Chapter 13

Empowering Faculty:
Building a Community of Learning

Current Dilemmas within Community Colleges
Empowering Faculty and Students: A Community
of Learning
The Building of Systems to Support Student Learning
Making it Work: Teaching the Teacher to Teach
Summary

*The term community should be defined
not only as a region to be served,
but also as a climate to be created.*

Building Communities, 1988.

13

*D*uring the last half of this century, much of the attention given to the status of education in North America and its relation to the world focused upon the recognition that monumental change was taking place in world order and that America was losing its pre-eminence among world powers. Other nations were not only competing, but actually beating us at our own game. Sputnik, launched in 1957, showed us that the space race was in the hands of the Russians. The debacle in Vietnam clearly demonstrated that military victory was not always achievable. The industrial expertise of Japan demonstrated to us that others could not only build better, more efficient cars, but they could also sell them more cheaply. In each of these situations, at the core of our introspection and re-examination of values and know-how was the sad state of American education. We were duly warned:

> Our once unchallenged pre-eminence in commerce, industry, science, and technological innovation is being overtaken by competitors throughout the world.... If an unfriendly foreign power had attempted to impose on America the mediocre educational performance that exists today, we might well have viewed it as an act of war.... We have, in effect, been committing an act of unthinking unilateral educational disarmament (*A Nation At Risk*, 1983, p.5).

This report detailed the failings of the American educational system and offered a series of recommendations that would "generate reform of our educational system in fundamental ways and ... renew the nation's commitment to schools and colleges of high quality throughout the length and breadth of our land."

The higher education version of *A Nation at Risk* was released in a report titled *Involvement in Learning: Realizing the Potential of American Higher Education* (1984). The goal of the study, sponsored by the National Institute of Education (NIE), was to examine the conditions of excellence in higher education. More specifically, the NIE wanted to know how current knowledge of higher education could be enhanced and how higher education actors could use research findings for improvement. The study director, Manuel Justiz, focused attention on the potential of higher education:

> The nation has been conducting a paradoxical debate on the quality of schooling. While all sides have assumed that we must become a society in which learning never ends, the debate always seems to stop at the border of high school graduation, as if learning itself ended at that point. But more than half of our students voluntarily cross that border, trusting that what awaits them on the other side is worthy. What they will find is a system of higher education that is by far the largest, most complex, and most advanced in the world. The nation has entrusted this system to extend both the franchise of learning and the frontiers of the universe itself. But our students will find that this great national resource has not realized its full potential (p. 1).

Involvement in Learning identified three conditions of excellence: student involvement, high expectations, and assessment and feedback. Student involvement refers to the amount of time, energy, and effort students devote to the learning process. The fact that more learning occurs when students are actively engaged in the learning process implies, among other things, that learning and personal development are directly proportional to the quality and quantity of student involvement, and that the effectiveness of any educational policy or practice is directly related to the capacity of that policy or practice to increase student involvement in learning. Suggestions from NIE include greater interaction between faculty and students, better advisement at all levels, and guiding students toward active modes of learning and toward taking responsibility for learning.

High expectations refer to the educational outcomes sought by students and institutions, including graduation requirements and standards. When realistically high expectations are clearly communicated to students, a high level of achievement tends to result. Suggestions include greater cooperation between faculty and administration for the development and implementation of programs, curriculum, and instructional philosophy that match knowledge, capacities, and skills expected of students. The NIE suggests that college leaders strive to ensure that the behavior of their institutions evidences the ideals of honesty, justice, freedom, equality, generosity, and respect for others.

Assessment and feedback means providing information about the teaching and learning process to students, faculty, and administrators in order to improve the effectiveness of their efforts. The use of assessment information to redirect effort is an essential ingredient in effective learning and serves as a powerful lever for involvement. Suggestions include not only assessment programs, but also a role for regular instructor and student input into the procedures and programs, which should be continuously developed and evaluated. Further, the NIE study encourages faculty and staff involvement in the decision making of colleges or universities, especially as decisions affect current students and the potential community of learners.

The exhortation of educational obligation and renewal found its community college emphasis in *Building Communities: A Vision for a New Century*. While the report did not have the dynamic impact of an *A Nation at Risk*, it did gain the attention of the 1,200-plus member colleges of the American Association of Community and Junior Colleges. The AACJC Commission on the Future of Community Colleges analyzed and made recommendations concerning issues dealing with the future of community colleges; and in keeping with the stated mission of community colleges, the teaching and learning process was reported as a central theme.

At their best, community colleges recognize and enhance the dignity and power of individuals. Students come to colleges to pursue their own goals, follow their own aptitudes, become productive, self-reliant human beings, and, with new knowledge, increase their capacity and urge to continue learning. Serving individual interests must remain a top priority of community colleges. But they can do much more. By offering quality education to all ages and social groups, community colleges can strengthen common goals as individuals are encouraged to see beyond private interests and place their own lives in larger context (1988, p.6).

Several of *Building Communities*'s recommendations dealt with the issues involving teaching and learning in the community college; these include: recruitment and retention of full-time faculty who represent the ethnic diversity of community college students and the curriculum; increasing the quality of our resources for faculty development (full- and part-time); developing a core curriculum and emphasizing the associate of applied science degree; making good teaching the hallmark of the community college movement; improving the quality of developmental study courses and programs; recognizing excellent teaching through salary increases and professional support; and emphasizing faculty self-evaluation and improvement through the development of classroom research.

Both the NIE and the *Building Communities* reports clearly make the point that faculty are essential in building a community of learning. Our study of award-winning instructors has convinced us of an extremely important concept: faculty play a crucial role in defining the culture of the college. They decide what is to be taught and how the curriculum will be implemented; and they screen, evaluate, and empower students. The faculty have enormous power. It is clear that teachers, regardless of their skills, are able to wield significant power in their jobs. In the final analysis, faculty determine the success or failure of the college because they determine the success or failure of the college's clients.

The award-winning instructors nominated by their CEOs to participate in this study are exceptional. They demonstrate mastery in involving students in active and exciting learning. They demonstrate that they possess high expectations for themselves and their learners. They naturally and normally employ effective assessment procedures and provide timely and accurate feedback to students. They, in effect, reflect many of the recommendations made by the study groups in *Building Communities* and *Involvement in Learning*. As well, many of the colleges nominated epitomize the recommendations of the study groups regarding institutional reorientation. Their recruiting and marketing plans are efficient and operational. Student orientation, assessment, and advisement procedures are mature, effective, and systematically evaluated. The curriculum is characterized by a general education core. Many of the colleges have computer-based student management processes. Early warning procedures designed to retain students involve a complex but cooperative relationship between faculty and student development personnel. Advising occurs so that students are constantly informed about their progress toward personal goals. Advising continues into the job-gaining and job-retaining aspects of students' lives. Attrition rates are changing as colleges and instructors pay particular attention to retention. If the student desires to transfer, all aspects of this complicated phenomenon are resolved through articulation plans with colleges and universities. In short, student motivation and success are managed through a process designed to propel the student as rapidly as possible along the path toward the student's educational or career goal.

In highly effective community colleges, the impending faculty crisis was recognized early, and faculty recruitment plans are now mature aspects of institutional functioning. In these colleges, enlightened leaders realized that full-time faculty selection involves a commitment of enormous resources. Some estimates support the claim that a full-time faculty member who is recruited with a master's degree and completes a career in college teaching will be paid in excess of a million dollars. For a multitude of reasons, effective colleges focus great energy on the recruitment, selection, socialization, assessment, development, reward, and celebration of their faculty. But what about the faculty and colleges who do not subscribe to these advancements?

CURRENT DILEMMAS WITHIN COMMUNITY COLLEGES

The literature supports the notion that many faculty have not attained recognition for excellent and exemplary teaching behaviors. Most institutions have not developed systems that ensure student success, and most institutions have not developed a process that puts energy and commitment to the idea of acquiring and developing a cadre of highly educated and trained teachers. The *Building Communities* commission found that community college faculty often felt overextended, typically teaching at least five courses per semester. Faculty reported that classes, especially in basic subjects, are too large, and that preparation time is too short. On many campuses the commission found a feeling of burn-out and fatigue among faculty. They concluded that such conditions yield a loss of vitality that weakens the quality of teaching. The commission was especially disturbed that 63 percent of community college faculty in a national survey rated the intellectual environment at their institution as "fair" or "poor." If the majority of the faculty in American community colleges believe that the intellectual climate is inadequate to support effective teaching, leaders can be assured that without effecting positive change, colleges will not be able to accomplish their goals.

Building Communities focused on the recruitment, selection, development, evaluation, reward, and retention of faculty. It was reported that in order for community colleges to mature into a viable force in higher education in the United States and Canada, effective teachers must be selected, developed, trained, and retained. These teachers must be those who believe community college learners must be developed and nurtured. They must believe in broadening the capacity of students to learn and be successful, and they must come to the community college because as excellent teachers the community college is their first choice.

The NIE report also points to warning signals of current and potential problems that must be recognized and addressed:

> Faculty are the core of the academic work force, and their status, morale, collegiality and commitment to their institutions are critical to student learning. When we

allow support for such a critical component of the enterprise to erode to the point at which the profession itself has become less attractive to our brightest students, we are compromising the future of higher learning in America (1984, p.11).

The NIE reports that many of our current faculty feel "stuck" in their careers. They have lost the traditional mobility and vision that motivated so many to strive for excellence in teaching and in research. The NIE also warns of the rapid increase in the proportion of part-time faculty whose situation brings strain on collegiality and may affect both the continuity in instructional programs and coherence in the curriculum. Its recommendations call for improvement of the institutional environment as a workplace for faculty, for renewal of faculty commitment to their institutions through new roles, and for the restoration of necessary support to keep the profession attractive and appealing as potential careers. These warnings are evident from other sources, as well. For example, the research literature posits a classic problem of professionals in the interpretation of a professional bureaucracy and the concept of pigeonholing clients. Mintzberg discusses this concept in *The Structure of Organizations:*

> The professional bureaucracy is unique among the five structural configurations in answering two of the paramount needs of contemporary men and women. It is democratic, disseminating its power directly to its workers (at least those who are professional). And it provides them with extensive autonomy, freeing them even of the need to coordinate closely with their peers, and all of the pressures and politics that entails. Thus, the professional has the best of both worlds: he is attached to an organization, yet is free to serve his clients in his own way, constrained only by the established standards of his profession (1979, p. 371).

Faculty members in community colleges are usually hired on the basis of the training acquired in a particular subject matter that is outside the control of their workplace. As experts in the subject matter, faculty members often tend to teach in the ways in which they themselves were taught and to behave toward students in ways similar to their own professors' behavior toward them. In many cases, this becomes the value base from which the instructor makes decisions in analyzing students and their competencies. Researchers talk about the necessity of a professional bureaucracy (Mintzberg, 1979) to develop autonomy as a means to perfect their skills free of interference—professionals are attached to their organization, yet they are free to serve clients (students) in their own way. Usually the only constraints on professionals are those established by the standards of their profession. But while we expect a greater degree of democracy and autonomy in the professional, we cannot overlook the traditional problems of a professional bureaucracy—such as pigeonholing or the categorizing of students' needs and the standardization of programs to meet those needs within predetermined categories (grouping according to knowledge, skills, and performance; allowing higher education admission based on standardized exams).

We know that teachers always find variability among students' abilities and accomplishments; as professionals they are required to handle day-to-day fluctuations in their instructional responses to students. We admit there is uncertainty in meeting our students' needs, but we try to contain that uncertainty by allowing discretion in our work. It is, however, this single variable in the teacher's professionalism that acts as a springboard to problems. Instructors' skills may vary considerably; for example, the new teacher may not have the experience to handle uncertainties, and the entrenched teacher may not want to "try anything new" to update his or her skills. Some teachers may value their income more than their students, some are so enamored of their skills that they forget about the real needs of students, and some teachers ignore the needs of their organization (they are loyal to the profession, but not the institution in which they work). Major innovation, which is necessary in this dysfunctional aspect of professionalism, is dependent on cooperation and new programs that must replace existing ones. There is, certainly, a call for agreement on institutional and professional values and a call for professionals to work cooperatively with each other and their institutions.

By increasing coordination among teaching faculty,

leadership of instructional units can be improved; curriculum reform might be initiated; and efforts such as mission development, institutional values, goal-setting, institutional effectiveness programs, program evaluation, and student development can be encouraged. A major challenge for the leadership of community colleges is to cause the faculty members to see themselves first as members of the college community and secondly as members of their specific professional community. From our perspective, community colleges cannot build communities with all that the concept implies without the loyalty of faculty, staff, and administration. Building the necessary "communities of learners" requires the development of unique strategies, the fully empowered participation of all members, and the understanding that overlapping individual values and commitment with organizational values and missions is an extremely complex and difficult task. But the final community is worth the effort.

A college's bureaucratic nature insists on a stable environment; programs are typically routinely set, with rules and regulations often imposed by state-level agencies. For example, studies indicate that as many as 75 percent of students who enter community colleges are more career motivated than academically motivated, and yet the typical approach is to move the student toward a two-year program. The thinking of the decision makers in community colleges is typically convergent. In problem solving, this convergence leads to old pigeon-holes to accommodate new demands. The solutions to building communities and effective teaching are more likely to be found in divergent thinking. New solutions are more likely found in inductive reasoning—that is induction of new general concepts, which help break away from old routines or standards rather than perfecting existing ones.

Cohen and Brawer (1989), who have been observing the community college for a quarter of a century, have painted a rather dismal view of the future of community colleges. They disdainfully view the abundance of commission reports based on what decision science calls a "rosy scenario;" rather, they believe the actual picture for the immediate future is rather dismal. They see faculty as clinging to their independent professional status and rejecting efforts at coordination; they believe that hiring practices show little sign of change and that progress in employing members of minority groups has been distressingly slow; and they note that although colleges will have to foster their own development, highly trained new faculty will not be prevalent. Nor do they believe that community college faculty meet all of the implicit tests of professional status: "While faculty have made great strides in extracting themselves from administrator-dominated paternalistic situations of a few years ago, they have far to go" (p. 372).

When professionals lose control over their work, they begin to exhibit behavior common among hourly employees, and they become passive. Faculty tend to empower their immediate leaders only to the extent that they can act as buffers between themselves and their administration. Cohen and Brawer point out, at this juncture, that two options are possible: the current trend toward public civil service, where control will ultimately come from outside the college; or a professional craft model where faculty collaborate within the academic unit to improve curriculum and instruction. Cohen and Brawer (1989) offer a model of faculty involvement, if not empowerment. They conclude that "a more desirable model is a faculty involved with curriculum planning in the broadest sense: reading and writing in their disciplines and the field of education; conducting research on students' exit and entrance abilities; and becoming program directors, laboratory managers, or curriculum coordinators" (p. 373).

Our study points out that faculty in effective colleges may and do play additional roles. While curriculum and instruction are the central tools of professional faculty, participation in governance is also critical. If faculty do not participate in making decisions about recruiting, assessing, placing, orienting, advising, and managing students, they certainly will not be able to see the larger picture of accomplishing the avowed mission of the community college. Faculty must participate in all aspects of developing human capital for the community and in helping students to accomplish their academic and career goals. For this to occur, both the faculty member and the college student must be empowered.

EMPOWERING FACULTY AND STUDENTS: A COMMUNITY OF LEARNING

We believe that empowerment is the key to change and that change evolves through a process of faculty and administration wanting to be changed. This can occur from external and internal sources; for example, universities can alter and shape the standards for the profession by changing who can enter the profession; and the workplace itself can redirect and empower faculty by changing how faculty are developed, recruited, selected, assessed, and rewarded.

The basic thesis of this chapter is that the community college will fail to achieve its mission of empowering students and communities unless it empowers faculty at the same time. Faculty must improve their skills, attitudes, beliefs, and expectations for students; and the college itself must improve the skills, values, and expectations related to its mission of developing human capital and the structures in which humans function. In our study we have observed individuals and community colleges that do not suffer from the limitations and generalizations made about community colleges. The study of award-winning instructors, and our own consulting and teaching, lead us to believe that there exists in the universe a population of colleges, CEOs, administrators, staff, and faculty who have broken out of the old "bureaucratic mold." These people and entities represent solutions to the problems of our young and struggling educational movement. Their new programs have often transformed structures through planned change and development. They have begun to recognize and challenge the idea of the professional at work.

> Change in the professional bureaucracy does not sweep in from new administrators taking office to announce major reforms, nor from government technostructures intent on bringing the professionals under control. Rather, change seeps in, by the slow process of changing the professionals—changing who can enter the profession, what they learn in its professional schools (ideals as well as skills and knowledge), and thereafter how willing they are to upgrade their skills. Where such changes are resisted, leaders may be best off to call on the professionals' sense of responsibility

to serve the students (Mintzberg, 1979, p. 379).

Empowerment of faculty is a double-edged sword. Leaders must organize for change with professional faculty at the center of the change. Reform efforts must be seen as a slow evolutionary process of changing colleges' behaviors, attitudes, and values, and then by changing their goals, programs, and procedures through a powerfully participative process. Yet the involvement must be mandatory. Leaders can be sure that professionals will not generally seek involvement but can become motivated to commit only through involvement. Resistance to change is normal; overcoming resistance is a task for visionary leaders, such as those described in *Shared Vision* (Roueche, Baker, and Rose, 1989).

Effective leaders build, through collaboration, action plans that capture the energy of college staff members. The president is the conceptual salesperson of any plan and must influence by first demanding and subsequently expecting collaboration between various divisions of the college. Our study of leaders in public schools and in community colleges validated a model of situational leadership, where leaders attempted to vary their behavior to fit circumstances. They sometimes emphasized mission; at other times, they emphasized morale and consideration of others: leaders were task-oriented in that they initiated structures for problem solving and decision making; people-oriented in that they were able to build a strong sense of institutional commitment through collaboration; and effectiveness-oriented in that they were able to provide both vision and direction for the college and its members through planning, organizing, and influencing the attitudes and values of individuals.

In our study of exceptional community colleges, we were surprised to find that in the more than 100 interviews we conducted, there was overwhelming consistency in the values and beliefs expressed by faculty and administration. We discovered that the college as a community had worked in various group processes for almost a decade to come to agreement on a set of philosophical values relating to the college's responsibility to student and community. Typical of these colleges are Humber College, Red Deer College, Jefferson State Community College, Maricopa County Community College District, DeAnza College, Foothill College,

Santa Barbara City College, Los Angeles Community College District, Miami-Dade Community College, St. Petersburg Junior College, College of DuPage, Johnson County Community College, Jefferson Community College, Howard Community College, Schoolcraft College, St. Louis Community College District, Monroe Community College, Genesee Community College, Suffolk County Community College, Central Piedmont Community College, Cuyahoga Community College, Linn-Benton Community College, Midlands Technical College, and Dallas County Community College District.

The analysis of our interviews supported the common view that both administrators and faculty at these colleges agreed that a direct relationship existed between student attendance and student success. College members articulated and communicated the belief to students that the primary purpose of financial aid was to increase students' academic success. College members spoke persuasively about the importance of student decision making and commitment to an educational goal as a prerequisite for success within a program. College members frequently reported that the college existed solely to successfully serve both students and community. This shared college philosophy relating to student socialization into the college was most interesting. College members believed that students must be guided firmly into making positive choices regarding their future. We found that the college held itself responsible for making the final decision as to where (at what level) the student would be placed into the curriculum. Once students are committed to an academic course of action, the college holds itself accountable to provide constant and accurate feedback on both student performance and progress.

THE BUILDING OF SYSTEMS TO SUPPORT STUDENT LEARNING

We know that having individuals believe that certain behaviors produce results and then building the systems to accomplish these results is the essence of successful leadership. Those who have studied leadership in a college setting have concluded that faculty are the key performers in the achievement of excellence. Effective colleges develop and task teams of individuals that cut across traditional functions. These individuals serve in traditional units of the college and serve on teams that solve problems, evaluate data, and make recommendations regarding systems developed to manage and motivate students. What follows is a brief discussion of the major aspects of the systems for success, aspects that we found in the exceptional community colleges and in our study of award-winning faculty.

Student Assessment: At excellent colleges the members of the academic team, including both faculty and administration, carefully develop a battery of tests to determine where students should be placed in the curriculum. Where the typical college is often unable to offer the number and types of courses that students need because of the unwillingness to require faculty to teach what students need, colleges have embedded the values and the expectations that the college must make the tough decisions necessary to meet student needs. Once individuals commit to the idea that resources must follow determined need, the resistance to change is significantly reduced.

Student Responsibility: When we speak with college presidents and administrators regarding a philosophy of firm and directive student management, they most often cite a view that adult students must take responsibility for their own behavior and actions. Thus, since mandatory assessment, placement, and the requirement to take remedial or developmental courses often violate this general principle, most colleges soften this perceived hard line of directive approach. Not only do faculty and administration at excellent colleges express strong support for the idea of directive, policy-based decision making, the institution is now able to produce ad hoc and longitudinal studies involving faculty to support the effectiveness of the college's strongly directive matriculation process.

Student Acquisition: Our study of exemplary teachers shows their active participation in recruitment, marketing, and articulation. Faculty show their leadership as colleges establish close and continuous relationships with business and industry and establish joint enrollment processes and articulation agreements with local high schools. These faculty also strategically serve the college and community by becoming involved in recruitment plans and by being familiar with admissions procedures allowing rapid development and retrieval of information pertaining to students and their performance and progress. Faculty involvement with student matriculation signalled to students the college's commitment to education and training.

Curriculum Integration: Whatever else colleges do, they must engage in reshaping their education and training programs to make them more effective in achieving both the goals of students and society. Exceptional colleges have gone beyond this need to examine the relationships between existing components of the curriculum. They have begun to identify and integrate, within the curriculum, essential skills for life.

Curriculum changes are requiring a battery of general education courses for every degree-seeking student along with minimum standards for academic performance. These changes have become the central focus of faculty input as they collaboratively develop goals that establish parameters for the requirements for successful educational reforms.

Developmental Studies: Most effective colleges see developmental studies as a foundation for successful completion of student academic goals; and perhaps as important, they see developmental studies as the linchpin of access and academic excellence. In order to ensure that these programs are able to salvage, redirect, and develop the skills and attributes students require for success, exceptional colleges staff, organize, and manage these programs as a top priority. We discovered that college administrators accomplish the leadership and management aspects of these programs, and faculty directly support the student development components, along with responsibilities of recruiting, assessing, placing, and managing student progress and performance.

Student Monitoring: The leadership of the community college must realize that leading and managing the multiple missions of the open-door college require a committed staff and management system that allows decision makers to employ student information in the development of policies and procedures. These policies and procedures, in turn, produce guidance and direction to college personnel as they work together to help students become successful in their career and academic pursuits. Informed and motivated faculty, along with leaders within each unit of the college, are the keystone to student management. Management procedures provide

298/ TEACHING AS LEADING

students with accurate and timely feedback regarding their progress and provide college personnel, especially faculty who work directly with students, with the effectiveness of policies and procedures for student monitoring. Student management also empowers the student into taking responsibility to meet with appropriate college personnel for counseling or when proper and corrective actions are needed.

Achievement and Graduation Information: One of the most important goals of excellent institutions is providing accurate and timely feedback on student performance, which moves students through the college cycle toward graduation. Exemplary instructors set great value on allowing students to link performance to their stated career and academic goals. Students and instructors are both empowered by being informed about students' progress. Immediate access and availability to students' performance records allow both faculty and students greater opportunities for currency about academic status and success in college.

Academic Standards: In our experience, one of the major obstacles to achieving access and excellence in open-door colleges is the unwillingness of the college and its leadership to establish academic standards—for fear that the uniform enforcement of such policies will adversely affect enrollment. If motivation is central to behavior, and purposeful behavior is central to success, then we must be able to create a climate that is perceived as supportive and that is maintained over time to permanently affect those who collaborate to make the student successful.

Academic standards consist of an integrated set of policies and procedures that communicate to all college personnel what is expected of students. Since educators are in the business of adding value and competencies to individuals, our study demonstrates that exceptional faculty communicate to students the consequences of failing to progress toward their stated goals. If the systems work, we must be convinced that properly placed students, properly developed curriculum, and faculty who believe that students can succeed will link effort to performance and performance to success. Academic standards should be incremental, allowing for initial warning, appropriate help, counseling, academic assistance, and reduction of academic loads. In cases where students do not respond to this intervention, the second level of academic standards is triggered.

Under these conditions, the student is placed on probation. Probation results in additional assistance, monitoring, and control to include possible course reduction. In exceptional cases where students do not respond to help, the third trigger is suspension for one semester. It is interesting to note that where academic standards are enforced, most students who have been suspended have re-enrolled at their first opportunity and as a group have been more successful in their second effort.

MAKING IT WORK: TEACHING THE TEACHER TO TEACH

We have identified the competencies that make excellent instructors; we have learned that the skills and expertise that excellent instructors employ are derived analytically and are operationalized until perfect. More important, we have seen leadership skills demonstrated in the classroom to the extent that empowerment of students can take place—students can take responsibility for their own learning, guided by the instructor who knows the value of situational teaching strategies and styles. So what?

That question obviously drove home the point that talent is a terrible thing to waste, and that the concept of leadership, motivation, and influence was not reducible only to the classroom course or the college environment. A good teacher can teach anywhere and with either traditional or nontraditional students in the classroom. Obviously, the community can profit from the expertise and talent of the exemplary teacher, but so can colleges and universities. Who better to teach teachers than the master teacher?

We propose that the exemplary teachers of community colleges not only be identified and celebrated, but that their skills become the vehicle by which a cadre of excellent teachers, apprenticed and mentored by the exemplary, award-winning instructor, is produced. In-service and pre-service classes in the college environment should be instituted for faculty development, and they should be taught by master teachers within that environment. Moreover, master teachers should be encouraged and rewarded by their colleges in this venture and toward the completion of higher degrees when appropriate. Exchanges among community college instructors should take place, and exemplary college faculty should be visiting scholars and practitioners at other institutions. Finally, senior institutions can profit from the experiences of exemplary instructors. Not only can they study and research exemplary instructors' efforts, but they can begin to incorporate what they have learned from them into formal courses in teaching effectiveness in the community college so that graduate students in all disciplines can profit by training for community college teaching at senior colleges and universities.

SUMMARY

It is not difficult to conclude that where academic alert, advising, and graduation information, feedback on performance, and the enforcement of academic progress standards are in place, a climate is created where students are able to see themselves as the centerpiece of the college. These are some of the essential elements of an empowered faculty who place their students at the center of their environment, who take seriously their responsibility for student success in an open-access college, and who are ably supported in their student-derived needs by an administration who also places great value in student and faculty success and strives to develop the community college into a complete learning community.

What leaders do, and how they interact with others, accounts for the critical difference between access with excellence and "the revolving door" among community colleges. The community college is an organization dedicated to serving students and the community; thus leaders must carefully and collaboratively build the unique structures and systems that accurately and innovatively meet the needs of their communities. Student success is the discovery of and commitment to the pursuit of career and educational goals, the achievement of which makes for responsible citizens in a democratic society.

We believe that community colleges, as new American educational institutions, have moved through the past 25 years building toward a maturity that promises upward mobility in and for our society. We look forward to a proud and equally exciting future for this unique contribution of higher education—the community college.

APPENDICES

Award-Winning Instructors In The American
Community College
Award-Winning Instructor's Project Worksheet
Student Questionnaire

Appendix 1

THE UNIVERSITY OF TEXAS AT AUSTIN COMMUNITY COLLEGE LEADERSHIP PROGRAM

"Award-Winning Instructors In The American Community College"

The Purpose of the Project

The Community College Leadership Program of the College of Education at The University of Texas at Austin is conducting a nationwide study of exemplary instructors in excellent American community colleges. These award-winning instructors will not only make valuable contributions to a new publication on community college teaching, but they will also be recognized and honored at a special awards ceremony at the 1989 NISOD International Conference on Teaching Excellence.

The Nomination Process

During the summer of 1988, nominations will be made by presidents and leadership teams who were identified in the recent national study of community college transformational leaders. The nominees must have received a national, regional, state or local award as an outstanding instructor within the last three years to be eligible. To be considered, nominations must be postmarked no later than September 1, 1988.

The Award

All instructors nominated will contribute to the national study on teaching excellence. In addition they will be recognized and honored at a special awards ceremony at the 1989 Annual International Conference on Teaching Excellence to be held in Austin, Texas in May.

The Criteria

Instructors will be asked to give specific examples of how they embody the following characteristics and behaviors in their classroom performance and their relationship with students.

Motivation	Interpersonal Skills	Intellectual Skills
Commitment	Objectivity	Individualized
Goal Orientation	Active Listening	perception
Integrated Perception	Rapport	Teaching strategies
Positive attitude	Empathy	
Reward orientation		

Exemplary Instructors Nomination Form

Instructions to the Nominator:

1. Please type all information.
2. Inform instructor they have been nominated.
3. Complete the form and **mail no later than October 1, 1988** to:

**Award-Winning Instructors' Project
Community College Leadership Program
EDB 348
Unviersity of Texas at Austin
Austin, Texas 78712**

Instructor/Nominee Information:

Name: _____

Academic Rank: _____

Teaching Field: _____

Teaching Awards: _____

Title of Award	Date Received
Title of Award	Date Received
Title of Award	Date Received

Personal Information:

Degrees   Field/Degree Awarded

_____   _____

_____   _____

_____   _____

Years of Teaching Experience _____ Gender _____ Ethnicity_____
Approximate Age _____Phone _____
Home Address _____
_____

Summer Address (if different from above)
_____
_____

President's Letter of Recommendation
(to be completed by President only)

PRESIDENT/NOMINATOR: Please use this page to write your
letter of recommendation. To help stimulate your thoughts, a
summary of teaching characteristics and behaviors is enclosed
within this packet of materials. Please do not share this packet of
materials with your nominees. Please type.

_____

Name of College   Address   City   Zip

_____

Name of President   Signature   Date

Appendix 2

AWARD-WINNING INSTRUCTOR'S
PROJECT WORKSHEET

Biographical Information

Age_____ Place of Birth_____Ethnicity_____Gender_____
Number of years' education: Father_____ Mother_____

Background and Work Experience

Degrees	Yr. graduated	Institution, Location	Major	Minor
_____	_____	_____	_____	_____
_____	_____	_____	_____	_____
_____	_____	_____	_____	_____

Number of years in college teaching _____
Years teaching (other than college) _____
(What? Where?) _____
_____

Faculty title _____Years in present position _____
Number of full-time faculty in your department _____
Department/Teaching field (specify developmental, if appropriate) _____
_____

Institutional Information

Total Class Assignments _____
Total number students taught per semester/qtr _____
Your average attrition rate? _____% Is there an institutional
attendance policy? Yes _____ No _____
   Effectiveness (circle one): excellent   good   fair   poor
Is there an institutional assessment policy? Yes_____ No _____
   Effectiveness: excellent   good   fair   poor
Is there an institutional advisement policy? Yes _____ No _____
   Effectiveness: excellent   good   fair   poor

Is there an institutional placement policy? Yes _____ No _____
    Effectiveness: excellent   good   fair   poor
Is there a faculty development program at your college? Yes ____
No _____. Circle the number of the aspects listed which apply to
your program: 1. selection of faculty; 2. evaluation of faculty; 3.
development of faculty; 4. promotion/tenure of faculty; 5. merit
rewards for faculty. Overall effectiveness of faculty development
program: excellent   good   fair   poor

Teaching Information

Which courses, formal or informal, were helpful in preparing you
to teach?_____

_____
Explain what you do in class early on to determine the readiness
of your students to learn_____

_____

_____

Time Use Information

Total hours spent in classroom/lab (weekly) _____ Total hours
(preparation time, weekly) _____ Office hours (weekly) _____
Other hours spent with students _____ Specify _____

_____

Other tasks (college- or student-related)_____

_____

_____

Conferences

Conferences attended during the last year related to improving
teaching (local, state, or national)_____

_____

_____

_____

Describe an incident or situation in your teaching experience in which you felt highly successful in motivating students to learn. What was the situation? What happened? What did you do? What was the student response? What was the overall outcome? What did you learn from the experience?

[Attach Extra Sheet if Necessary]

Describe an incident or situation in your teaching experience in which you felt you were unsuccessful in motivating your students to learn. Describe that situation. What happened? What did you do? What was the student response? Overall outcome? What did you learn from the experience?

[Attach Extra Sheet if Necessary)
IMPORTANT INFORMATION ON NEXT PAGE

As fully as you care to, explain your personal philosophy of the role of the teacher in enabling student learning.

Descriptors: Excellent Teachers

Adjectives (words) you would use to describe excellent teachers (list as many as you think apply):_____

_____

_____

_____

_____

_____

Appendix 3

STUDENT QUESTIONNAIRE

Instructions

Purpose: The purpose of this questionnaire is to determine how you feel about the instructor in this course. This information will be used for research purposes only.

I. Please rate your instructor on the following descriptive statements by assigning a number based on the following scale:

1 Strongly Disagree 2 Disagree 3 No Opinion 4 Agree 5 Strongly Agree

In the spaces below, write in numbers from 1 to 5 to demonstrate how you feel about your instructor:

_____ The instructor motivated me to do my best in this course.
_____ A key reason I have worked hard in this course is due to my instructor's behavior toward me.
_____ What I have gained from this course has been important to me.
_____ This instructor has made a positive difference in my life.
_____ The instructor is committed to my learning.
_____ I have discovered a relationship between my needs and what I have learned in this course.
_____ What I have learned in this course is an adequate reward for my efforts.
_____ My instructor went beyond what I expected to help me to learn.
_____ I expect to earn the grade I deserve in this course.
_____ The instructor has taught me to take responsibility for my own learning.
_____ The instructor has used practical teaching methods in this course.

II. Place a check by the words which best describe your instructor:

_____ Motivator	_____ Innovator	_____ Leader
_____ Learner	_____ Optimistic	_____ Giving
_____ Achiever	_____ Intellectual	_____ Positive
_____ Persuasive	_____ Dependable	_____ Ethical
_____ Accessible	_____ Unselfish	_____ Listener
_____ Scholarly	_____ Dynamic	_____ Committed
_____ Helpful	_____ Inspirational	_____ Forceful

_____ Organizer	_____ Creative
_____ Confident	_____ Humorous
_____ Obliging	_____ Competent
_____ Eloquent	_____ Honorable
_____ Successful	_____ Enthusiastic
_____ Interesting	_____ Energetic
_____ Sympathetic	_____ Compassionate

III. In this space provided, describe a situation in which your instructor was successful in motivating you to learn. (Include in your response the following: a short description of the situation, an explanation of what the instructor did, an explanation of what you did, and a discussion of the outcome of this situation.)

_____

_____

(if necessary, continue on the back of this page)

Student Information (Check of fill in the blank as appropriate):

Male _____Female _____ Age___ Ethnicity_____ Number
of semesters/qtr in college _____
Instructor's name: _____Course name:_____
I am taking this course in order to (check all that apply): transfer
to another college ____; complete a degree at this college ____;
improve personal/professional skills ____; get a new job ____; I
have no specific educational goal at this time _____.

REFERENCES

AACJC Commission on the Future of Community Colleges. 1988. *Building communities: A vision for a new century.* Washington, DC: American Association of Community and Junior Colleges.

Astin, A. 1975. *Preventing students from dropping out.* San Francisco: Jossey-Bass.

Astin, A. 1978. *Four critical years.* San Francisco: Jossey-Bass.

Baker, G. A. 1982. *Analyzing the learner's motivational problems.* Monograph. New York: Media Systems Corporation, Harcourt Brace Johanovich.

Baker, G. A. 1989. *Teaching as leading inventory.* Community College Leadership Program: The University of Texas at Austin.

Bass, B. M. 1985. *Leadership and performance beyond expectations.* New York: Free Press.

Bean, J. 1986. Assessing and reducing attrition. In *Managing college enrollment,* 53, San Francisco: Jossey-Bass.

Bennis, W., and Nanus, B. 1985. *Leaders: The strategies for taking charge.* New York: Harper and Row.

Biddle, B. J., and Anderson, D. S. 1986. Theory, methods, knowledge, and research on teaching. In M.C. Wittrock (Ed.), *Handbook of research on teaching* (3rd ed.). New York: Macmillan Publishing Company.

Blake, R., and Mouton, J. 1964. *The managerial grid.* Houston, TX: Gulf.

Blocker, C. E., Plummer, R. H., and Richardson, R. C. Jr., 1965. *The two-year college: A social synthesis.* Englewood Cliffs, NJ: Prentice-Hall, Inc.

Brophy, J. E., and Good, T. L. 1986. School effects. In M. C. Wittrock (Ed.), *Handbook of research on teaching* (3rd ed.). New York: Macmillan Publishing Company.

Brown, E. N. 1987. *The relationship of student success to the education goals of community college students.* Unpublished doctoral dissertation, The University of Texas at Austin.

Burns, J. M. 1978. *Leadership.* New York: Harper and Row.

Cazden, C. B. 1986. Classroom discourse. In M. C. Wittrock (Ed.),*Handbook of research on teaching* (3rd ed.). New York: Macmillan Publishing Company.

Chickering, A. 1977. *Experience and learning: An introduction to experiential learning.* New Rochelle, NY: Change Magazine Press.

Cohen, A. M., 1968. *Focus on learning—preparing teachers for the two-year college.* (ERIC Document Reproduction Service No. ED 019 939).

Cohen, A. M., and Brawer, F. B. 1977. *The two-year college instructor today.* New York: Praeger Publishers.

Cohen, A. M. and Brawer, F. B. 1987. *The collegiate function of community colleges: Fostering higher learning through curriculum and student transfer.* San Francisco: Jossey-Bass.

Cohen, A. M., and Brawer, F. B. 1989. *The American community college* (2nd ed.). San Francisco: Jossey-Bass.

Corno, L., and Snow, R. E. 1986. Adapting teaching to individual differences among learners. In M. C. Wittrock (Ed.),

Handbook of research on teaching (3rd ed.). New York: Macmillan Publishing Company.

Cronbach, L. J. 1975. Beyond the two disciplines of scientific psychology. *American Psychologist.* 30(2): 116-127.

Cross, K. P. 1971. Access and the accommodation in higher education. Paper presented to White House Conference on Youth. *Research Reporter.* Berkeley, CA: Center for Research and Development in Higher Education.

Cross, K.P. 1976. *Accent on learning.* San Francisco: Jossey-Bass.

Cross, K.P. 1978. *The missing link: Connecting adult learners to learning resources.* New York: Future Directions for a Learning Society, The College Board.

Cross, K. P. 1981. *Adults as learners: Increasing participation and facilitating learning.* San Francisco: Jossey-Bass.

Cross, K.P. 1984. *Societal imperatives: Needs for an educated democracy.* Paper presented at National Conference on Teaching Excellence, Austin, TX, May 23, 1984.

Cross, K. P. 1989. Teaching for learning. *AAHE Bulletin.* April: 3-7.

Cutherbertson, P. 1982. *The effects of contingency variables on leadership style.* Unpublished doctoral dissertation. The University of Texas at Austin.

Denzin, N.K. 1978. *The research act: A theoretical introduction to sociological methods* (2nd ed.). New York: McGraw-Hill.

Dressel, P. L. 1982. *College teaching as a profession: The doctor of arts degree.* East Lansing: Michigan State University. (ED 217 750).

Easton, J. Q. 1984. *National study of effective community college teachers.* (ERIC Document Reproduction Service No. ED 245 740).

El-Khawas, E., et al. (Ed). 1988. *Community college fact book.* New York: AACJC and American Council on Education/ Macmillan.

Erikson, E. 1959. Identity and the life cycle. *Psychological Issues* 1.

Erickson, F. 1986. Qualitative methods in research on teaching. In M. C. Wittrock (Ed.), *Handbook of research on teaching* (3rd ed.). New York: Macmillan Publishing Company.

Evans, M. G. 1970. The effects of supervisory behavior on the path-goal relationship. *Organizational Behavior and Human Performance.* 55: 277-298.

Fenstermacher, G. D. 1986. Philosophy of research on teaching: Three aspects. In M. C. Wittrock (Ed.), *Handbook of research on teaching* (3rd ed.). New York: Macmillan Publishing Company.

Fisher, J. L. 1984. *Power of the presidency.* New York: American Council on Education/Macmillan.

Fisher, J. L., Tack, M. W., and Wheeler, K. J. 1988. *The effective college president.* New York: American Council on Education/Macmillan.

Flanagan, J. C. 1954. The critical incident technique. *Psychological Bulletin.* 51(4): 327-358.

Flanders, L. R. 1982. *Senior executive service and mid-managers' job profiles.* Washington, DC: U.S. Office of Personnel Management.

Flanders, N. 1970. *Analyzing teacher behavior.* Reading, MA:

Addison-Wesley.

Gates A., and Creamer D. 1984. Two-year college attrition: Do student or institutional characteristics contribute most? *Community/Junior College Quarterly.* 8: 39-51.

Giroux, R. 1989. *Human resource development.* Humber College, Ontario.

Gleazer, E. J. 1980. *The community college: Values, vision, and vitality.* Washington, DC: American Association of Community and Junior Colleges.

Goodwin, L. D., and Goodwin, W. L. 1984. Qualitative vs. quantitative research or qualitative and quantitative research. *Nursing Research.* 33 (6): 378-380.

Greene, M. 1986. Philosophy and teaching. In M.C. Wittrock (Ed.), *Handbook of research on teaching* (3rd ed.). New York: Macmillan Publishing Company.

Greenleaf, R. 1973. *Servant as leader.* Newton Center, MA: Robert K. Greenleaf Center.

Guskey, T. R., and Easton, J. Q. 1983. The characteristics of very effective teachers in urban community colleges. *Community/Junior College Quarterly.* 7(3): 265-274.

Hall, J. 1973. Communication revisited. *California Management Review.* 56-67.

Halpin, A. 1955. The leader behavior and leadership ideology of educational administrators and aircraft commanders. *Harvard Educational Review.* 25: 18-32.

Halpin, A. 1956. *The leader behavior of school superintendents.* Columbus OH: College of Education, Ohio State University.

Herndon, S. 1984. Factors that differentiate between persisters and dropouts among recipients of financial aid. *Journal of College Student Personnel.* 25(4): 367-368.

Hersey, P. 1984. *The situational leader.* Escondido, CA: Center for Leadership Studies.

Hersey, P., and Blanchard, K. H. 1982. *Management of organizational behavior: Utilizing human resources* (4th ed.). Englewood Cliffs, NJ: Prentice-Hall.

Herzberg, F. 1968. One more time: How do you motivate employees? *Harvard Business Review.* 9: 203-210.

Herzberg, F. 1976. *The managerial choice.* Salt Lake City, UT: Olympus Publishing Company.

Heverly, M.A. 1987. *Community college student persistence: Longitudinal tracking of multiple cohorts.* Kansas City, MO: Association for Institutional Research.

Hillway, T. 1958. *The American two-year college.* New York: Harper and Brothers.

Hirst, W. A., and Bailey, G. D. 1983. *A study to identify effective classroom teaching competencies for community college faculty.* (ERIC Document Reproduction Services No. ED 227 890).

Houle, C. O. 1984. *Patterns of learning: New perspectives on life-span education.* San Francisco: Jossey-Bass.

House, R. 1971. A path-goal theory of leader effectiveness. *Administrative Science Quarterly.* 16: 321-339.

House, R., and Mitchell, T. 1974. Path-goal theory of leadership. *Contemporary Business.* 3 (Fall): 81-98.

Huff, S., Lake, D., and Schaalman, M. 1982. *Principal differences:*

Excellence in school leadership and management. Boston: McBer.

Hunter, M. 1982. *Mastery teaching.* El Segundo, CA: TIP Publications.

Jago, A. G. 1982. Leadership: Perspectives in theory and research. *Management Science.* 28: 315-336.

Jenrette, M. 1988. *The teaching and learning project.* Miami, FL: Miami-Dade Community College.

Jick, T. 1979. Mixing qualitative and quantitative methods: Triangulation in action. *Administrative Science Quarterly.* 24: 602-611.

Jung, C. 1977. *Psychological Types.* R.F.C. Hull, trans., Collected Works of C.G. Jung, Vol. 6. Bollingen Series XX, Princeton University Press.

Kanter, R. 1983. *The change masters: Innovation for productivity in the American corporation.* New York: Simon and Schuster.

Kerr, C. 1984. *Presidents make a difference: Strengthening leadership in colleges and universities.* Washington, DC: Association of Governing Boards of Universities and Colleges.

Klemp, G. O. 1977. Three factors of success. In D. W. Vermilye (Ed.), *Relating Work and Education.* San Francisco: Jossey-Bass.

Klemp, G. O. 1979. Identifying, measuring, and integrating competence. In P. Pottinger and J. Goldsmith (Eds.)., *Defining and measuring competence.* San Francisco: Jossey-Bass.

Klemp, G. O. 1982. Assessing student potential: An immodest

proposal. In C. Taylor (Ed.), *New directions for experiential learning: Diverse student preparation: Benefits and issues.* San Francisco: Jossey-Bass.

Klemp, G. O., Huff, S. M., and Gentile, J. G. 1980. *The guardians of campus change: A study of leadership in nontraditional college programs.* Boston: McBer and Company.

Knowles, M. 1983. *Andragogy in action.* San Francisco: Jossey-Bass.

Knowles, M. 1989. *The making of an adult educator: An autobiographical journey.* San Francisco: Jossey-Bass.

Kolb, D. 1984. *Experiential learning: Experience as the source of learning and development.* Englewood Cliffs, NJ: Prentice-Hall, Inc.

Koos, L. V. 1949. Programs of junior-college teacher preparation. *Junior College Journal.* 19: 333-346.

Kramer, G. 1985. Why students persist in college: A categorical analysis. *NACADA Journal.* 5(2): 1-17.

Lewin, K. 1951. *Field theory in social science.* New York: Harper and Row.

Light, R., and Pillemer, D. 1982. Numbers and narrative: Combining their strengths in research review. *Harvard Educational Review.* 41: 429-471.

Likert, R. 1967. *The human organization.* New York: McGraw-Hill.

Linthicum, D. 1989. *The dry pipeline: Increasing the flow of minority faculty.* Washington, DC: National Council of State Directors of Community and Junior Colleges.

Losak, J. 1986. President's forum: What constitutes student success in the college? *Community College Journal for Research and Planning.* 5: 1-15.

Luft, J. 1961. The Johari window. *Human Relations and Training News.* January: 6-7.

Martin, J. 1982. Excluding women from the educational realm. *Harvard Educational Review.* 52 (2): 133-148.

Maslow, A. 1954. *Motivation and personality.* New York: Harper.

Matlock, K. 1988. *Student services and retention in Texas two-year colleges.* Unpublished doctoral dissertation, University of Texas at Austin.

McCabe, R. 1988. Educational programs of the American community college. In J. Eaton (Ed.), *Colleges of Choice.* New York: American Council on Education/Macmillan.

McClelland, D. C. 1972. What is the effect of achievement motivation training in the schools? *Teacher College Record.* 74 (2): 129-145.

McClelland, D. C. 1978. *Guide to behavioral event interviewing.* Boston: McBer and Company.

McClelland, D. C. 1982. *Motivation in society.* San Francisco: Jossey-Bass.

Menges, R. J., and Mathis, B. C. 1988. *Key resources on teaching, learning, curriculum, and faculty development: A guide to the higher education literature.* San Francisco: Jossey-Bass.

Mintzberg, H. 1979. *The structure of organizations.* Englewood Cliffs, NJ: Prentice-Hall, Inc.

Monroe, C. 1972. *Profile of the community college.* San Francisco:

Jossey-Bass.

Naylor, J., Pritchard, R., and Ilgen, D. 1981. *A theory of behavior in organization.* New York: Academic Press.

Neumann, L. 1984. Equity theory and students' commitment to their college. *Research in Higher Education.* 20 (3): 269-280.

Noel, L., et al. 1985. *Increasing student retention.* San Francisco: Jossey-Bass..

Omaha Boy, N. 1985. *Teaching behaviors of excellent instructors at Miami-Dade Community College.* Unpublished doctoral dissertation, University of Texas at Austin.

Ottinger, C. 1987. *Fact book on higher education.* Washington, DC: American Council on Education/Macmillan.

Pascarella, E. 1986. Orientation to college and freshman year persistence/withdrawal decisions. *Journal of Higher Education.* 57 (2): 155-175.

Pate, H. P. 1990. *Relationship of effective teaching characteristics to methods of faculty evaluation in two-year colleges.* Unpublished doctoral dissertation. The University of Texas at Austin.

Peters, R. 1965. Education as initiation. In R. Archambault (Ed.), *Philosophical analysis and education.* London: Routledge and Kegan Paul.

Peters, T. J., and Waterman, R. H., Jr. 1982. *In search of excellence: Lessons from America's best-run companies.* New York: Harper and Row.

Peters, T. J. 1987. *Thriving on chaos: Handbook for a management revolution.* New York: Alfred A. Knopf.

Piaget, J. 1971. *Psychology and epistemology*. Middlesex, England: Penguin Books.

Polit, D., and Hungler, B. 1987. *Nursing research: principles and methods* (3rd ed)., Philadelphia: Lippincott.

Porter, L., and Lawler, E. 1968. *Managerial attitudes and performance*. Homewood, IL: Richard Irwin.

Riesman, D. 1980. *On higher education*. San Francisco: Jossey-Bass.

Rogers, C. 1961. *On becoming a person*. Boston: Houghton Mifflin.

Rosenthal, R., and Jacobson, L. 1968. *Pygmalion in the classroom*. New York: Rinehart and Winston.

Roueche, J. E. 1968. *Salvage, redirection or custody? Remedial education in the junior college*. Washington, DC: American Association of Junior Colleges.

Roueche, J. E. 1972. Accountability for student learning. *Interamerican revista/review*. (November): 6-14.

Roueche, J. E. 1982. Don't close the door. *Community/Junior College Journal*, January:17-23.

Roueche, J. E., and Baker, G. A. 1983. *Beacons for change*. Iowa City: American College Testing Service.

Roueche, J. E., and Baker, G., A., 1986. *Profiling excellence in America's schools*. Arlington, VA: American Association of School Administrators.

Roueche, J. E., and Baker, G. A. 1987. *Access & excellence: The open-door college*. Washington, DC: Community College Press.

Roueche, J. E., Baker, G. A., and Brownell, R. L. 1971. *Accountability and the community college: Directions for the '70's.* Washington, DC: American Association of Junior Colleges.

Roueche, J. E., Baker, G. A., and Rose, R. R. 1989. *Shared vision: Transformational leaders in American community colleges.* Washington, DC: Community College Press.

Roueche, J. E., Baker, G. A., and Roueche, S. 1984. *College responses to low-achieving students: A national study.* Orlando: HBJ Media Systems Corporation.

Roueche, J. E., and Mink, O. G. 1976. *Impact of instruction and counseling on high-risk youth.* Austin, TX: National Institute of Mental Health Grant No. R01MH2259.

Roueche, J. E., and Mink, O. G. 1980. *Holistic literacy in college teaching.* New York: Media Systems Corporation.

Roueche, J. E., and Roueche, S. 1977. *Developmental education: A primer for program development and evaluation.* Atlanta: Southern Regional Education Board.

Roueche, J., and Snow, J. 1977. *Overcoming learning problems.* San Francisco: Jossey-Bass.

Schneider, C., Klemp, G. Jr., and Kastendiek, S. 1981. *The balancing act: Competencies of effective teachers and mentors in degree programs for adults.* Chicago: Center for Continuing Education, University of Chicago, and Boston: McBer and Company.

Smith, A. 1983. Discriminating factors among college student persisters and nonpersisters. *Journal of College Student Personnel.* 24 (1): 77-8.

Smith, J. K. 1983. Quantitative versus qualitative research: An attempt to clarify the issue. *Educational Researcher.* 12 (3): 6-13.

Stogdill, R. 1948. Personal factors associated with leadership: A survey of the research. *Journal of Psychology.* 25: 35-71.

Stogdill, R. 1974. *Handbook of leadership: A survey of theory and research.* New York: Free Press.

Tannenbaum, R., and Schmidt, W. 1958. How to choose a leadership pattern. *Harvard Business Review.* 36: 95-101.

Tinto, V. 1982. Defining dropout: A matter of perspective. *Studying student attrition.* San Francisco: Jossey-Bass.

Tinto, V. 1987. *Leaving college: Rethinking the causes and cures of student attrition.* Chicago: University of Chicago Press.

Tough, A. 1977. *Major Learning Efforts: Recent research and future directions.* Toronto: Ontario Institute for Studies in Education.

Valek, M. 1988. *Teaching as leading in the community college: An analysis of faculty competencies developed through path-goal theory.* Unpublished doctoral dissertation, The University of Texas at Austin.

Vaughan, G. B. 1986. *The community college presidency.* New York: American Council on Education/Macmillan.

Villela E. 1986. The environmental factors in influencing attrition. *Journal of General Education.* 38 (3): 221-231.

Vroom, V.H. 1964. *Work and motivation.* New York: Wiley.

Vroom, V.H. 1976. Can learners learn to lead? *Organizational Dynamics.* Vol. 4, No.3.

Walberg, H. J. 1986. Syntheses of research on teaching. In Wittrock, M. C., *Handbook of research on teaching* (3rd ed.). New York: Macmillan Publishing Company.

Weinstein, C. 1982. Training students to elaboration learning strategies. *Contemporary Educational Psychology.* 7: 301-311.

Weinstein, C. E., and Mayer, R. E. 1986. The tracking of learning strategies. In Wittrock, M. C., *Handbook of research on teaching* (3rd ed.). New York: Macmillan Publishing Company.

Willett, L. 1983. One-stop or stop-out? *Community/Junior College Quarterly.* 7 : 333-341.

Wittrock, M. C. 1986. *Handbook of research on teaching* (3rd ed.). New York: Macmillan Publishing Company.

Wlodkowski, R. J. 1985. *Enhancing adult motivation to learn.* San Francisco: Jossey-Bass.

Yukl, G. A. 1989. *Leadership in organizations.* Englewood Cliffs, NJ: Prentice-Hall, Inc.

INDEX

Easton, J.Q., 57, 77, 93, 99, 101, 125
El-Khawas, E., 74, 85
El Paso Community College (TX), 230
Ellison, N.M., 106
Emerson Electric Company, 268
Erickson, F., 50-51
Erikson, E., 59, 120
Equal Opportunities Commission, 71
Essex Community College (MD), 14
Estes, Y., 178
Evans, M.G., 53, 58

Felos, C., 235
Fenstermacher, G.D., 8-10
Fisher, J.L, 41
Fite, B., 208
Flaherty, J., 181, 183
Flanagan, J.C., 53, 64
Flanders, N., 50, 64
Fletcher, M.J., 18-19
Florida Community College at Jacksonville (FL), 33, 147, 149, 162
Flynn, R., 229
Foothill College (CA), 147, 294
Foothill-DeAnza Community College District (CA), 273
Ford, J., 34
Foreman, L., 225
Foy, S., 217, 235
Frakes, G., 200
Frazier, K., 223
Frederick Alliance for Creative Education (MD), 267
Frederick Community College (MD), 267

Gadsden State Community College (AL), 202
Gallagher, P., 233
Gates, A., 78
Genesee Community College (NY), 295
Gentile, J.G., 65
Gentry, J., 207